# THE YEAR OF VOTING DANGEROUSLY

**Also by Maureen Dowd:**

*Bushworld*
*Are Men Necessary?*

# THE YEAR OF VOTING DANGEROUSLY

*Maureen Dowd*

TWELVE

*New York   Boston*

*To Kevin and Peggy, my awesome siblings and irksome
sparring partners*

---

Twelve
Hachette Book Group
1290 Avenue of the Americas, New York, NY 10104
twelvebooks.com
twitter.com/twelvebooks

First Hardcover Edition: September 2016

Twelve is an imprint of Grand Central Publishing. The Twelve name and
logo are trademarks of Hachette Book Group, Inc.

The publisher is not responsible for websites (or their content)
that are not owned by the publisher.

The Hachette Speakers Bureau provides a wide range of authors for
speaking events. To find out more, go to www.hachettespeakersbureau.com
or call (866) 376-6591.

Library of Congress Control Number: 2016945297

ISBNs: 978-1-4555-3926-0 (hardcover), 978-1-4555-4159-1 (large print)
978-14789-6433-9 (audio book downloadable), 978-1-4789-6432-2
(audio book cd), 978-1-4555-3924-6 (ebook)

Printed in the United States of America

RRD-H

10  9  8  7  6  5  4  3  2  1

# Contents

# Acknowledgments

I'm lucky enough to work with best—and most generous—journalists in the world at *The New York Times*. I am also lucky enough to be friends with many dazzling journalists and historians outside the *Times*, all of whom have helped me decipher history as it is being made.

I thank all of you.

My fairy godfathers on my *New York Times* column are Carl Hulse, our Chief Washington Correspondent, who knows more about politics than most senators; Leon Wieseltier, who knows more about everything than anyone; and Andy Rosenthal, the former editorial page editor who is now a fellow *Times* columnist.

I am especially grateful to Sean Desmond, my No. 1 at Twelve and one of the best editors I've ever worked with; and Alex Thompson, who is a meticulous researcher, savvy political observer, loyal friend, and really cool dude.

And a big shout-out to Rita Beamish, my friend with the finely tuned moral compass, who interrupted a safari with her husband, Paul, in Tanzania to hunt for Wi-Fi and roar at Trump.

# Introduction

## *Escalator to Bedlam*

When you have lived through extraordinary history—watching a president get impeached, covering father-son presidencies, chronicling a cooked-up war, seeing the wacky woman from Wasilla go rogue, savoring the election of the first black commander in chief—you don't expect to be exponentially more astonished.

Indeed, you might find yourself becoming a jade, thinking you'd seen it all.

But then America got mad—and went mad.

Donald Trump glided down that escalator and promised to build that wall and bragged about his manhood and dissed the Pope and politics vaulted past parody.

We are watching the most epic battle of the sexes since Billie Jean King faced off against Bobby Riggs. The former first lady and first woman ever to run for president as the nominee of a major party is going up against a thrice-married Rat Pack reality TV star who still calls women "sweetheart" and rates their racks.

What could go wrong?

On previous wild political rides, we were still operating within the usual boundaries and hoary traditions. That's why McCain aides called it "going rogue" when Sarah Palin tried to dart away from typical campaign mores.

But 2016 is a dizzying dive through the looking glass and into Donald Trump's Narcissus pool—and must-follow Twitter feed.

"It's as though Trump blew up the science lab, exposing the raw nerve of America's stream of consciousness," says Jon Meacham, the presidential historian.

The Republican Party, held hostage to the whims of its 70-year-old high-chair king, is imploding. The Democratic Party, held hostage to the Clintons' bizarre predilection for arrogant and self-defeating behavior just when things are going well, had to stitch itself back together after its unexpected civil war.

Tectonic plates are grinding. Gatekeepers, old rules and old media are vanishing.

We have an out-of-control id taunting a tightly controlled super-ego. We have the king of winging it versus the queen of homework. She says he's too unpredictable to be president, he says she's too predictable. Trump can excite his crowds but falters on substance; Hillary has substance but falters on exciting her crowds. "The boor versus the bore," *Time*'s Charlotte Alter call it.

He's anti–political correctness and she's always overcorrecting. He does the post-ideological shuffle and she does the whatever-it-takes-to-win slide. The Republican nominee trashes the press but constantly engages with us and the Democratic nominee praises the press but routinely hides from us. Oddly, the Trumpster, as he calls himself, at times sounds like more of a dove than the Warrior, as Hillary's friends call her.

We have two candidates with the highest unfavorables ever recorded and a majority of voters who feel stuck voting against, rather than for, someone. Both parties nominated the only person who could possibly lose to the other. Voters are agonizing about whether they can trust either candidate. Will Trump, who has scant impulse control and who's willing to say the most insulting, provocative things that people wouldn't say at a dinner party much less a global forum, get into a tweet battle with a madman and start a world war?

Will Hillary ever seem on the level? Or will she always be surrounded by a cordon of creepy henchmen and Clinton Inc. sycophants, shrouded in a miasma of money grabs and conveniently disappearing records and emails?

Both candidates have a Nixonian streak and a fluid relationship with the truth, and both love to play the victim. Trump whinges and sends out self-pitying tweets about how the press and fellow Republicans are being unfair to him and not giving him enough credit. Hillary always does best when she's up against a bunch of pasty-faced, hectoring white male Republicans determined to bring her down—or just a sole taunting Tang-colored one.

The 2016 race quickly became the nastiest in modern history, vicious and salacious. "You have to go all the way back to 1884 to find a choice between two candidates who had big liabilities the way Hillary Clinton and Donald Trump do," says John Dickerson, the host of CBS's *Face the Nation*. "Grover Cleveland had fathered a child out of wedlock and James G. Blaine was dogged by a series of scandals in office."

As Dickerson notes, Lord James Bryce wrote that the race became "a contest over the copulative habits of one and the prevaricative habits of the other." And Blaine supporters chanted "Ma, Ma, where's my Pa?" to which Cleveland's supporters responded "Gone to the White House. Ha, ha, ha!"

The flashes of violence at Trump rallies were acid flashbacks to the '68 Democratic convention in Chicago. Republican officials cringed but Trump didn't mind. He told me it added a frisson of excitement. His Cleveland convention featured a brass-knuckles law-and-order message. Trump's most loyal supporters were angry white men and Hillary's most ardent were black women.

"This is a deeply, deeply polarized country not just by party but by class," David Axelrod, former senior advisor to President Obama, told me. While Obama's attention to nuance and emphasis on diplomacy was seen by many as a strength after the bellicose, black-and-white W., Axelrod said, now some find those qualities a weakness and yearn for a strongman.

"There was a susceptibility to a guy like Trump coming along," he said. "Trump is the perfect antithesis of Barack Obama. He's defiantly, gleefully anti-intellectual, anti–'political correctness.' He is just as bombastic as Obama is deliberate. As much as anybody since George Wallace or Pat Buchanan, he has overtly sent dog whistles of race out to white working-class voters. That gratuitous defamation of group after group, person after person, is just anathema to Obama. He genuinely believes this guy would be a calamity for the country."

Unlike the Bushes, who outsourced their political thuggery, Donald Trump does his own wet work.

"He has ripped away what was left of the fiction that the candidates themselves are above the game they were in," says Howard Fineman of *The Huffington Post*. "Not to credit Donald Trump, because he's crude and combative and an egomaniac, but in a weird way, he's at least being candid. And I guess there's something oddly thrilling about a guy who rips the mask off it all and is standing there as the naked id of politics. He is the destroyer of the old world."

The Don Rickles act may wear thin, but the Republican nominee does have a bat-like sonar for sniffing out weak spots in opponents and political and policy arguments. "Trump has an intuitive ability to put his jam-smeared finger on things," Meacham says dryly.

When I asked Bill Maher if he had a good title for this book, chronicling Trump's rampage through the Republican Party, the host of HBO's *Real Time* replied with a reference to the Leonardo DiCaprio mauling in *The Revenant*: "Call it *Raped by a Bear*."

Or to borrow a different animal metaphor from the late, great columnist Mary McGrory, the Republicans' attempt to tame Trump reminds you of a very small man trying to walk a very large dog. Trump is so thin-skinned that he is just as determined to bite Republicans who have rejected him as he is Democrats.

The race becomes even nuttier when you consider the candidates' past parallels and intersections. Both are larger-than-life New Yorkers and members of famous dynasties: an ex-senator and secretary of state living in Chappaqua and a real estate developer born in Queens. Trump is a former Democrat and donor to Hillary's campaigns and the Clinton family foundation while Hillary and Bill were guests at Trump's wedding reception to Melania. And their daughters, Ivanka and Chelsea, are pals.

Bill Clinton was one of the last pols to speak to Trump before he jumped into the race and some Republicans have voiced suspicions that Trump is a Manchurian candidate, unleashed to sabotage the Republican Party and ensure Hillary's election.

The race is rife with racism, sexism, tribalism, jingoism, anti-intellectualism, anti-Semitism, gladiatorial bloodlust, conspiracy theories, federal investigations, hooliganism, xenophobia, puerile name-calling and, most absurdly, penis and "schlong" taunts.

Political campaigns have always been about throwing gorilla dust, as Ross Perot memorably put it, jockeying to see who can prove more alpha. But this year the metaphor turned real. Inevitably, given Trump's obsession with skyscrapers, Amazonian women, large crowds and poll numbers, size mattered. Americans watched the jaw-dropping spectacle of Marco Rubio and Donald Trump trading barbs about the size of Trump's manhood on stage. Mirabile dictu, indeed.

And, perhaps even more amazing, what were the odds that Hillary would find an opponent whose blond hair was a matter of greater obsession in the press than hers?

Out of all the things I've covered in politics over the years, watching Donald Trump morph from a Gotham toon into a presidential nominee is one of the most astounding.

I had covered him as a "short-fingered vulgarian," as *Spy* magazine called him, and as a blingy playboy ("Best Sex I've Ever Had," trumpeted the *New York Post*, purportedly quoting his mistress and later wife, Marla Maples). He was a beauty pageant and casino owner peacocking with beautiful women. His favorite movie is *Citizen Kane*, about a would-be politician who lived in a castle, perhaps because Trump has his own Florida Xanadu, perhaps because he does not realize that the 1941 film about William Randolph Hearst's shame spiral is Orson Welles's indictment of acquisitiveness or perhaps because he knows it's lonely at the top.

Once Trump began campaigning for president with a burst of bigotry about Muslims and Mexicans, he took a reputation as a huckster and turned it into a reputation as Hitler. He also elicited comparisons to Mussolini, Idi Amin, Hugo Chávez, a Marvel comic villain and an orange clown puffer fish.

By far the most shocked person watching Donald Trump's progress—the yuge crowds at stadiums and the Secret Service around Trump Tower on Fifth Avenue—was Donald Trump.

Trump scrambled the Republican Party dogma, presenting himself as an isolationist protectionist rather than an interventionist globalist free-trader, and breaking Ronald Reagan's commandment about never speaking ill of fellow Republicans. Trump dismissed the last Republican nominee, Mitt Romney, as a "choker," and rightly excoriated the last Republican president, W., for missing signals before 9/11 that Osama was going to attack and for taking us into a stupid war.

Through the primaries, everything that should have brought Trump down—when he mocked John McCain for being captured or a *Times* reporter for his disability, and when it came out that he had pretended to be his own PR man under assumed names on phone calls with reporters—bounced off.

I've seen lots of bad moments wipe out candidates, like Michael Dukakis looking goofy in the tank and Poppy Bush checking his watch and Al Gore sighing and John Kerry windsurfing and Rick Perry forgetting the three federal agencies he wanted to close and Marco Rubio acting like a malfunctioning robot.

But now, in the fever dream atmosphere of Trump and a freakingly fast news cycle, gaffes don't matter and neither does telling the truth.

"I could stand in the middle of Fifth Avenue and shoot somebody and I wouldn't lose any voters," Trump marveled at an Iowa rally.

The TV boss was so disoriented at his succès fou that he could not get it together to gather an A team or stop doing stuff like his embarrassing taco bowl tweet on Cinco de Mayo.

During a lunch interview at Trump Tower, as he crossed his arms over uneaten meatballs, he made a face when I asked him whether he would "pivot." He did not seem interested in raising his game beyond Twitter insults and ill-advised retweets (including one about Megyn Kelly as a "bimbo" and some that originated on white-supremacist message boards). Even the quietly supportive Melania told Donald to knock off the retweets.

He seemed to be constantly squandering his opportunities. When he tried to stop his always riveting and sometimes inflammatory riffs and use the teleprompter, he came off, as commentator Matthew Dowd said, like a tranquilized circus lion. Ignoring Lee Atwater's maxim to get out of the way when your opponent is self-destructing, Trump stumbled even on a day in July when he should have been triumphant.

After FBI chief James Comey chided Hillary over classified emails, saying she had been "extremely careless" and making it clear that she had been untruthful, Trump managed to get headlines for praising Saddam Hussein for killing terrorists without reading them their rights. The lugubrious Paul Ryan, the Irish undertaker of the

Trump campaign, once more stepped in to object, telling Megyn Kelly about Saddam Hussein: "He was one of the twentieth century's most evil people."

Trump lives and dies by the numbers. Would all his misfires add up? As Bush senior's pollster, the late Robert Teeter, once told me, public opinion is like confetti: Little pieces of paper float down and eventually form patterns on the ground. Opinion takes time to coalesce, but once it does, it can be hard to change.

In addition to the wickedness, there have been moments of wicked fun with Trump. He made monkeys out of a lot of people who had it coming, and he gleefully exposed the hypocrisy, the fund-raising excesses and professional political vultures. Given the electoral history of the Republicans since Nixon's Southern Strategy, winning races by stirring up racist, homophobic and misogynist feelings, it was rich to see them criticizing Trump for those qualities. They simply wanted a nominee who would be a more subtle bigot, as party tradition demands.

The megalomaniacal Trump made an unlikely David, but when the Goliath of the GOP primaries, Jeb Bush, spent $130 million on his campaign, it was stunning to see Trump beat him with free TV, social media and trucker hats—on his own dime.

"What Donald Trump has done is turn the party apparatus and professional campaign whores on their greedy heads," one veteran Republican strategist told me. (But as his operation grew, he hired one of them, Paul Manafort, a lobbyist and political consultant whose firm had a lot of experience advising dictators around the globe, including Ferdinand Marcos in the Philippines and Vladimir Putin's puppet in the Ukraine.) Like many other Republicans, this strategist is holding her nose, waiting for Trump to crash and burn, and hoping that the bonfire of the vanities brings a fresh start.

"If the party repositions itself as the party of principle on taxes, government and opportunities with a young, dynamic leader, it can redefine itself," she says. "We have to move away from the NRA financing campaigns and go to tech and other businesses."

I interviewed Trump when he made earlier feints at the brass ring.

Back in 1999, I flew on his plane—stocked with gilt fixtures, a double bed and French impressionist paintings—when he went to his first presidential rope line and made his maiden foreign policy speech in Miami. He bashed Castro, much to the delight of the Cuban-Americans in the crowd. He looked shy when he came face to face with the Trump 2000 posters.

In many ways, Trump hasn't changed. As a friend of his once told me: "He transmits; he doesn't receive."

Then, as now, he had no PC restraints, the zingy put-downs were flying and numbers were the sentinels of his success: how many magazine covers Melania had been on; how many men lusted after her; how many zoning changes he had finagled; how many stories he had stacked on his building near the UN; how many times he had stamped the Trump name on the General Motors building; how high his ratings were on Larry King.

He complained, only half-joking, that he didn't want to be interviewed by me while my column was running in the Saturday paper; he wanted to wait until I was back in the higher-circulation Sunday paper.

"I am just very popular with the black populace," he told me then. "When Puff Daddy has a party, when Russell Simmons has a party, I'm the person they call." This past summer, some swing-state polls showed him attracting zero percent of black voters, which meant his only black supporters might be Dr. Ben Carson and the random guy at a California rally he pointed to and hailed as "my African American."

Trump was a caveman in how he talked about women, airing his views to me and on *The Howard Stern Show*, but he broke barriers for women in the construction business.

"Women are much tougher and more calculating than men," he told me. "I relate better to women. I go out with the most beautiful women in the world. Certain guys tell me they want women of substance, not beautiful models. It just means they can't get beautiful models."

Even though he was friendly with the Clintons back then, he said he thought that Bill had handled the Monica affair "disgracefully."

"People would have been more forgiving if he'd had an affair with a really beautiful woman of sophistication," Trump asserted. "Kennedy and Marilyn Monroe were on a different level."

In the spring, Trump stretched the gender gap like it was taffy. When I asked him during the primaries how he could win if 73 percent of women disliked him, he murmured, "sixty-eight percent," citing a different poll.

Given the changing population of the country and how he was anathema with Latinos, a fast-growing demographic, Trump, like Mitt Romney before him, seemed to be running not so much for the presidency as the presidency of white men, conjuring a vision of the good old days that were not coming back.

\* \* \*

Speaking of the good old days, I was also with Hillary Clinton at the beginning of her sojourn at the White House. We had dinner in May 1992 at a revolving restaurant in Covington, Kentucky. She was relaxed and interesting. As we sipped white wine, she told me about a summer job she had while she was at Yale Law School, scooping out fish entrails in a makeshift salmon factory in Valdez, Alaska. She began to get worried about the fish quality.

"They were purple and black and yucky-looking," she recalled. She confronted the owner about how long the fish had been dead and he tried to shut her up. But she wouldn't give up on it so he fired her.

"I found another job," she shrugged.

I was impressed. It showed her strong will and her desire to make the world a better place, even one fish at a time.

I was sympathetic to Hillary's desire to bring the antiquated role of first lady into modernity. The job is a ridiculous tightrope, with women like Hillary and Michelle Obama, who have the exact same education and credentials as their husbands, having to deal with china while the president deals with China.

Still, I was dubious about her role shepherding health care in her husband's administration. Was it wise to put the spouse of the president in charge of 13 percent of the economy, given the fact that people in the administration might be afraid to push back or be honest with her?

However, covering Hillary when she came to present the emerging health-care plan to Congress, I proclaimed her appearance "bravura," "polished" and brimming with "crystal clarity." I wrote that she and Bill at the outset were doing "an elegant tango" on health care, avoiding all the possible pitfalls.

But Hillary ended up tanking health-care reform with her secretive, my-way-or-the-highway approach. That stubborn secrecy would come back to haunt her again and again.

Her husband, who has more nimble political instincts, did not intervene to insist that Hillary compromise on the plan, and some advisers believed that he felt too beholden to his wife for putting up with—and publicly defending—all his shenanigans. "She has a hundred-pound fishing wire around his balls," one of her top health-care deputies told me at the time.

Hillary was seen as so controlling by many voters that she tended to be at her most popular when she was losing control. She won her Senate seat in 2000 after being embarrassed by her husband over Monica and crowded in a debate by Rick Lazio. She got a wave of sympathy in 2008 after the New Hampshire debate with Obama when she was asked why she was not as likable as her younger rival and Obama ungraciously chimed in, not even looking at her: "You're likable enough, Hillary." She went on to pull out New Hampshire after she choked up at a Portsmouth café, frustrated by spending years in the shadow of one Natural from Arkansas only to be suddenly eclipsed by another from Chicago.

Over the years, I have written about the duality in Hillary that disturbs even many Democrats. She has the bright, idealistic public service side but it is offset by a dark ends-justify-the-means side. She's confident and capable but she can also make decisions from a place of insecurity and paranoia. The Clintons swept into the White House on a populist platform that people who play by the rules should get ahead. But then they don't always deign to play by the rules.

They offer a Faustian deal and it's purple and black and yucky-looking: You want progressive policies for women? Ignore Bill's unseemly affair with a 22-year-old intern and his hiding behind the skirts of his top women cabinet officials who came out to defend his lies. Ignore the Clinton attack dogs' efforts to smear Monica Lewinsky as a loony stalker.

You want a Supreme Court that's not retrogressive? Ignore Hillary's greedy Goldman Sachs speeches and the tangled web of monetary self-interest between donors to the Clinton Foundation and people doing business with Hillary's State Department.

You want to stop the Neanderthal Trump and put the first woman in the White House? Then swallow her extremely careless handling of classified information.

After turning the White House into Motel 1600, with a revolving door for donors, she and Bill left Pennsylvania Avenue like grifters, taking a truckload of gifts—sofas, rugs, a table, chairs, a DVD player. They gave some items back and paid back $85,966 after people complained that their gifts had been intended for the permanent White House collection. As she left the White House, Senator-elect Clinton eluded the Senate gift ban by quickly scarfing up expensive gifts worth tens of thousands of dollars from wealthy Hollywood and New York supporters to appoint her Washington house.

As a top Clinton aide once astutely put it: "Hillary, though a Methodist, thinks of herself like an Episcopal bishop who deserves to live at the level of her wealthy parishioners in return for devoting her life to God and good works." Or as *The Onion* put it, her campaign slogan is "I deserve this."

What prompted Hillary to make three Goldman Sachs speeches for $675,000 on the cusp of a presidential campaign where the electorate was clearly in a pitchfork mood about bankers, after the Clintons had already earned $150 million in speaking fees and tens of millions more in book profits?

Trump mocks Hillary for a lack of stamina, but she has tremendous endurance. She has been on the national stage for a very long time, often defending herself or her husband, which must be draining. This is, after all, someone who has had Secret Service protection for 24 years. She admitted in one speech that she hadn't driven a car since 1996.

Tina Fey fought for Alec Baldwin for *30 Rock*, knowing that working with him would make her a better actress. But despite a lifetime spent with the two most gifted politicians of her era, Bill and Barack, Hillary never learned how to master the stagecraft of politics. "If you could just sit down and have a drink with her, you would love her," a former Clinton White House aide told me recently. Her boosters say that so often, to offset her guarded demeanor and distaste for the press, that it has become a punch line in our office: She's a hoot in private.

After waiting eight years for her delayed coronation, Hillary was barely able to fend off a 74-year-old Democratic socialist with a slim Senate record and a brusque demeanor. It must have been awful for her to lose all the excitement to usurpers twice, one a fresh face and rare talent, but one Bernie Sanders.

The Vermonter became an unlikely youth idol and money raiser on the Internet, attracting the young women who were expected to thrill to Hill. Clinton played Katy Perry and Taylor Swift at her relatively small, subdued campaign events, but most young women were feeling the Bern. Gloria Steinem told Bill Maher dismissively that girls were going to Bernie events merely to meet boys, and Madeleine Albright chastised young women who preferred Bernie as ungrateful for all she and other women had done. These comments drew sharp rebukes from young women, who correctly pointed out that moving beyond identity politics and feeling free to choose a candidate of either sex was a positive evolution, exactly what older feminists had fought for.

Multitudes of young women told interviewers that they weren't driven by a now-or-never feeling about a woman becoming president. They knew a woman would be president. They just weren't sure they wanted this woman. They agreed with Jon Stewart, who told David Axelrod on *The Axe Files* podcast that Hillary seems to be "a bright woman without the courage of her convictions because I'm not even sure what they are. . . . Maybe a real person doesn't exist underneath there."

Young people wanted to vote for someone they felt passionate about—and it was the old guy with the rumpled hair and crumpled suit railing against Big Money and offering a lot of free stuff.

As Olivia Sauer, an 18-year-old college freshman and Bernie supporter from Ames, Iowa, told the *Times* during the Iowa primary: "With Hillary, sometimes you get this feeling that all of her sentences are owned by someone."

Everyone questions Hillary's authenticity but no one questions her toughness, even neocons. She can pull the trigger. But does she know where to aim?

I would feel more confident in her judgment if she ever talked about acquiring wisdom from her stumbles on health care, Iraq and the lack of planning after the NATO-led intervention in Libya and dislodging of Muammar el-Qaddafi. (President Obama told Fox's Chris Wallace that this inadequate preparation was the worst mistake of his presidency.) Or if Hillary said she had learned anything from her misadventures hiring scummy strategists like Dick Morris and Mark Penn; her spendthrift, botched campaign in 2008; her outrageous homebrew server fiasco or her moneygrubbing.

Even President Obama poked fun at Hillary at the White House Correspondents' Dinner, saying: "If this material works well, I'm going to use it at Goldman Sachs next year, earn me some serious Tubmans."

Hillary apologizes only when backed into a corner, and even then conveys the attitude that she merely regrets being caught, not the actual mistake.

\* \* \*

This bumfuzzling race of 2016 will be remembered as the year politics utterly fused with entertainment and social media. As James Gleick, the author of *Chaos*, says, "Running for president is the new selfie."

There have long been elements of show business: Joe Kennedy purveying the glossy dream of the perfect American family, all thick hair and flashing white teeth and Hyannis Port and Newport mansions. And supporting Hollywood player Ronald Reagan turning the presidency into the leading-man role of the century.

But *The Apprentice* boss torqued up and dumbed down the presidential contest into the ultimate reality show. Trump is the Kim Kardashian of American politics, replacing substance with solipsism and issues debates with Twitter feuds, and showing a rare talent for grabbing the attention of an ADD nation round the clock as he tries to be Troll in Chief.

"Celebrity is the iron ore of our age," Howard Fineman told me. "It's the raw material that gives people platforms and power that they then look to use in some way. Before, presidents came to power through political or military accomplishment. Even Ronald Reagan had two terms as a governor. But we're entering a new age where social media gives this colossal megaphone to people who are famous. You're not a complete Hollywood person now unless you have a political cause."

In 2009, Desirée Rogers, President Obama's first social secretary, caught flak when she told *The Wall Street Journal* that she was in charge of promoting the Obama brand. David Axelrod got annoyed and told her that the president "is a person, not a product."

How quaint.

Trump is brazenly all about the brand, sporting his own clothing line on the trail, hawking the quality of Trump wines and Trump steaks and Trump vitamins and Trump buildings and Trump women. But renting out his name ended up whipsawing him. He spread his name too thin, without proper quality control. The accusations of fraud and con artistry at Trump University and Trump Institute were damaging, as was his insistence that the judge in the Trump University case, who was of Mexican descent, couldn't be fair because of Trump's call for the wall.

Hollywood, as William Goldman memorably said, is a place where nobody knows anything. Now Washington has become a place where everybody knows nobody knows anything.

Even the Nate Silver big-data experts, who boasted that they could predict races using math without regard to the human element, have been flummoxed and apologetic.

"The most surprising thing is how utterly irrelevant we all are in a way worse than we all feared," Jake Tapper, the anchor of CNN's *The Lead*, told me. "Over forty-five percent of the country could not care less what we find important, those standards needed to uphold a great democracy. We can tell them all we want whether or not it's appropriate to attack somebody's wife for not being hot or that it's not okay to attack somebody's father and replace conspiracy theories with facts. They've rejected not only you and me but Mitt Romney and Paul Ryan and everyone in the gang—big media, Wall Street, the Washington establishment. It's sobering."

Republican strategist Alex Castellanos concurs with a chuckle: "The powdered-wig crowd is having a hard time."

On the left and right, voters were pumped for revolutions. Many people think that a Hillary win will only delay the revolution for the Democrats, similar to the meltdown Republicans are going through.

"For all their faults, Bernie Sanders and Donald Trump ripped the scab off the system and showed it for what it was: a completely rigged system and not democratic at all," Matthew Dowd, the strategist who worked for W. and became disillusioned by the Iraq war, told me. "It looked like nobody was looking out for the average person." A few Democratic Party caucus sites in Iowa got decided by a coin toss.

"The voters sit there and trust and trust and trust, almost like a battered spouse," he said. "All of a sudden, they realized they were codependent and battered and they said, 'I'm done.'"

For many, the American dream—work hard and play by the rules and your life and your children's lives will get better—has curdled.

"Nobody trusts anybody," Meacham says. In polls, the number of people who believe that the federal government will do the right thing some or most of the time is at an all-time low.

"We're like *Downton Abbey*," *Politico*'s Glenn Thrush says. "The silverware still gets polished and we still wear fancy clothes. The edifice is still there but the infrastructure is collapsing."

*The Guardian* reported that "rage rooms" have opened across the country in cities where manufacturing jobs are vanishing, with people paying to shred a teddy bear or smash a TV with a baseball bat or lead pipe.

Now Trump is the baseball bat or lead pipe the working class can use to smash Washington. Hillary is attacking Trump about unsavory business practices, but Trump fans shrug that it takes a thief to catch a thief.

"We on the East Coast might think 'Get over it,'" Chuck Todd, the host of NBC's *Meet the Press*, told me. But he tries to channel how people feel outside the elitist bubble: "In the last ten years, we've told all these working-class people, 'Suck it up and be bilingual; suck it up and allow men to marry each other and women to marry each other even though you go to church and hear it is a sin; suck it up and salute a black president, and oh, by the way, that great job your parents had? You can't get it anymore.' Nobody knows what a middle class looks like anymore. What the hell is a gig economy? All this, while everyone else, including Bruce Jenner, is a protected, special class of citizen."

Our leaders and law enforcement agencies did not connect the dots that could have stopped the attacks on 9/11. With a lot of mumbo jumbo about WMDs, a nonexistent Saddam-Osama alliance and the known unknowns, the country was deceived into a bloody, costly war without end in Iraq by Bush 43, Dick Cheney, Donald Rumsfeld, Paul Wolfowitz and assorted neocons. Thirteen years later, American troops are still dying in Iraq. W. mountain biked as Katrina bore down on the Big Easy.

After 15 years in Afghanistan, President Obama announced in July that he could not keep his promise to extricate us from that war. Obama ran in 2008 promising to get us out of Iraq, Afghanistan and Gitmo. He's still working on all three.

The economy nearly tanked because of Wall Street greed and derivative shell games and none of the top bankers paid for it; indeed, some CEO bonuses are bigger than ever. Globalization gutted the working class and trade deals worked out better for multinational corporations than for many Americans, who watched helplessly as special interests paid Washington to let millions of jobs go overseas. The touted retraining for the gig economy never seems to gear up. "Is there anything to do when Nabisco moves jobs to Mexico except stop eating Oreos?" asked Tapper, who reported that, for all Trump's China and outsourcing bashing, Trump and Ivanka manufactured a lot of the clothing for their companies in China.

Ted Cruz tried to burn down the Capitol where he worked, seeking to turn Washington into his own personal Thunderdome. Mitch McConnell made it his life's work to thwart Obama at every turn. After eight years of an African American president who was expected to bridge the red/blue and white/black divides, the divisions by ideology and race have gotten worse.

\* \* \*

Obama's 2008 win was a vivid reflection of changing demographics, a moment for many to celebrate that America is no longer a country that will be run by a clique of white, Protestant men. But, as Thrush notes, Obama's "blackness was disruptive in a deep psychic way even for people who aren't overtly racist. There's a sense he doesn't look like the people on the coins."

Once Obama was not The One, once the 2008 tulip craze passed, once things got tough with obnoxious, obstructionist Republicans, Obama had no LBJ elbow grease or appetite for the fight. He didn't even want to go to the LBJ play *All the Way* on Broadway because he knew it would evoke the obvious negative comparison.

He made a rational decision on issues and then expected people to come around to his righteous point of view, lecturing them as the constitutional law professor he once was. As a top adviser to the president bemoaned, he'd "rather be right than win."

"The whole point of politics," Fineman says, "is to rope people who don't like you and oppose you into doing what you want."

But Obama was a proud and diffident debutant, a solitary cat who preferred to stay above the fray, even though politics is the fray. As Neera Tanden so vividly put it, "My analogy is that it's like becoming Bill Gates without liking computers." James Carville echoed that, telling me, "It's like if you found out that Peyton Manning didn't like to play football."

The president is a decent man with an exemplary family and no personal shadows, a welcome relief from the Clinton ethical laxity and conjugal mishegoss. But Obama was too cool for school. Americans elected him because they had a hunger for dramatic change, while the first black president mistakenly assumed he was all the change they could handle.

When he was running in 2008, Obama promised to make government "cool" again. But it just became more dysfunctional. He promised to get us out of Middle East chaos, but we are in just as much quicksand as ever. He is transformational simply because of who he is—and that's no small thing.

After he started with a bang—pushing through an economic stimulus package and then enacting his health-care initiative without a single Republican vote—Obama ended up preferring to be careful and solitary, making his mark with executive orders and moves he could do on his own, like deals with Cuba and Iran and, on climate change, with China.

The *Times*'s Michael Shear wrote a feature this summer about how President Obama is a night owl who likes to read, work and watch ESPN alone after an early dinner with his family. He stays up until the wee hours but only allows himself one treat at night: seven lightly salted almonds. He seems eager to be done with the Oval, joking that after all the thorny decisions, he wants to open a shack in Hawaii stocked with T-shirts in one color (white) and one size (medium).

One of the most eloquent presidential candidates ever seemed to lose the narrative thread and empathetic voice that got him into the Oval Office in 2008 with such a slender résumé and exotic name.

During the 2012 reelection bid, Obama delegated selling his agenda to the man who had once disdained him, Bill Clinton, naming him "Secretary of Explaining Stuff." The president scorned salesmanship and easy emotion and had a hard time articulating and soothing American jitters on terrorism and racial tensions. He complained privately that people should not get so alarmed because you were more likely to die from a lightning strike or a fall in the bathtub than be killed in a terrorist attack.

"Obama is an arch-pragmatist who will tell you that the spot on your lung will kill you in two weeks," Thrush says.

His mother was an anthropologist and there was a lot of that in Obama, observing at a remove. "There's no doubt there's a theatrical nature to the presidency that he resists," Axelrod told *Businessweek* about his old boss. "Sometimes he can be negligent in the symbolism." Obama conceded this to Chuck Todd, saying, "It's not something that always comes naturally to me."

The president was steely about killing Osama bin Laden and raining drones. In some ways the detached, sleek, precisely targeted Obama recalls a drone. But he seemed more comfortable as the Nobel Peace Prize–winning global citizen than the forceful American leader in the world. And that laid the groundwork for Trump, who mined the feeling that America wasn't tough enough and wasn't taking what's ours.

Yet Obama's approval ratings rose above 50 percent as people watched the 2016 mudfest.

"The squalid nature of the campaign has lifted him up in people's eyes," Axelrod told me. "And he's been very much going his own way, speaking his mind, doing things he wanted to pursue, acting freer and that allowed people to reconnect with the guy they elected in the first place."

* * *

When this campaign started, I assumed that I would be covering two "Just Trust Us" dynasties who, as Martin O'Malley said, had been passing the crown back and forth for decades.

But like Ramsay Bolton, Trump shockingly and quickly flayed Jeb Bush. "And low energy, that term just hit, it's amazing," Trump boasted to me, sounding as feral as the *Game of Thrones* fiend. "It was over. That thing, that was a one-day kill. Words are beautiful."

It turned out that Jeb, the Good Son who was designated as the presidential prospect in the family, was introverted and rusty from being out of politics for so long. And he did not have W.'s sharp political instincts. He did not comprehend the bristling public mood and was finished almost before he started when he argued that illegal immigrants come to the United States out of "an act of love" and pleaded with one tepid audience in New Hampshire, "Please clap."

With House Bush out of the *Game of Thrones*—until George P. runs against Chelsea—I wanted to do some fresh reporting on the family I'd covered for 32 years. When I started covering Bush senior's White House, he came across like P. G. Wodehouse's Bertie Wooster, and I despaired, wishing I had a more complicated, Shakespearean family to cover.

But when his son was elected and the country was scarred by 9/11, the Bush family story grew more complicated, and parlous. Just as with the Clintons and health care, the public welfare began to be affected—and undermined—by family dynamics.

I talked to top advisers to both Bushes and sifted through the letters Poppy Bush sent me over the decades-long expanse of what he jokingly calls "our love-hate relationship." We had our differences, but as a president he was a beacon of civility and bipartisanship in a world where those qualities are disturbingly rare. I tried to do a definitive essay on the braiding of love and competition between the father-and-son presidents that led inexorably—and Oedipally—to the invasion of Iraq, which W. biographer Jean Edward Smith calls "easily the worst foreign policy decision ever made by an American president."

\*　　\*　　\*

When I started working on presidential politics, I worried that the biggest story I would cover was that George Bush Sr. showered with his spaniel, Millie. Now I worry that I am living through so much amazing history, I'll never be able to record it all. (If the country is lucky, the father-and-son presidency won't be followed by a husband-and-wife impeachment—despite what some Republicans seething about Hillary's email transgressions are muttering.)

Sometimes voting, as Samuel Johnson said of second marriages, can seem like the triumph of hope over experience. Hopefully, this book can entertain and illuminate, serving as a guide for desperate voters in a year when more Americans than ever are disturbed and flummoxed by their choices.

It seems strange, but even though we spend years exploring every aspect of presidential candidates, holding them up to the light at every angle, asking what kind of ice cream they eat and what TV shows they watch and sometimes even what underwear they prefer, we can never really know what kind of president they will be. "You never can tell what's going to happen to a man until he gets to a place of responsibility," Harry Truman said after his presidency. "You just can't tell in advance." Or as the former British prime minister Harold Macmillan once said when asked what disrupted his best-laid plans: "Events, dear boy, events." The capacity for perverse and self-destructive behavior among alphas is boundless and mind-boggling. Leaders are often confronted by events that were never part of the campaign conversation. And sometimes presidents are borne back ceaselessly into the past.

W. promised a humble foreign policy. Obama promised to unite red and blue and extricate us from the Middle East. Just at the moment when the winner of the White House should feel most ratified by the awesome prize of the job, the awesome responsibility of the job intensifies insecurities and pathologies.

Arthur Schlesinger Jr., the historian and JFK aide, suggested in his memoirs that several modern presidents were mentally unbalanced and that top aides to LBJ debated whether the president was clinically paranoid or manic-depressive. Alex Thompson reported in *Politico* that recently released documents reveal that Kennedy and Nixon clandestinely kept psychotropic drugs in their medicine cabinets. Unlike on *The West Wing*, there is no White House shrink, and as Schlesinger wrote, there is no procedure in the Constitution "for dealing with nuts."

Then, on top of any gremlins that get exacerbated by living in the White House, which has been described as so disorienting to work in that it's like being on a submarine, history slaps the chief executive with wind-shear shocks such as the Bay of Pigs, Cuban Missile Crisis, the Iranian hostages, 9/11, Katrina and mass shootings, and the president either rises to the occasion or drags the country down. Either the president gets the best of those gremlins or they haunt us.

Chasing nine presidential campaigns has made me realize the complexities of predicting who will be a good president. President Obama promotes Hillary on the trail by saying "there has never been any man or woman more qualified for this office." But as we learned with Nixon and Kissinger, and later with Cheney and Rumsfeld, the longest résumés in the world and decades of service in top jobs do not ensure that you won't cause disaster. Absolute power blinds. And just as getting the job at a more tender age, as with JFK and W., can lead to tyro errors, sometimes being steeped in the past can fog your thinking or leave you with scores to settle.

We can mine the past for prologue, starting with Hillary Clinton and Donald Trump on the trail back in the '90s, and tracing their progress—sometimes soaring and sometimes stumbling—as they reach the pinnacles of their parties. We can follow the triumph, tragedy and ultimate fall of the House of Bush.

One of Poppy Bush's winning qualities was that he was a magic aficionado. Shortly before his inauguration, the president-elect showed off his bag of tricks, including a crystal ball with a disembodied voice that gave Delphic answers to questions such as queries about tax increases: "The images are cloudy. Have someone else ask."

The crystal ball for presidents is always cloudy given history's tricks. But because the politicians on these pages have shaped, and will shape, the national character, we must try to fathom their characters. And then we must hope that the worst of the job brings out the best in our next president.

# 1

# "Here's the beauty of me."

# Trump the Disrupter

I've been hesitant to start writing about Donald Trump.

I was worried that if I wrote something that made him mad, he would send out one of his midnight mordant tweets about me, something like "She started as a 3. Now she's a 1."

I'd be upset, of course. And relieved that I wasn't a 0. But I've known Trump a long time. That's how he talks about women. I remember when he sadly broke the news that Heidi Klum was no longer a 10.

He offered this clinical breakdown about Halle Berry to Howard Stern: "From the midsection to the shoulders, she's a 10. The face is a solid 8. And the legs are maybe a little bit less than that."

As he once told me: "Certain guys tell me they want women of substance, not beautiful models. It just means they can't get beautiful models."

So when Fox News's Megyn Kelly grilled Trump during the Republican debate, asking him about his sometimes vicious Twitter account and noting, "You've called women you don't like 'fat pigs,' 'dogs,' 'slobs' and 'disgusting animals,'" I knew what the glamorous former litigator was up to.

It was Tom Cruise taunting Jack Nicholson in *A Few Good*

*Men.* Kelly was trying to get Trump to lash out in a misogynist way. But he restrained himself in the hall, staying away from the slob-to-supermodel rating system he likes to use. He showed his irritation later, tweeting that the anchor "bombed" and was "totally overrated" and "angry," and he retweeted a post calling her a "bimbo."

There was something amusing about Fox News, which is a daily Miss Universe pageant, chock-a-block with glossy beauties as anchors, reporters and even "experts," giving The Donald a hard time about focusing on women's looks.

I came away from the debate thinking three things: Roger Ailes is a television genius. It's no coincidence that he presided over the ninth-most-viewed show ever on cable, after college football, with the extra kick of eclipsing his nemesis Jon Stewart's big finale.

Kelly has a lot of Tim Russert in her: She knows how to set up mesmerizing gunfights at the O.K. Corral, loaded for a follow-up after every salvo.

And Trump is, as always, the gleefully offensive and immensely entertaining high-chair king in the Great American Food Fight. He is, as Kurt Andersen wrote in 2006, "our 21st-century reincarnation of P. T. Barnum and Diamond Jim Brady, John Gotti minus the criminal organization, the only white New Yorker who lives as large as the blingiest, dissiest rapper—de trop personified."

The novelist Walter Kirn tweeted post-debate: "Trump is simply channeling the bruised petty enraged narcissism that is the natural condition of Selfie Nation." After all, as James Gleick has tweeted, "Running for president is the new selfie."

I enjoy Trump's hyperbolic, un-PC flights because there are too few operatic characters in the world. I think of him as a toon. He's just drawn that way. And his Frank Sinatra lingo about women aside, he always treated me courteously and professionally.

Back in 1999, when he was flirting with a presidential run, I asked the ladies' man how he would do with the women's vote.

"I might do badly," he said with a smile. "They know me better than anybody else. Women are much tougher and more calculating than men. I relate better to women."

This campaign is more raw and rude than usual, reflecting the off-with-their-heads Twitter sensibility. But it can not only be wickedly fun but wildly useful to have an id agitating amid the superegos.

After covering nine presidential races, I have concluded that it is really hard to know who you're electing—even after attenuated campaigns with an absurd amount of exposure for candidates.

That's because you can't foresee what crises will crop up, or what gremlins of insecurity and perversity the White House will inevitably elicit in presidential psyches.

You can have a candidate like W., after sincerely telling us he will have a "humble" foreign policy, proceed to stumble jejunely into decades-long wars in the Middle East. You can have a charming newcomer like Barack Obama, ascending like a political Pegasus, who loses altitude because it turns out he disdains politics.

It's always a pig in a poke. So why not a pig who pokes?

It will cause winces and grimaces at times and Trump can go badly astray, as he did with the president's birth certificate. His jibes at women may hurt the Republican Party with some women.

His policy ideas are ripped from the gut instead of the head. Still, he can be a catalyst, challenging his rivals where they need to be challenged and smoking them out, ripping off the facades they've constructed with their larcenous image makers. Trump can pierce the trompe l'oeil illusions, starting with Jeb's defense of his brother's smashing the family station wagon into the globe.

Consider how Trump yanked back the curtain Thursday night explaining how financial quid pro quos warp the political system.

"Well, I'll tell you what, with Hillary Clinton, I said be at my wedding and she came to my wedding," he said. "You know why? She had no choice because I gave. I gave to a foundation that, frankly, that foundation is supposed to do good. I didn't know her money would be used on private jets going all over the world."

Sometimes you need a showman in the show.

## Postscript

After this column went to press Friday night, Trump had his full-blown Jack Nicholson "You need me on that wall" meltdown over Kelly. He went on CNN and complained about her "ridiculous" questions, telling Don Lemon that "You could see there was blood coming out of her eyes, blood coming out of her wherever."

Erick Erickson, who has been criticized himself for insensitivity toward women, quickly disinvited Trump from a gig at the RedState Gathering, inviting Kelly instead, and blogging "I just don't want someone on stage who gets a hostile question from a lady and his first inclination is to imply it was hormonal."

Trump made a stab at defending himself in a tweet, indicating that he had meant blood might also come out of Kelly's nose. He also huffily tweeted about "so many 'politically correct' fools in our country."

In a post headlined "Turns out Megyn packs kryptonite," *Politico*'s Mike Allen noted that Trump's deputy, Michael Cohen, retweeted a tweet (from an account called "surfersfortrump") with the hashtag "boycottmegynkelly" and the message "we can gut her."

Even in opéra bouffe, showmen can get thrown out of the show if they cross certain boorish lines. Trump just can't stop himself. Or doesn't want to. As Carly Fiorina tweeted: "Mr. Trump: There. Is. No. Excuse." Congratulating his Fox debate anchors in a tweet, Rupert Murdoch had some choice words for his billionaire frenemy: "Friend Donald has to learn this is public life."

# Introducing Donald Trump, Diplomat

Donald Trump gives me his Grumpy Cat look.

I'm sitting in his office in Trump Tower high above Fifth Avenue, next to a wall plastered with framed magazine covers giving the effect of an infinity mirror, his face endlessly multiplying—including an old *Playboy* with the real estate mogul slyly smiling next to a comely bunny.

"I could put up forty of those walls," he says. "I have covers in warehouses. It's crazy."

I'm trying to tell the freshly minted pol that Megyn Kelly had the right to ask him a question in the debate on how he talks about women, and that she should be tough on the front-runner.

He's not buying it. In fact, in his stubborn "I win, you lose" way, he has an assistant come over to hand me a printout of Gabriel Sherman's *New York* magazine piece headlined "How Roger Ailes Picked Trump, and Fox News' Audience, Over Megyn Kelly."

But the 69-year-old is trying hard not to bare his claws at any women right now. His wife, Melania, and his daughter Ivanka have told him they don't want him to come across as a misogynist when they don't see him that way.

"I have many women executives and they are paid at least as much as the men," he said. "I find women to be amazing."

The billionaire braggart known for saying unfiltered things is trying to be diplomatic. Sort of.

It has suddenly hit Trump that he's leading the Republican field in a race where many candidates, including the two joyless presumptive nominees, are sputtering. He's got the party by the tail—still a punch line but not a joke.

The *Wall Street Journal* huffed that Trump's appeal was "attitude, not substance," and the nascent candidate is still figuring out the pesky little details, like staff and issues, dreaming up his own astringent campaign ads for Instagram on ISIS and China.

The other candidates, he says, "have pollsters; they pay these guys $200,000 a month to tell them, 'Don't say this, don't say that, you use the wrong word, you shouldn't put a comma here.' I don't want any of that. I have a nice staff, but no one tells me what to say. I go by my heart. The combination of heart and brain. When Hillary gets up there she reads and then goes away for three days."

As he headed off this weekend to see the butter cow in Iowa—"Iowa is very clean. It's not like a lot of places where you and I would go, like New York City"—Trump is puzzling over a conundrum: How does he curb the merciless heckler side of himself, the side that has won over voters who think he's a refreshing truth teller, so that he can seem refined enough to win over voters who think he's crude and cartoonish?

How does he tone it down when he's proud of his outrageous persona, his fiery wee-hours Twitter arrows and campaign "gusto," and gratified by the way he can survive dissing John McCain and rating Heidi Klum when that would be a death knell for someone like Scott Walker?

"Sometimes I do go a little bit far," he allowed, adding, after a moment: "Heidi Klum. Sadly, she's no longer a 10."

He could act more refined, he muses over spaghetti and meatballs, with a side of pulled pork, in the Trump Tower restaurant, as fans gawk and wait for selfies, but that would make for a boring lunch.

He relishes giving me a play-by-play of the Kelly and Rosie O'Donnell donnybrooks as though he's talking about Pacquiao-Mayweather. He beams with pride when he talks about Rush Limbaugh marveling about how much "incoming" he can take.

"I'm a counterpuncher," he said. "I can't hit people who don't hit me. Maybe that's my weakness. Perry started it. Lindsey Graham started it. This moron Rand Paul just started it because he is mired in twelfth place and he's a U.S. senator."

He said Rosie was a bully and the only way to beat bullies is to smack them in the nose.

So he doesn't think of himself as a bully?

He looks hurt. "Oh, no, the opposite," he said. "In fact, I'll go a step further. The way to do best with me is to be really nice to me."

I mention that George Will has written a column demanding that Republican leaders renounce Trump as a cynical opportunist "deranged by egotism."

"So George Will came to Mar-a-Lago ten years ago and made a speech," Trump said. "I refused to go because he's a boring person." Trump said he stayed on the patio and had dinner and that offended Will. (Will says he has "other and better reasons for thinking it might not be altogether wise to entrust him with the nation's nuclear arsenal.")

I tell Trump that he has transcended the level of narcissism common in a profession full of narcissists. He is, after all, wearing a red tie with a label by "a wonderful guy named Trump," as he wryly puts it, with his Brioni suit. In the latest *Time*, Jeffrey Kluger, the author of *The Narcissist Next Door*, said "people at ease inside their skin just don't behave the way Trump does."

I ask if he was always like this, boasting that he had the best baby food and the best high chair?

"Honestly, I don't think people change that much," Trump said. "I'm a solid, stable person." Knocking on the wooden restaurant wall, he added: "I am a man of great achievement. I win, Maureen, I always win. Knock on wood. I win. It's what I do. I beat people. I win."

No insecurities?

"I don't know how you would define insecurity as it pertains to me," he replies.

He does have a germ phobia and carries packs of germicidal disposable wipes. He describes how a man came out of a restaurant bathroom the other night with wet hands wanting to clasp his hand. "So what do I do?" Trump asked. "I don't eat. That's OK."

I note that many people still think his bid is more runaway Macy's Thanksgiving Day balloon than a run on meaningful issues.

He says it's real, noting: "I was with Carl Icahn yesterday and I said, 'Carl, if I get this thing you are going to represent me on China. Maybe I'll even give you China and Japan.' You know, the money they are ripping from us."

He is trying to be a bit more low-key. He says he thought it would be "cool" not to put his name on some of his "Make America Great Again" caps. But it's hard to imagine Trump implementing impulse control.

What if, I ask him, he fires off a nuclear tweet at Vladimir Putin insulting his pecs or Kim Jong-un calling him a "fat little slob"?

"I'll only do it for a purpose," he said. "I have total control. I will get along great with these people. I'm a dealmaker. I'm the best dealmaker there is."

How will he deal with Carly Fiorina, who is being hailed as the one to slay Trump after she excoriated him, interpreting his blood "wherever" remark as being about Kelly's period?

"Carly has to be a little bit careful," he warned.

What if he bursts into Trumpian analysis of how Carly and Hillary look?

"Oh, I would never talk about their looks," he replied primly. He did, however, imitate how his ears felt ("Eeeeeeeeee") when he hears Carly's "staccato bing, bing, bing" voice and delivery.

How important are women's looks to him?

He said he has found looks can hold you back, that "some of the great-looking men and women, they've never had a problem getting a date, they've never had a problem in life, now they get into a world which is a cruel place and they don't fight as hard."

I ask Trump if he can at least admit that President Obama was born in this country.

The Grumpy Cat face comes back. "No comment," he murmurs.

# Donald Trump Struts
# His Own Pageant

Some blondes have all the fun.

As Hillary Clinton and Jeb Bush get more testy, Donald Trump gets more chesty. And more blond.

It's mind-boggling to contemplate a President Trump trying to make peace between North and South Korea, even as we watch the pugnacious Candidate Trump trolling poor Jeb on Twitter and predicting that poor Hillary would have to run the country from Leavenworth.

But, as Trump would say, deal with it.

The pol who refused to identify himself as a pol on his jury duty questionnaire has utterly scrambled American politics. And he has trademarked the phrase "Make America Great Again."

"I was surprised it was available," he told me.

Certainly, Trump could explode at any moment in a fiery orange ball. But meanwhile, he has exploded the hoary conventions, money-grubbing advisers and fund-raising excesses of the presidential campaign, turning everything upside down, inside out, into sauerkraut.

It is a fable conjured up in several classic movies: A magnetic, libidinous visitor shows up and insinuates himself into the lives of a bourgeois family. The free spirit leaves, but only after transforming the hidebound family, so that none of them can see themselves the same way again.

That is the profound metamorphosis Trump has wrought on the race. The Don Rickles of reality shows is weirdly bringing some reality to the presidential patty-cake.

The Donald's strange pompadour and Hillary's strange server have eclipsed all the usual primary permutations.

Because Trump is so loud, omnipresent, multiplatform and cutting, he's shaping the perception of the other candidates. Once he blurts out the obvious—Jeb is low energy, Hillary is shifty, Mitt choked—some voters nod their heads and start to see his targets in that unflattering light as well.

Trump has trapped his Republican rivals into agreeing with his red-meat opinions on immigration or attacking him, neither of which are good options. Trump bluntness only works for Trump, and getting into a scrap with him is like being tossed into a bag of badgers.

Mike Murphy, the chief strategist of Jeb's super PAC, went on the record in a *Washington Post* story with a veiled message to Jeb to stop taunting Trump.

"Trump is, frankly, other people's problem," Murphy said.

Jeb stooped to conquer Trump, echoing his use of the phrase "anchor baby," only to have the news spilled that Jeb had co-chaired a group that advised politicians not to say "anchor baby."

The real estate developer has turned a fetish for the biggest and the best—in everything from dinner rolls to skyscrapers—into a presidential vision for "the silent majority." He's tapped into a hunger among those who want to believe that America is not a shrinking, stumbling power passed like a pepper mill between two entitled families.

Indeed, in interviews, voters who like Trump often use an anatomical variation on the word brass.

The shame spiral and money pit that followed the false Iraq narrative W. and Dick Cheney put into play to remove the strongman Saddam Hussein—the identity crisis that came with the knowledge that America can no longer whip or outfox anybody—has led many Americans to want a strongman.

"Trump is the proverbial strongman," David Axelrod says. "There's no one more opposite to Obama. Bush had been impulsive and reckless, so voters wanted someone who was thoughtful and deliberative. Now they've had enough of gray and they want to go back to black and white, and that's Trump. He knows nothing else."

It's mesmerizing to watch Trump try to turn himself into a real candidate in real time.

He was mocked when he said that he got his national security advice from watching "the shows" on TV. But voters know that top diplomats, spooks and generals led presidents down the tragic paths to the Bay of Pigs, Vietnam and Iraq. Jeb Bush gets his advice from Paul Wolfowitz, who naïvely bollixed up Iraq and gave us ISIS. And Hillary and top Republicans say they get valued counsel from Henry Kissinger, who advised Nixon to prolong the Vietnam War for political reasons even though he thought it might be unwinnable.

The neophyte pol belatedly realized that he could not glide past the horror of two Boston thugs accused of laughingly beating a homeless Hispanic with a pole and peeing on him in Trump's name.

He lives beyond parody. There's very little difference between the old Darrell Hammond duck-lipped impersonation of the Trumpster and Trump, the presidential candidate.

Both dwell on how "huge" and "big" his projects are and how "great" his ratings are and how much square footage he has.

(Unlike the Hammond impersonation and Trump's turn as *SNL*

host, the presidential candidate shies away from boasting about hot women.)

There is nothing that excites Trump the candidate more than crowing that he has a great big crowd and Jeb has a teeny-weeny crowd. He sounded orgasmic as he described to the New Hampshire town hall that his Alabama event this weekend had to be moved from a room that held 1,000 to a room that held 2,000 to a convention center to a stadium.

So Trump should appreciate the task ahead: It's huge.

As Axelrod puts it: "In a parlance Trump would appreciate: We're still in the swimsuit competition. It gets harder in the talent rounds."

# Bush and Clinton Dynasties Hit Trump Bump

Pity Poppy.

When I went down to Houston a few years ago to eat pizza with the former president, he was his usual gracious self, speaking fondly about President Obama and his new pal Bill Clinton.

But there was one person who got dismissed with a brusque obscenity: Donald Trump.

It was at the height of Trump's birther madness and Bush was disgusted by it.

So I can only imagine 41's dismay and disbelief—and acid flashbacks to spoiler Ross Perot—now that Trump has popped up to block the path of the son who Poppy desperately wants to see as 45, restoring the family name after 43's spiral.

The New York wheeler-dealer, who held a fund-raiser at his Trump Tower apartment for gubernatorial candidate Jeb at Poppy's request back in 1997, has had a devastating and disorienting effect on Jeb's presidential candidacy.

The Trumpster has suckered Jeb! into scraps that have ended up backfiring on Jeb and elevating Trump. And he has trumpeted a lethargic, insubstantial image of Jeb that is at odds with the perky red "Jeb!" campaign logo.

In a *Washington Post* story last week about the fractious relationship, Trump ridiculed Jeb's investment banking work at Lehman Brothers and later Barclays. Trump suggested that the millions Jeb was paid were a reward for steering Florida state funds to Lehman. "Why would you pay a man $1.3 million a year for a no-show job at Lehman Brothers—which, when it failed, almost took the world with it?" Trump asked.

In a bank shot, Trump dragged in the Democratic front-runner, noting, "That's a Hillary Clinton kind of situation."

It's deeply weird, but the jeering billionaire reality star seems authentic to many Americans. Trump is a manifestation of national disgust—with the money that consumed politics, with the dysfunctional, artificial status quo and with the turgid return to a Bush-Clinton race, with a less adept Bush and Clinton.

"The prospect of Hillary and Jeb as the nominees created a huge opening for something like this," said former W. strategist Matthew Dowd. "The American public looked at it and said, 'I do not want that.'"

Dowd said Friday that everyone should stop being in denial and start accepting that Trump could be the nominee.

"Do I think that Trump should be president?" Dowd asked. "No. Do I think he can be the badly needed match that burns down the status quo? Yes. Do I think he could precipitate an advent of a real third party? Yes."

He thinks the other candidates don't know how to deal with Trump. "They should treat him like an alien visitor," he said, "and, like judo, use his own weight—in this case, his self-absorption and hair-trigger reactions—against him. He doesn't care if you say he's not a real conservative."

Trump's "gusto," as he likes to call it, has thrown into sharper relief the grinding-it-out, impatient entitlement, the overthinking and overcorrecting of Jeb and Hillary.

Both campaign like they are owed, not because of their great national achievements, but because of their byzantine family dynamics.

Jeb feels he is owed because his brother sneaked in and snatched the presidency that his parents had designated for the Good Son, and because he was pressured to help W. purloin Florida in 2000.

And Hillary feels she is owed because she moved to Arkansas and then stuck it out with Bill through an anachronistic first lady job and Monica; because she was a team player and bided her time in the Senate and as secretary of state; because a whippersnapper named Barack sneaked in and snatched the presidency that should have been hers.

Funnily enough, the biggest narcissist in the race—and possibly the universe—has the one slogan that refers to the desires of voters: "Make America Great Again!" Hillary has "Hillary" with an arrow pointing at it. And Jeb has "Jeb!" with an exclamation point that represents the only fizz in his campaign.

Each one of this trio has a dilemma.

Because she is seen as domineering and distant, Hillary is most popular—and becomes most human—when she is brushed back. When she is pushed against the wall, she gets better. But how can she win if she can only convey authenticity when she is losing?

She is so coiled about losing again—carrying her front-runner status around like a Fabergé egg—that she screws up and starts losing. Her server, meant to shield her image and protect her from investigation, ends up sparking an investigation and damaging her image.

Jeb has to avoid the towel-snapping tone of his brother, because that overcompensating testosterone led to tragedy. But how does he convey strength to voters fretting that America is weak and prevent Trump from painting him as a milquetoast?

Trump knows he has a dilemma as well. His hyperbolic style and instinct for the jugular have propelled him to the front of the pack—a fact that has stunned even him. But how does he keep the colored lights going while conveying requisite dignity?

Even Joe Biden, padding around the edge of the campaign, has a dilemma: How does he honor the wish of his late son, Beau, to run when the death of Beau has left him so depleted he may not be able to run?

Matt Dowd thinks Biden would do well in this field: "Trump's the only one who can make Biden seem disciplined."

# Here's the Beauty of Trump

The White House has a strange, mind-warping effect on its occupants.

Presidents are exalted and fawned over. Their every whim is indulged and their image is endlessly and lovingly replicated on every wall. Reaching the pinnacle of power, raised up on the shoulders of Americans to the highest office often has the perverse consequence of making presidents more paranoid, introverted, insecure, reckless or downright nuts.

So what would happen if Donald Trump, a clinical narcissist with a thin skin, touchy temperament and taste for flattery, got into the Oval Office?

I call Trump to tell him my fears. Given that he already likes to start sentences, "Here's the beauty of me," wouldn't we be risking a narcissistic explosion at 1600 Pennsylvania Avenue?

I remind him that Dick Cheney and Donald Rumsfeld could manipulate W. into the Iraq invasion because they played on W.'s fear of being labeled a wimp, as his father had been. I note that when Vladimir Putin called Trump "an outstanding and talented personality," Trump was so impressed that he called the ruthless former KGB officer "highly respected within his own country and beyond."

So, I ask him, couldn't people manipulate you based on your ego? Given that you get easily swayed by what people say about you, pro and con, wouldn't you be malleable?

"I am malleable," Trump said, taking it as a compliment, more like I've called him flexible. He sounds sleepy, calling at 7 a.m. Friday from his Versailles-like Fifth Avenue penthouse, where he went for a nap after his veterans event in Des Moines Thursday night, before returning to New Hampshire and Iowa. He is still so new at politics that he coyly uses the phrase "being on the trail, as they say."

He says about his chances in Iowa that he's a good "closer": "Even in golf, I've won a lot of club championships that way. Closing is not an easy thing."

He rejects the idea that he's too easily swayed by compliments or slights, too easily prone to pouts and feuds.

"Putin said Donald Trump was absolutely brilliant and would win the election," he said. "My rival wanted me to disavow it. The head of Russia calls me brilliant and you want me to disavow it? What are you smoking?"

Trump is a Yugely exaggerated version of us all. We like the people who like us and don't like the people who don't. But as he says, he's got the microphone to punish the people who, in his view, act like "dirty" dogs.

I ask how he could ever be president given his insane—and sometimes hilarious—fusillade of insults online and off. How on earth could you run the country that way? "I'm the king of Palm Beach," he replied, which at first sounds like a non sequitur. But then he explains that when he's at Mar-a-Lago he gets along great with all the fancy, Waspy Palm Beach society women at charity balls, the Mrs. Hetherington III types. "I leave and they say, 'He's the most politically correct young man we've ever seen.'" At the same time, he says, he gets along great with construction workers.

So he is claiming that he knows how to act properly and flexibly when he needs to. But right now, he doesn't need to, so he goes back to bragging and insulting.

Using his usual ego arithmetic, he calculates that his gamble to skip the debate on Fox News and throw together a veterans fund-raising rally nearby has worked out great. He says it made over $6 million—money instantly ponied up by him, his business partners and golf buddies. And he boasts that he had more cameras at his event and a higher number of journalists.

"We had 400," he said. "They had 350."

Who knows? Trump tosses out numbers with the same gleeful abandon as John Iselin, the ambitious senator running for president on an anti-Communist platform in *The Manchurian Candidate*.

Maybe because Trump is so easily aggrieved himself, he has bonded with legions of aggrieved Americans. While others cast him as a bully, Trump cast himself Friday at a New Hampshire rally, with an Adele soundtrack, as a tender soul trying for self-actualization. "When somebody doesn't treat you properly," he said, talking about Fox News, "you gotta be tough, you gotta be strong. You can't let them push you around."

The prolix plutocrat told me he tried to watch some of the debate after his event. "Without Trump, the debate is boring," he said. "Everything became about Jeb." And you know he thinks that's boring. "I fell asleep."

I note that Fox's Charles Krauthammer told the moderator Megyn Kelly that it was a relief to hear a palaver that was not full of ad hominem and insults.

"He's a moron," Trump says.

And certainly the candidates were relieved not to have Trump coiled like a cobra, with resting bitch face, looking for the right moment to spew venom. Jeb seemed comfortable for the first time with no Trump there "to steal his lunch money," as Fox News's Chris Stirewalt put it.

I ask what he thought of Ted Cruz mimicking him at the start of the debate, saying, "Everyone on this stage is stupid, fat and ugly, and Ben, you're a terrible surgeon." Trump demurs about Carson: "I never said he was a bad doctor. I just said he was not as good as people thought."

Did he notice that Kelly was very tough on all the other candidates, too, I ask. Shouldn't he stop using words in tweets and retweets like "bimbo" and "lightweight" about Kelly and stop retweeting pictures of her in provocative glamour shots or risk losing the support of some women? After all, his own wife, Melania, was a model who did those kinds of shots.

"Megyn's a broadcaster," he replied briskly.

Wouldn't it be smarter to move beyond this feud? "I'm really rich and successful," he replied. "I don't have to make up with everyone."

I tell him that Newt Gingrich, who has praised him in the past, told Bill O'Reilly that people want to assess how stable a president will be when hit with crises, and Trump's petulance about an admittedly juvenile Fox news release could "shrink" him. "Newt said that?" Trump said, sounding hurt.

He's a very sensitive guy, for a guy who can be very insensitive.

# Chickens, Home to Roost

Here's why the Trump campaign is wicked fun:

I watched Donald Trump in New York for decades, as a bachelor swanning, a party fixture mingling, a master of bling and bluster.

I went with him on his art-filled plane in 1999 as he dipped his toe in the presidential pool and saw him shyly approach his first political rope line, even as he bragged that other candidates didn't draw as many cameras or have a supermodel by their side.

So I can assure you of two things. No one is more shocked at how far, how fast, Trump has come than Trump.

Watching him morph into a pol in real time and wriggle away from the junior-varsity GOP chuckleheads trying to tackle him is hypnotic. He's like the blond alien in the 1995 movie *Species*, who mutates from ova to adult in months, regenerating and reconfiguring at warp speed to escape the establishment, kill everyone in sight and eliminate the human race.

The other thing I know is that Trump really wants to be president. It isn't a joke anymore. People who are told that they should be president get infected. The less qualified and prepared they are, like Dan Quayle and W., the less they worry. And the more qualified and prepared they are, like Colin Powell and Mario Cuomo, the more they can tie themselves in Jesuitical knots.

The most enjoyable thing about the Trump phenomenon has been watching him make monkeys out of a lot of people who had it coming.

Marco Rubio, a frothy focus-grouped concoction whose main qualifications to be president consist of a nice smile and an easy wit, has been mocking Trump as a con man.

Real estate developers are con men by nature, trying to get what they want at the lowest price and sell it at the highest price, over-promising how great it's going to be.

As Maria Konnikova, the author of *The Confidence Game*, notes, con men are created by the yearning of their marks "to believe in something that gives life meaning.... Their genius lies in figuring out what, precisely, it is we want, and how they can present themselves as the perfect vehicle for delivering on that desire."

It's delicious watching the neocon men who tricked the country and gulled the naïve W. into the Iraq invasion go ballistic trying to stop the Gotham con man.

Bill Kristol of *The Weekly Standard* wrote an outraged column about why there wasn't more outrage at Trump, who correctly pointed out that Americans were deceived into a catastrophic war.

Kristol, the midwife to three debacles—Dan Quayle, Iraq and Sarah Palin—solicited suggestions for the name of the new party that Republicans will have to start if Trump secures the nomination. How about "Losers"?

Eliot Cohen, a former W. State Department official who pushed to "liberate" Iraq, said Trump would be "an unmitigated disaster for American foreign policy." And Robert Kagan, who backed the Iraq war, said "the only choice will be to vote for Hillary Clinton." Max Boot concurred.

It's amazing, having been tainted by the worst foreign policy disaster in American history, that the Republican national security intelligentsia would unite against a Trump presidency in an open letter, charging that he would "make America less safe" and "diminish our standing in the world." Sort of like the Iraq invasion?

Even though he made some good points, especially about the Trump Steaks shame spiral, it's pretty rich to have Mitt Romney, the man who called on 11 million people to "self-deport," talking about Trump's bigotry.

Trump was right about Romney. When you lose a race that you should have won by being an inept phony, you can't call this year's front-runner an inept phony.

It's delightful to see the encrusted political king-making class utter a primal scream as Trump smashes their golden apple cart. He's a real threat to the cozy, greedy, oleaginous cartel, their own Creature from the Black Lagoon.

For all the Republican establishment's self-righteous bleating, Trump is nothing more than an unvarnished, cruder version. For years, it has fanned, stoked and exploited the worst angels among the nativists, racists, Pharisees and angry white men, concurring in anti-immigrant measures, restricting minority voting, whipping up anti–Planned Parenthood hysteria and enabling gun nuts.

How lame was it that after saying he was a crazy choice, Rubio, Ted Cruz, Paul Ryan and John McCain turned around and said they will support Trump if he's the nominee?

After watching Hillary Clinton, for whom campaigning is a nuisance, and Barack Obama, who disdains politics, it's fun to see someone having fun. Like Bill Clinton, Trump talks and talks to crowds. They feed his narcissism, and in turn, he creates an intimacy even in an arena that leaves both sides awash in pleasure. It's easy to believe him when he says that, unlike President Obama, he would enjoy endlessly negotiating with obstructionists and those on the other side of the aisle.

That's the wicked fun part. But then there's the simply wicked part.

Trump wants to be seen as Ronald Reagan but often he's more like Pat Buchanan, playing to the crowd's prejudices just to hear the bloodthirsty roar, evoking memories of Molly Ivins's observation about Buchanan's 1992 culture wars speech, that it was translated from the original German.

Trump, who was slow to disavow David Duke and the Klan, stokes the gladiatorial fever, leading to minorities being roughed up and the press being bullied. His mocking of a *Times* reporter with a disability was grotesque.

He has a tenuous relationship with the truth and an inch-deep understanding of policy. Although it is compelling when he says he would surround himself with an A team in the White House, his campaign is not chock-a-block with A-team players. On Friday, his team put out a press release saying Trump would campaign this weekend in a town called "Witchita" in the state of "Kanasas." And he has not brought on heavyweights who could bring him up to speed on substance.

He has a nasty gift for dragging everyone down to his own vulgar level. Presidential campaigns should not be about belittling people's appearances or bragging about your own appendages. Whatever his flaws, President Obama has reinforced our desire for class in presidents.

After doubling down on his outrageous statements and saying he would force the military to follow his orders to break international laws involving torture and murdering terrorists' families, Trump said on Friday that he would not do that. Good to know.

In a rare show of regret, he said he does "understand that the United States is bound by laws and treaties and I will not order our military or other officials to violate those laws and will seek their advice on such matters."

Trump sees his egregious positions on immigration, torture and terrorism revenge as opening bids. After Super Tuesday, he told reporters that while they might be surprised, he would be a "unifier, once we get all of this finished."

But he should take a lesson from Condi Rice. She went along with the Iraq invasion, thinking she could reposition W. on the side of diplomacy afterward. But some positions are so extreme, there's no coming back. Your deal with the devil is sealed.

# Will Trump Be Dumped?

Most people would be upset to be at the center of an agitated national debate about whether they were more like Hitler, Mussolini, Idi Amin, George Wallace or a Marvel villain.

Not Donald Trump.

He doesn't like invidious comparisons but he's cool with being called an authoritarian.

"We need strength in this country," he told me Friday morning, speaking from his Fifth Avenue office. "We have weak leadership. Hillary is pathetically weak.

"She got us into Libya and she got us into Benghazi and she's probably got forty eggheads sitting around a table telling her what to do, and then she was sleeping when the phone call came in from the ambassador begging for help. You know, the 3 a.m. phone call?"

I asked the brand baron if he's concerned that his brand has gone from fun to scary, from glittery New York celebrity to *SNL* skits about him featuring allusions to the KKK and Hitler. He blamed a "disgustingly dishonest" press.

I wondered about ex-wife Ivana telling her lawyer, according to *Vanity Fair*, that Trump kept a book of Hitler's speeches by his bed. Or the talk in New York that in the '90s he was reading *Mein Kampf*. *Nein*, he said. "I never had the book," he said. "I never read the book. I don't care about the book."

All over town, even in the building where I'm writing this column, freaked-out Republicans are plotting how to rip the nomination from Trump's hot little hands.

How does it feel to be labeled a menace, misogynist, bigot and xenophobe by your own party? "Honestly," he replied, "I'm with the people. The people like Trump."

Since he prefers to rely on himself for policy advice, is he seeking out expert help on the abstruse delegate rules? "Yeah," he said, "I have people, very good people, the best people." No details, as usual.

Won't a contested convention require more of a campaign than *après moi le déluge*? "I have an organization but it's largely myself," he said.

More heavyweights are jumping in to stomp Trump, including Elizabeth Warren. Asked about her jabs, he pounced: "I think it's wonderful because the Indians can now partake in the future of the country. She's got about as much Indian blood as I have. Her whole life was based on a fraud. She got into Harvard and all that because she said she was a minority."

Told that President Obama was mocking his wine as $5 wine marked up to $50, Trump shot back, "My wine has gone through the roof."

What about Mitt Romney, who's pushing for an open convention? "He's a jealous fool and not a bright person," Trump said. "He's good-looking. Other than that, he's got nothing."

Paul Ryan, who will be leading the GOP convention in Cleveland, says there could be a floor fight. But he protested that he would, no, no, never take it himself, just as he once said about the speakership.

Ryan snickered at the idea that Mexico would pay for the wall and chided Trump for warning that there would be riots at the convention if the Gasping Old Party tried to snatch the nomination. Was the speaker interested in seizing the crown himself?

"I don't think so," Trump said, noting that he liked Ryan and that they'd talked. "All that matters is the votes. I see people making statements about me that are harsh and yet they are calling me on the other line saying, 'Hey, when can we get together?'"

Mitch McConnell also urged Trump to ratchet down the ferocity. Trump insisted that "the violence is not caused by me. It's caused by agitators." He added that "Hillary is the one disrupting my rallies. It's more Hillary than Sanders, I found out." The Clinton campaign called this "patently false."

But shouldn't parents be able to bring children to rallies without worrying about obscenities, sucker punches, brawls and bullying? "The rallies are the safest places a child could be," Trump replied primly.

Didn't the man rushing the stage give him pause? "I got credit for that because it looked like I was moving toward him," he said.

Trump said that when the "agitators" scream and the crowd screams back, "Frankly, it adds a little excitement." But there must be a safer, saner way to get some oomph.

I wondered if he realized that, in riling up angry whites, he has pulled the scab off racism. "Obama, who is African American, has done nothing for African Americans," he replied.

He said he would soon unleash the moniker that he thought would diminish Hillary, the way "Little Marco" and "Lyin' Ted" torched his Republican rivals; "I want to get rid of the leftovers first."

When he mocks Hillary, as he does in a new ad that shows her barking, it may backfire. Due to his inability to let go of his chew toy Megyn Kelly, Trump drew a remarkable rebuke Friday night from Fox News after he called for a boycott of her show and tweeted that she was "crazy" and "sick." Fox painted Trump as a stalker, saying he had an "extreme, sick obsession" with the anchor. Unable to resist, even though he knows I respect Kelly, he also described her to me as a "total whack job" with "no talent."

He has a history of crude remarks about women from his visits to Howard Stern's show that could be used in Hillary ads. A conservative anti-Trump super PAC is running an ad with women repeating his coarse remarks.

"All of these politicians have said far worse than that," Trump said, "drunk, standing in a corner."

Joe Scarborough said that just as FDR was the master of radio and JFK of television, DJT is the titan of Twitter. The titan agreed, gloating about how his tweets to his seven million followers, sometimes penned in his jammies, become cable news bulletins. "Yeah," he said, "I'll do them sometimes lying in bed."

Not exactly a fireside chat. But it sure started a fire.

# Trump Does It His Way

You could hear how hard it was for Donald Trump to say the words.

"Yeah, it was a mistake," he said, sounding a bit chastened. "If I had to do it again, I wouldn't have sent it."

I was telling him he lost my sister's vote when he retweeted a seriously unflattering photo of the pretty Heidi Cruz next to a glam shot of his wife, Melania.

He repeated his contention that he didn't view the Heidi shot "necessarily as negative." But I stopped him, saying it was clearly meant to be nasty.

Trump also got into his schoolyard excuse of "he did it first" and "that wasn't nice," insisting that Ted Cruz wrote the words on the digital ad put up by an anti-Trump group aimed at Utah Mormons; it showed Melania in a 2000 British *GQ* shot posing provocatively and suggested that it was not first-lady-like. Cruz denies any involvement.

Truth be told, Trump said he "didn't love the photo" of Melania. "I think she's taken better pictures," he said, also protesting: "It wasn't a nude photo, either. It wasn't nude!"

It's ridiculous how many mistakes Trump has made in rapid

order to alienate women when he was already on thin ice with them—and this in a year when the Republicans will likely have to run against a woman.

He did a huge favor for Hillary, who had been reeling from losing young women to a 74-year-old guy and from a dearth of feminist excitement. And for Cruz, who started promoting himself as Gloria Steinem, despite his more regressive positions on abortion and other women's issues.

Wouldn't it have been better, I asked, if Trump campaign manager Corey Lewandowski had simply called the reporter Michelle Fields and apologized for yanking her arm?

"You're right, but from what I understand it wouldn't have mattered," Trump said.

In an MSNBC interview with Chris Matthews, the formerly pro-choice Trump somehow managed to end up to the right of the National Right to Life Committee when he said that for women, but not men, "there has to be some form of punishment" if a President Trump makes abortion illegal.

Trump quickly recanted and even told CBS's John Dickerson that "the laws are set. And I think we have to leave it that way."

"This was not real life," he told me. "This was a hypothetical, so I thought of it in terms of a hypothetical. So that's where that answer came from, hypothetically."

Given his draconian comment, sending women back to back alleys, I had to ask: When he was a swinging bachelor in Manhattan, was he ever involved with anyone who had an abortion?

"Such an interesting question," he said. "So what's your next question?"

I pressed, how could he possibly win with 73 percent of women in this country turned off by him?

He chose another poll, murmuring, "It was sixty-eight percent, actually."

Trump doesn't have a plan to turn it around with women, except to use Ivanka as a character witness and to chant that "nobody respects women more than I do."

"I'm just going to be myself," he said. "That's all I can do."

I asked how he would get past the damage done by his insults about women's looks.

"I attack men far more than I attack women," he said. "And I attack them tougher."

Besides, he noted, he gets attacked on his looks, too. "My hair is just fine, but I get attacked on my hair," he said. "But if I attack someone else on their hair, they'd say, 'Oh, what a terrible thing to do.'"

How do you rate your own looks? I asked.

"Phenomenal," he said with a trace of self-deprecation. "Hey, it's worked. What can I say?"

He was trying to be careful—an unfamiliar approach—in talking about women.

When I told him that Hillary called him "an id with hair" at a New York fund-raiser, he was subdued. "Yeah, what is that all about?" he said. "Huh?"

And Rosie O'Donnell was there and compared him to a Harry Potter villain. "Give me a break, Rosie," he said. "I won't comment on Rosie. I wish her the best. See? In the old days—tell your sister, I'm making progress."

I mentioned that Megyn Kelly wants him on her show. "I think I'd probably do it," he allowed.

The front-runner has a right to be paranoid, with everyone plotting to steal his prize. He said he doesn't want to "act like someone overly aggrieved," but he was stewing in aggrievement about how "unbelievably badly" he gets treated by the press. The brand expert knows his brand is not so shiny these days.

"It's a very interesting question because I do enjoy life a lot and I have fun with life and I understand life and I want to make life better for people, but it doesn't come out in the media," he said.

Has he missed the moment to moderate, to unite, to be less belligerent, to brush up on his knowledge about important issues?

"I guess because of the fact that I immediately went to No. 1 and I said, why don't I just keep the same thing going?" he mused. "I've come this far in life. I've had great success. I've done it my way."

He added: "You know, there are a lot of people who say, 'Don't change.' I can be as presidential as anybody who ever lived. I can be so presidential if I want."

Then start.

# Donald the Dove, Hillary the Hawk

It seems odd, in this era of gender fluidity, that we are headed toward the most stark X versus Y battle since Billie Jean King and Bobby Riggs.

Donald Trump exudes macho, wearing his trucker hat, retweeting bimbo cracks, swearing with abandon and bragging about the size of his manhood, his crowds, his hands, his poll margins, his bank account, his skyscrapers, his steaks and his "beautiful" wall.

He and his pallies Paul Manafort and Roger Stone seem like a latter-day Rat Pack, having a gas with tomatoes, twirls and ring-a-ding-ding. The beauty pageant impresario's coarse comments to Howard Stern, rating women on their breasts, fading beauty and ability to take the kids off his hands, reverberate through the campaign.

In Indiana, Trump boasted that "Iron" Mike Tyson and "all the tough guys" had endorsed him. The chair-throwing Bobby Knight backed Trump with the brass-knuckles encomium that Trump, like Harry Truman, would have the guts to drop the bomb. When his rallies become Fight Club, Trump boasts that it adds a little excitement.

Hillary Clinton's rallies, by contrast, can seem like a sorority rush reception hosted by Lena Dunham, or an endless episode of *The View*, with a girl-power soundtrack by Katy Perry, Taylor Swift and Demi Lovato. The ultimate insider is portraying herself as an outsider because she's a woman, and the candidate who is considered steely is casting herself as cozy because she's a doting granny.

Her website is chock-a-block with empowerment gear, from a hot pink "woman's card" to a "Make Herstory" T-shirt to a "Girls Just Wanna Have Fun-damental Rights" tote bag to a "A Woman's Place Is in the White House" throw pillow. She says her favorite shows are *The Good Wife*, *Madam Secretary* and *Downton Abbey*, and she did a guest shot on *Broad City*.

Trump's most ardent supporters, white men, are facing off against Hillary's most loyal supporters, black women.

Clinton and Trump have moved on to their mano a womano fight, leaving behind "the leftovers," as Trump labels deflated rivals.

Already, it's unlovely.

"It's going to be nasty, isn't it?" says Obama Pygmalion David Axelrod. "Put the small children away until November."

A peeved Jane Sanders called on the FBI to hurry up with the Hillary classified email investigation. A desperate Ted Cruz cut a deal with John Kasich, who then put a bag over his head and acted as if he didn't know Cruz. Then Cruz latched on to Cruella Fiorina, accomplishing the impossible: finding a Potemkin running mate who's even more odious. We can only hope that Cruz, who croons Broadway show tunes, and Carly, who breaks into song at the lectern, will start doing duets from *Hamilton*.

In one of the most gratifying moments of an unhinged campaign, former Speaker John Boehner told Stanford students that Cruz was "Lucifer in the flesh." Satanists immediately objected, saying it was unfair to their deity.

Even though Trump is the one who has no governing experience, he will suggest that the first woman at the top of a major party ticket is unqualified by charging that she lacks "strength" and "stamina" and claiming that if she were a man, she would not get even 5 percent of the vote.

During his unburdening at Stanford, Boehner imitated Clinton, saying, "Oh, I'm a woman, vote for me."

But such mockery merely plays into Clinton's hands. As former Jeb Bush super PAC strategist Mike Murphy told MSNBC, "Her big judo move is playing the victim." And as former Jeb aide Tim Miller noted to CNN, Trump's numbers with women are so bad that the only way he can win is if he manages to repeal women's suffrage before November.

Once you get beyond the surface of the 2016 battle of the sexes, with its chest-thumping versus maternal hugging, there's a more intriguing gender dynamic.

On some foreign policy issues, the roles are reversed for the candidates and their parties. It's Hillary the Hawk against Donald the Quasi-Dove.

Just as Barack Obama seemed the more feminized candidate in 2008 because of his talk-it-out management style, his antiwar platform and his delicate eating habits, always watching his figure, so now, in some ways, Trump seems less macho than Hillary.

He has a tender ego, pouty tweets, needy temperament and obsession with hand sanitizer, whereas she is so tough and combat-hardened she's known by her staff as "the Warrior."

The prime example of commander-in-chief judgment Trump offers is the fact that, like Obama, he thought the invasion of Iraq was a stupid idea.

He can sound belligerent, of course, saying that he would bomb the expletive-deleted out of ISIS and that he would think up new and imaginative ways to torture terrorists and kill their families.

But he says that in most cases he would rather do the art of the deal than shock and awe.

"Unlike other candidates for the presidency, war and aggression will not be my first instinct," he said in his maiden foreign policy speech in Washington last week, adding, "A superpower understands that caution and restraint are really truly signs of strength."

These Kumbaya lines had the neocons leaping into Hillary's muscular embrace.

If the neocons get neophyte Republicans on the presidential ticket, they prefer ones like Dan Quayle, W. and Sarah Palin, who are "educable," as Bill Kristol, the editor of the *Weekly Standard*, once said of Quayle.

Trump may have a lot to learn about the issues, but he's not malleable.

In his new book, *Alter Egos*, *Times* White House correspondent Mark Landler makes the case that the former Goldwater Girl, the daughter of a Navy petty officer and a staunch Republican, has long had hawkish tendencies, reflected in her support for military action in Iraq and Libya and a no-fly zone in Syria.

"It's bred in the bone," Landler told me.

"There's no doubt that Hillary Clinton's more muscular brand of American foreign policy is better matched to 2016 than it was to 2008," Jake Sullivan, Hillary's policy adviser both at the State Department and in her campaign, told Landler.

But Hillary never expected to meet this mix of dove, hawk and isolationist. She thought she would face Marco Rubio, a more traditional conservative who would out-hawk her. Instead, she's meeting Trump, who is "a sheep in wolf's clothing," as Axelrod put it. Like a free-swinging asymmetric boxer, Trump can keep Hillary off-balance by punching from both the left and the right.

You can actually envision a foreign policy debate between Trump and Clinton that sounds oddly like the one Obama and Clinton had in 2008, with Trump playing Obama, preening about his good judgment on Iraq, wanting an end to nation-building and thinking he could have a reset with Russia.

Despite gossip when she was first lady that she did not like people in uniform, the truth is the reverse. She gravitates toward "nail-eaters," her aides told Landler, and loves the gruff, Irish, bear-like demeanor of Jack Keane, a retired four-star general and resident hawk on Fox News who helped define her views on military issues and is still in touch.

As secretary of state, she hit it off with General Stanley McChrystal and David Petraeus. And she loved to have a stiff drink with Bob Gates and John McCain.

She has a weakness for big, swaggering, rascally he-men.

Like Donald Trump.

*May 7, 2016*

# Donald Trump or Paul Ryan: Who's King of the Hill? (A Satire)

Paul Ryan and Donald Trump sit down at Republican National Committee headquarters on Capitol Hill to hash out a couple of little things, like who is running the party and who is the actual Republican.

"Welcome to Washington, Donald," Ryan says, shaking hands with the presumptuous nominee. "Reince says you're far more gracious in private than in public and I sure hope that's true."

Trump smirks and pulls out his bottle of industrial-strength sanitizer, squirting a prodigious amount on his hands.

Trying to thaw the chill, the House speaker displays his best ingratiating Irish undertaker air. "Hey," he says, "thanks for not calling me Lyin' Ryan."

"I never use the same adjective twice," Trump replies coolly. "As you know, I do have killer instincts. That's how I knocked out sixteen losers. So let's try a few names for kicks. Pious Paul? Pompous

Paul? Phony Paul? Backstabbing, blindsiding Paul who hung me out to dry to protect his own presidential ambitions for 2020?"

Ryan blanches, protesting: "No, no, I just want us to come together with a positive vision."

"I am positive," Trump says, manspreading as party aides cower in the corners. "I'm positive that what you did was terrible. You're just giving cover to more traitors, like that reject Lindsey Graham, who I beat like a toy drum. Now Nasty Lindsey's on TV spewing hate and saying my convention should be held in Area 51. The only number he needs to remember is zero—the number of votes he got."

Ryan puts on his best altar-boy demeanor, which annoys Trump.

"Look at that face!" the billionaire mocks. "Or should I say two? Two-faced Paul. You're just mad because you and Mitt wanted to lead white male America and instead I'm going to. Romney choked. And what about that time you lied about how fast you ran a marathon? Cheatin' Ryan. A choker and a cheater."

"Now Donald, be reasonable," Ryan says. "I'm just trying to figure out how to endorse you and not put my own majority at risk. We can't be a bigoted, angry party. You just make our problem with Hispanics worse when you tweet a picture of yourself eating a taco bowl on Cinco de Mayo."

"No way, José," Trump says. "That got 80,000 retweets and 100,000 likes. *Muy bueno*. I have eight million Twitter followers. You have, like, one million and need two accounts to get there."

Ryan rolls his eyes. "Thousands of those retweets were by people you offended," he says. "You can't judge everything by numbers. We have to maintain American values. Banning Muslims is not what we stand for. Try to be more like Reagan."

"Fine," Trump shoots back. "I'll start my campaign in Mississippi Klan territory like Reagan. You establishment guys are such phonies. You wanna use race as a wedge issue but be subtle about it.

I AM NOT SUBTLE. I have brought millions of people into the party and you have been unbelievably unfair to me. I am the greatest political phenomenon in history."

"Donald, you need to rein it in," Ryan persists. "Your volatility scares people. Everyone is shuddering at the thought that you are about to get classified intelligence briefings and at your bromance with Putin. No one believes that you're a genuine conservative. You support Planned Parenthood, raising the minimum wage and some higher taxes on the wealthy, our people. You're Bernie Sanders with even weirder hair."

"Well, Two-Face," Trump retorts, "if you're such a big-deal conservative, why did you push for that budget increasing spending by billions, funding Obama's executive amnesty program, relocation of terrorist refugees and sanctuary cities—but somehow no money for the border fence? You're a white Obama. Bad! Sad!! The nuns said your budgets were so mean and un-Christian they wanted to beat erasers around your head."

"Donald, the party is off the rails," Ryan says. "Ordinarily, people who hate each other always pretend not to once the nomination has been clinched. Jeez, the Bushes are boycotting your convention."

Trump harrumphs. "Well, I have Four-Eyes Rick Perry doing a groveling about-face to support me. Who wants the Bushes, that pathetic dynasty? Sour grapes because I called out W. on his horrible war and Jeb on his terrible campaign. No low energy in Cleveland! My convention is going to rock with celebrities and hot women. We're going to have Mike Tyson and that tiger. We're going to have Bobby Knight and Miss Aruba emceeing. We might even have a beauty pageant with Gary Busey judging. Carly won't be in it. But your wife—"

Ryan interrupts quickly, "Donald, you have to stop insulting women. You're starting to make Todd Akin sound like Lena Dunham."

"Women love me!" Trump objects. "Didn't you see that famous *New York Post* headline quoting Marla, my second wife, saying, 'Best Sex I've Ever Had'? I love the women who vote for me—even the poorly educated, flat-chested ones."

Ryan, beaten down and late for his P90X workout in the House gym, gives it one last shot.

"Donald, you need to stop quoting the *National Enquirer* and do some homework," he pleads. "You can't suggest we are going to slough off our debt, even though that's what you did with your creditors when you kept going bankrupt. And you should remember that I'm the senior elected Republican in the country."

"For now," Trump murmurs, taking out his hair spray for a spritz before he walks past the press octopus. "What I will remember is that you sabotaged me when I should have been savoring my success. And you should remember the number one rule from *The Art of the Deal*: There can be only one Number One, Two-Face."

# The Mogul and the Babe

We are in one of those rare unharmonic convergences when reality is more absurd than satire.

So I decided to dispense with satire and simply call Donald Trump at Trump Tower on Friday to hear about his trip to survey the damage from the volcanic eruption of his imminent nomination.

Not since Pompeii have there been so many people caked in muck and frozen in varying poses of horror.

Trump told me that when he came to tour the ruins of the Republican Party here in Washington on Thursday, he and Paul Ryan asked if everyone would clear the room.

They let Reince Priebus stay. "He's a hard worker and a good guy," Trump said. And the New York billionaire was clearly in need of new buttling, after his former butler at Mar-a-Lago, Anthony Senecal, got caught last week with past Facebook posts about how President Obama should be dragged from the "white mosque" and hanged.

So, with the soul of the party at stake, the two most powerful—and polar opposite—men in the GOP got down to it.

What were Speaker Ryan's demands?

"We talked about the success I've had," Trump replied. "Paul said to me that he has never seen anything like it because I'm a non-politician and I beat very successful politicians. He was really fascinated by how I won. I said, it's just like I have good ideas and I've bonded with the people and my people are very loyal. They will stay through thick and thin, whereas the people that support Marco and Cruz wouldn't. If Jeb sneezed, they'd leave."

No doubt Ryan was furiously taking notes for 2020, in case Trump loses big, which is a nearly unanimous expectation in the nation's capital.

So Ryan didn't ask Trump to stop making remarks that alienate women? "No," Trump said, "he wants me to be me." So much for the showdown.

When I asked if he had been chided by any Republicans for his Twitter feud with Elizabeth Warren, he replied, "You mean Pocahontas?" So much for reining it in.

I noted that John Cornyn said he gave Trump some tips on how to discuss illegal immigration more sensitively to woo Hispanic voters. "I love getting advice," Trump deadpanned. "It's just what I need, just what I need is more advice. The seventeen people I beat are still giving me advice."

Trump also briefly saw Poppy Bush's guru, James Baker. "I was more interested in asking him about Ronald and Nancy Reagan and the whole Reagan era than I was in terms of getting advice currently," Trump said.

As usual in Trumpworld, there was good news. Trump enjoys the status that comes with a Secret Service code name: "Mogul." Ryan was friendly, if noncommittal; Lindsey Graham called to talk ISIS and Syria; nine House committee chairmen endorsed Trump; and a Quinnipiac poll popped up showing Trump effectively tied with Clinton in the swing states of Florida, Ohio, and Pennsylvania. "It means I'm going to win the election," Trump said. The man with no pollster mused, "I think I've increased the value of polls."

And, as is usual in Trumpworld, there was swarming craziness and chaos. When ABC News's George Stephanopoulos quizzed Trump about his tax rate and about why he hasn't released his tax returns yet, pointing out that Richard Nixon released his while under audit, Trump shot back, "It's none of your business."

The candidate who's under fire for his own tone told me he was offended by Stephanopoulos's tone. Trump said he's not afraid that people will find out he's not as rich as he says. "Tax returns don't show that," he said. "They would show, do I use Cayman Islands stuff? And the answer is no, I can tell you right now. Am I ensconced in some of the crazy countries where you keep money and avoid taxes? The answer is no, I don't do that."

*The Washington Post* revived a story, with a new damning audio, about how Trump had masqueraded as his own publicists, named John Barron and John Miller, to boast about himself back in the '70s, '80s and '90s. Trump admitted in court testimony in 1990 that he had used the name John Barron as an alias. Former *Times* editor Joe Sexton told me that he thought he interviewed Trump-as-Barron in 1985 while working as a sportswriter with UPI and chasing a story about the New Jersey Generals. The *Post* audio on "John Miller" contained classic Trumpisms like "That I can tell you." CNN interviewed a forensic audio specialist who believed that Trump was posing as Miller. But Trump insisted to me that the *Post* recording was not his voice. "Do you know how many people I have imitating my voice now? It's like everybody."

I asked how voters could trust him when he has been shifting positions so much lately, even saying that the temporary Muslim ban was just a "suggestion." (In *The Art of the Deal*, he called his technique of self-promotion "truthful hyperbole.") "I didn't shift on that," he said. "But we have to talk about problems, and if we don't talk about the problems we're never going to solve the problems, and that is a real problem, in case you haven't noticed."

While many Republicans are expressing how scared they are to be handcuffed to someone so erratic, Trump is almost feral in savoring his victory. "They say it was the roughest primary in memory, in history," he said proudly. Recalling trouncing Jeb Bush, he noted, "Low energy, that term just hit. That thing, that was a one-day kill. Words are beautiful."

No one marvels more at his success than Trump. "Don't analyze it," he said. "Just do it. The other players would come up to Babe Ruth and say, 'Babe, how do you hit the long ball?' And he said, 'I don't know, man. I just hit it.' There's a little bit of truth in that."

# Trump in the Dumps

He won't pivot. So I have to.

Having seen Donald Trump as a braggadocious but benign celebrity in New York for decades, I did not regard him as the apotheosis of evil. He seemed more like a toon, a cocky huckster swanning around Gotham with a statuesque woman on his arm and skyscrapers stamped with his brand. I certainly never would have predicted that the Trump name would be uttered in the same breath as Hitler, Mussolini and a scary menace, even on such pop culture staples as *The Bachelorette*.

Trump jumped into the race with an eruption of bigotry, ranting about Mexican rapists and a Muslim ban. But privately, he assured people that these were merely opening bids in the negotiation; that he was really the same pragmatic New Yorker he had always been; that he would be a flexible, wheeling-and-dealing president, not a crazy nihilist like Ted Cruz or a mean racist like George Wallace. He yearned to be compared to Ronald Reagan, a former TV star who overcame a reputation for bellicosity and racial dog whistles to become the most beloved Republican president of modern times.

Trump was applying his business cunning, Twitter snarkiness

and bendy relationship with the truth to his new role as a Republican pol. The opposition was unappetizing: Cruz, a creepy, calculating ideologue; Marco Rubio, a hungry lightweight jettisoning his old positions and mentor; Chris Christie, a vindictive bully; Jeb Bush, a past-his-sell-by-date scion.

When Trump pulled back the curtain on how Washington Republicans had been stringing their voters along for years with bold promises, like repealing Obamacare, that they knew had no chance, it was a rare opportunity to see them called out. And when Trump was blunt about how cheaply you could buy and sell politicians in both parties, it made this town squirm.

His obnoxious use of ethnicity only exposed the fact that Republicans had been using bigotry against minorities and gays to whip up voters for decades. The GOP would love to drop Trump now because it prefers a candidate in the party's more subtle racist traditions. (Or even a candidate savvy enough to heap disdain on the 47 percent of government freeloaders at a ritzy fund-raiser without having a bartender tape it and leak it.)

The neocons calling Trump a fascist would certainly prefer a more militaristic candidate. Trump realized the Iraq war was misbegotten long before much of the media cognoscenti in New York, and he was willing to hold W. accountable for being asleep at the switch before 9/11 and using a bait and switch on Iraq. Even though he ranted about the press, he was also far more available to the media than the cloaked Hillary Clinton, who has yet to give a news conference this year. But he undermines his accessibility when he incites nastiness against reporters at his rallies and revokes the *Washington Post*'s credentials for a headline he doesn't like.

Before his campaign became infused with racial grievance, victimhood and violence, Trump told me, "I have fun with life and I understand life and I want to make life better for people." If he had those better angels, he didn't listen to them. Seduced by the roar of the angry crowd, Trump kept dishing out racially offensive comments about "my African American," a black man he spotted at a California rally, the "Mexican" judge on the Trump University case and the "Afghan" who committed the atrocities in Orlando. Mitt Romney is right that Trump's rhetoric causes "trickle-down racism" and misogyny. The *Washington Post* had a front-page story on Friday about the vulgarities freely directed at Hillary Clinton by men and women at Trump rallies.

Trump told me he could act like the toniest member of high society when he wanted, and he would as soon as he dispatched his GOP rivals. He said his narcissism would not hinder him as he morphed into a leader. But he can't stop lashing out and doesn't get why that turns people against him. Everything is filtered through his ego. He reacted to Orlando not as a tragedy so much as a chance to brag about "the congrats" he got for "being right on radical Islamic terrorism."

The presumptive but now tenuous nominee seemed bereft at a Dallas rally on Thursday night when he could no longer brag about his polls, which are shattering records for negativity. Finally, on Friday, Trump couldn't stop himself from tweeting out a poll, even though it was one that showed him behind Hillary.

Trump has made his campaign all about his ability to win. So if he stops winning, what's his raison d'être?

Trump's pledges to release his tax returns and to surround himself with an A team fell through. A month after his hostile takeover of the Republican Party, he's got a skeletal operation a few floors below his office suite in Trump Tower.

Trump shocked himself by shooting to the top of the Republican heap. It was like watching a bank robber sneak into a bank, only to find all the doors unlocked. But like Dan Quayle and Sarah Palin, Trump refused to study up on policy. So he has been unable to marry his often canny political instincts with some actual knowledge.

He has made some fair points. A lot of our allies do take advantage of us. Our trade deals have left swaths of America devastated. And it was a positive move to propose a meeting with the NRA on gun control for people on the terrorist watch list. But his fair points are getting outnumbered by egregious statements and nutty insinuations, like suggesting that President Obama is tolerant of ISIS attacks, an echo of the kooky birther campaign that he led, suggesting that Obama wasn't qualified to be president.

Now Trump's own behavior is casting serious doubt on whether he's qualified to be president.

# Interlude

## *Making America Grate Again (the quotable DJT, part 1)*

*Because it's hard to contain the Vesuvial Donald Trump in the 1,300 words of my column, we did a round of questions about his rivals and a few other boldface names in the news this week. Here are Trump's rapid-fire impressions, delivered over the phone and over lunch at the restaurant in Trump Tower—the art of the meal with the birther of a nation.*

**On President Obama**
"Obama is going to like me very, very much because when he's done with his term, he will be at my golf courses because I have the best golf courses in the world. He's going to go off to greener pastures, I guess."

"Putin hates Obama. We don't get along with anybody, every country hates Obama. They don't like his attitude. They don't like his style. They don't like him, they don't like that he's not available."

**On Carly Fiorina**

"She's a fine woman but it's not gonna happen. She was viciously fired from Hewlett-Packard and the company still hasn't recovered. The stock went down to nothing."

**On Joe Biden**

"A person who was very loyal to the president, which I respect. I'd love to run against him because it's going to be an election based on competence and I'm really competent."

**On Hillary Clinton**

"Highly complex person who can't help going over the edge. She just can't stay true to herself. She has a real bad thing going with the emails. I'm not talking politically. That's one thing and it's going to be a disaster. But what she did was illegal. She could be having more fun. But this is no fun for her. The FBI is checking everything."

**On Why He Invited Hillary to His Wedding**

"I was a businessman, if I ever should need something."

**On Jeb Bush**

"He's a stiff. The guy can't even talk. He has zero energy. You would fall asleep interviewing him."

Jeb said this week that he listens to Paul Wolfowitz's advice on foreign affairs, that he would not rule out the use of torture and that "taking out Saddam Hussein turned out to be a pretty good deal." On Jeb bizarrely cleaving to his brother on Iraq, Trump had this to say:

"It's so sad what a brotherly relationship will do to one's mind. We were a hell of a lot better off with Saddam Hussein holding that crazy country together than we are now with it split up into ISIS and five other factions. If only we could have Saddam back, as bad as he was, rather than two trillion dollars spent, thousands of lives lost and all these wounded warriors. Maybe his brother said, 'Hey, listen, that's my legacy. Don't kill me.'"

**On Elizabeth Warren**
"She's caught a little wave. Perhaps it's her Indian upbringing."

**On Bill de Blasio**
"He's having an awfully hard time being the mayor of New York and people are very upset. There is a lot of restlessness with crime, squee-gees all of a sudden, and we are seeing things that we haven't seen for a long time."

**On Bernie Sanders and His Confrontation with the Black Lives Matter Activists**
"I thought it was a disgrace for him to let that microphone be ripped out of his mouth."

**On John Kerry**
"Iran is going to go down as one of the worst deals in history. Our chief negotiator goes into a bicycle race at 73, falls down and breaks his leg. These people are incompetent." [Kerry is 71.]

**On Howard Schultz**
"He's impressive on television. He's done a great job. What's he worth? It takes guts to run. He told me once that the Starbucks in Trump Tower made more money than any of the others."

**On Al Gore**
"It's a tough path for him to get in the race right now. He won the election, the popular vote by 600,000, but he can never be president. There was that mix-up in Palm Beach, a place I know very, very well,

where people accidentally voted for Pat Buchanan. Pat Buchanan has been really supportive of me."

### On Scott Walker

"He gave me a plaque and everything is nice. And I like him. And then about a week ago one of his guys came up and said that Donald Trump is full of it. I said, 'Thank you so much. Now I can hit him.' I hit Scott so hard. I said his state was a disaster. So there's a lot of power there. He went from number one to number four in Iowa. I went to number one."

### On Lindsey Graham

"He has registered zero in the polls after a vicious attack on me, and I think he's a totally irrelevant person."

### On Chris Christie

"He's a friend of mine but he missed his time. If he would have done it four years ago he would have beaten Romney and he could be president right now. But this is a different time."

### On Marco Rubio

"Don't know Rubio. Got to know him behind the lectern. Really nice guy. Highly thought of. Very young. But I have better hair than he does."

### On George Pataki

"He's at zero. Who has zero? He doesn't have one vote. He was a terrible governor who did a terrible job in New York State."

### On Mitt Romney

"He was so disappointing to me. He choked, in sports they choke, can't sink a three-pointer to win the tournament. The great ones can, the bad ones can't, that was an election that should have been won."

**On Sarah Palin**
"A really fine woman, badly mistreated by the press. And she has been so supportive of me."

**On John Kasich**
"He's been very nice to me. It's hard for me to hit somebody who's not hitting me."

**On Ted Cruz**
"He's been terrific to me, so supportive."

**On Bobby Jindal**
"Bobby Jindal, the governor of Louisiana, said the worst thing anyone can do is ask Trump a tough question, a mean question, because that's when he performs best."

**On Jim Gilmore**
"Him, I don't know."

**On Sharon Stone and her nude photo in _Harper's Bazaar_**
"She looked great. She's always been nice to me."

**On Ben Affleck and the Hot Topic of Whether Couples Should Hire Attractive Nannies**
"I'd say it was an extra level of risk."

**On the Police**
"I'm a huge fan of the police. But it's amazing some of the things I've seen. What amazes me, why aren't they shooting at the legs? It's so bad for the police, for the image of the police. The choking incident with Eric Garner was terrible, I thought."

**On Twitter**
"The nice thing about Twitter, in the old days when I got attacked it would take me years to get even with somebody, now when I'm attacked I can do it instantaneously, and it has a lot of power. You see some genius statements on Twitter. You see some statements coming out which are Ernest Hemingway times two."

**On Climate Change and Bill Maher's Fear That Trump Believes Global Warming Is a Chinese Hoax Designed to Destroy American Manufacturing**
"Well, I don't actually think it's a Chinese hoax, but I'm not a believer in man-made climate change. And again I had uncles at MIT and stuff. By the way, many smart people agree with me."

**On Roger Stone**
"Ever since I fired him, he's been on TV saying nice things about me. I should have fired him sooner." (Stone says he quit.)

**On Iraq**
"I was against that war from the beginning. That's a big thing because that shows judgment."

**On Bill Clinton**
"Too thin. He used to be a friend of mine, now we can't be friends."

# 2

# High Rise of the Short-Fingered Vulgarian (DJT from back in the day ... )

# Living la Vida Trumpa

Melania Knauss pulls up her black Calvin Klein sheath to show off her supermodel knees.

"I never wear skirts this long," says the girlfriend of Donald Trump with a pretty grimace, standing in the aisle of his plane, stocked with gilt fixtures, French impressionist paintings, a double bed and the creme-filled finger cookies the real estate king decrees "the greatest."

But politics requires sacrifices. And Monday's trip to Miami was a dress rehearsal for Mr. Trump's potential White House bid. So the amiable Miss Knauss was doing her bit, wearing conservative gray and black Calvins chosen by a publicist for the Trump modeling agency. But the Slovenian's stilettos by Manolo Blahnik gave her away as someone blissfully unfamiliar with rope lines.

Mr. Trump was making his maiden foreign policy speech to Cuban Americans who adore his Castro-bashing. "I'd have, personally, two words for him: 'Adios, amigo!'" he told a large, cheering crowd, adding that he wanted the first hotel in free Cuba.

The flirtation of the Trumpster, as he calls himself, is the apotheosis of our Gilded Age. Our politics is warped by money, celebrity, polling and crass behavior, and our culture is defined by stock-market high-rolling, boomer narcissism, niche marketing mania, rankings and a quiz show called *Who Wants to Be a Millionaire?*

"I love Regis," Mr. Trump says.

Why shouldn't billionaires play *Who Wants to Be a President?*

"I've already got my own airplane," he says. "We could save money on Air Force One."

You gotta love a guy whose economic platform runs all of a page and a half and is a $5.7 trillion squeeze-the-rich tax plan that would make The Donald at least $750 million poorer. And there are more provocative plans to come.

Oddly, given so many years of Trump plastering TRUMP on every available surface, the builder and casino owner actually looked a bit shy when he saw the Trump 2000 posters, with his own pouty kisser staring back, and Cuban American fans at the Bay of Pigs Museum yelling "Viva Donald Trump!"

He gave a tentative wave to his first rope line, but soon recovered enough to note that Steve Forbes never had so many cameras at the airport or a supermodel by his podium.

Mr. Trump does not live an examined life. He lives a quantified life. He keeps track of all numbers, the sentinels of success—the number of magazine covers his girlfriend is on this month and the number of men who are dripping with lust for her; the number of zoning changes he has finagled; the number of stories he was able to stack on his building near the UN; the huge amount of money he was paid to do a clever ad for an online company, in which he looks down a girl's shirt, and the short amount of time it took him to do it; the number of favorable mentions in a Palm Beach publication about a club he has started at Mar-a-Lago; the number of working-class guys who call out to him.

"I am just very popular with the black populace," he says. "When Puff Daddy has a party, when Russell Simmons has a party, I'm the person they call."

He uses a kind of ego arithmetic. About the candidates, he demands: "Did they make billions of dollars in a short period of time? No. Could they...? No." And: "Hey, look, what's so good about these people? I do *Face the Nation, Meet the Press, Larry King.* I think I do better than they do. They're boring as hell. They get no ratings and everybody turns off the set."

He refers to W. as the anointed "son of the president who should have finished the war" and says he looks "vacuous." He thinks Bill Bradley is "not exactly Cary Grant." Al Gore has made "dreadful mistakes," including Alpha Girl. (Author Naomi Wolf, who coached Vice President Al Gore on how to be less beta and more alpha.)

At the end of his first day as an exploratory guy, Mr. Trump was very tired. Almost too tired to brag. But he rallied enough at midnight, in a limo from the airport back to Trump Tower, to check out a big poster with his name on it and to muse about how much of Third Avenue he had built.

"I think the only difference between me and the other candidates," he summed up, "is that I'm more honest and my women are more beautiful."

# Trump Shrugged

Greed is good, again.

Gordon Gekko's *Wall Street* homily and Ayn Rand's paeans to selfishness are the manifestos of our giddy materialism.

As a young capitalist in Ms. Rand's novel *Atlas Shrugged* explained: "When I die, I hope to go to heaven. . . . So I want to be prepared to claim the greatest virtue of all—that I was a man who made money."

Now it's not only Wall Street that is go-going; it's Main Street. Everybody wants to spin that wheel and make a mil—on TV, on the Internet, on stocks and on the playing field.

Donald Trump is talking about ponying up $100 million to run for president. So, in this season of giving some and getting more, I asked the high-rolling plutocrat, spending the holiday weekend at his Mar-a-Lago mansion in Palm Beach, for a soliloquy on the subject of greedisgood.com.

"It really is not very different than the eighties," Mr. Trump says. "In the eighties, people had limos. Now they have all-terrain vehicles, which cost more than the limos.

"There was an anti-eighties feeling for a while, everyone cutting back, but now the mood is 'Let's just do it!' I just got back from a golf course I built in Florida. It costs $300,000 to join. In the eighties, there was no such thing. Rich people are handing me checks like Godiva chocolates.

"Greed is not good. The line played well in a movie. But a lot of things play well in words—like 'All men are created equal'—that sound magnificent and beautiful, but that doesn't necessarily make them so. Greed is the bad part of success. And people have wanted to be successful from the beginning of time.

"My entire life, I've watched politicians bragging about how poor they are, how they came from nothing, how poor their parents and grandparents were. And I said to myself, if they can stay so poor for so many generations, maybe this isn't the kind of person we want to be electing to higher office. How smart can they be? They're morons. There's a perception that voters like poverty. I don't like poverty. Usually, there's a reason for poverty. Do you want someone who gets to be president and that's literally the highest-paying job he's ever had?

"You don't need money to get beautiful women. All my life, I've had friends who were successful and can't get a date, let alone a date with a beautiful woman. I have watched men worth hundreds of millions who have all the trappings—a G5 Gulfstream jet, the Fifth Avenue apartment, the Palm Beach estate, and they cannot get a date. They're sitting at home watching television. They're brilliant all day long and at night, they don't have a clue.

"These people who eat people alive for a living, come seven o'clock, they see a girl who's a solid 5—not supermodels, 10's—and they look at her in awe, but they develop lockjaw.

"I fixed up a very well-known powerful, rich man with a very nice and very beautiful woman he'd been trying to meet for a year and a half. She called me the following day and said, 'Don't ever do that to me again,' and an hour later he called me and said, 'It was unbelievable. Could you call her and arrange a second date?'

"Ultimately, a woman can't make love to a G5.

"People believe there's more glamour to being a very wealthy person, but there really is a lot of work. Once, a very rich guy calls me up and asks if I can get him reservations that night for Le Cirque. He can't get in. So I got him in, and he calls the next day and says: 'You got me the best table. But how do you deal with all that publicity?' Look, what's the point of being successful if nobody knows who you are?

"This dot-com nonsense? I think a lot of it will go away. Maybe it's all a mirage. It's pretty fragile. Every single IPO coming out goes through the roof. I just don't see anything tangible. I like to see and feel and touch something—bricks, mortar.

"A friend called me up the other day and talked about investing in a dot-com that sells lobsters. Internet lobsters. Where will this end? The next day he sent me a huge package of lobsters on ice. How low can you stoop?

"Bradley would be bad for the economy. He's a Marxist. As far as he's concerned, Communism is just fine.

"When the market goes down, we'll all be cleansed and brought back to reality. If I'm president, it won't happen for a long time. If I'm not, it will happen immediately."

*September 19, 1999*

# Trump l'Oeil Tease

Donald Trump is not so egotistical. Sometimes he actually goes off the record to brag about himself. And he promises that, if elected president, he would not change the name of 1600 Pennsylvania to the Trump White House or build a bronze and glass tower over the West Wing.

He would probably stock the joint with supermodels, though, and keep the hot tub President Clinton installed on the South Lawn.

"We would have a lot of fun," says the man who always seems to be having fun, except when ex-wives or bankers pester him for gazillions.

Once The Warren (as in Beatty) began toying with a presidential run, could The Donald be far behind?

Never underestimate a guy who pulls himself out of a $9.2 billion hole. Why should his legacy be a skyscraper that casts a shadow on the UN when he could cast a shadow on the world?

"To be blunt, people would vote for me," Mr. Trump says. "They just would." Why? "Maybe because I'm so good-looking," he banters. "I don't know. Larry King calls and says, 'Do my show. I get my highest ratings when you're on.'"

The man is pure id, no trepidation, no guilt, no PC restraints. (As a friend of his says: "He transmits; he doesn't receive.") His only fear: "I photograph short. I'm six foot three." In a landscape of black-and-white candidates, he's Technicolor.

The rakish plutocrat thinks he could do better with the working class and minorities than "my own people." He says: "Rich people who know me love me. Rich people who don't know me hate me. The working man loves me."

And how would the famous ladies' man do with the women's vote?

"I might do badly," he kids. "They know me better than anybody else. Women are much tougher and more calculating than men. I relate better to women. I go out with the most beautiful women in the world. Certain guys tell me they want women of substance, not beautiful models. It just means they can't get beautiful models."

He does not think Americans would mind a twice-divorced play-boy in the White House. "Actually, I think people like it," he says about his racy love life. "It's a fantasy.

"Of course, if necessary, I could be married in twenty-four hours," he adds. "It would be very easy. Believe me."

Mr. Trump has a new book, *The America We Deserve*. Everyone else is mistaking a campaign for a book tour, so why not mistake a book tour for a campaign?

Jesse Ventura, who doesn't want the jagged-edge Pat Buchanan to be the Reform Party candidate, is wooing Mr. Trump, a registered Republican who describes himself as an independent tilting liberal on social issues. The two men met 12 years ago when Mr. Ventura appeared in *WrestleMania* at a Trump casino-hotel in Atlantic City. Now all politics is *WrestleMania*.

Things Trump told me:

On Pat Buchanan: "He's medieval."

On Bill Bradley: "He puts me to sleep. And he was the architect of a tax plan that cost many more billions than it saved. He suffers from a lack of common sense. He didn't run again in New Jersey because the polls were showing him in deep trouble, not because of any great moral reason."

On Al Gore: "Highly underrated."

On W.: "He escaped from the drug issue, but his answers didn't give people a lot of comfort."

On Bill Clinton: "He handled the Monica situation disgracefully. It's sad because he would go down as a great president if he had not had this scandal. People would have been more forgiving if he'd had an affair with a really beautiful woman of sophistication. Kennedy and Marilyn Monroe were on a different level. Now Clinton can't get into golf clubs in Westchester. A former president begging to get in a golf club. It's unthinkable."

On the Clinton Chappaqua house: "Very overpriced. I could have gotten him that house for $600,000 less."

On Ken Starr: "Starr's a freak. I bet he's got something in his closet."

On Hillary: "The concept of the listening tour is ridiculous. People want ideas. Do you think Winston Churchill, when he was stopping Hitler, went around listening?"

On Rudy: "He's made New York the hottest city in the world. If he gets beaten, it's virtually unfair. Hillary should run in New Jersey."

On Tina Brown's *Talk*: "The magazine looks terrible. Elizabeth Taylor on the cover? Crazy. At least they didn't use a current picture of her."

On plastering the name TRUMP all over the General Motors building: "It's only on there five times. But I haven't done the back of the building yet, on Madison Avenue."

# Trump Fired Up

Donald Trump gives me an interview, though he has his doubts. "I would like the interview to be in the Sunday paper," he says.

He can't be worried about his exposure, so it must be his boundless appetite for bigger/taller/glitzier that makes him yearn for the larger readership of Sunday.

"Me, too," I reply. "But the only way that's going to happen is if I give Frank Rich my notes and let him write the column."

"I like Frank Rich," he says, his voice brimming with appreciation for a man whose circulation is bigger than mine. "Me, too," I say.

Kurt Andersen, who jousted with The Donald as an editor at *Spy*, celebrates the "Daffy Duck" of deal making in *New York* magazine this week as one of the "Reasons to Love New York," calling him "our 21st century reincarnation of P. T. Barnum and Diamond Jim Brady, John Gotti minus the criminal organization, the only white New Yorker who lives as large as the blingiest, dissiest rapper—de trop personified."

When I call De Trop Trump at Mar-a-Lago, he's still ranting about "that big, fat slob Rosie O'Donnell." When he granted Tara Conner, the naughty beauty queen, a second chance this week, Rosie made a crack on *The View* about an oft-married snake-oil salesman not being the best person to pass moral judgments. He slimed back, and the Great American Food Fight was on.

This past year was rife with mistakes—global mistakes, bigoted tirades, underwear mishaps. Winding up 2006, I asked the celebrity arbiter of who-can-stay and who-must-go about redemption.

In the case of Hollywood's overexposed and underdressed young ladies of the night, Mr. Trump judiciously notes that in some cases, carousing is good for your career. His rule is, the more talented you are, the less you should mindlessly party. But if mindlessly partying is your talent, go for it.

"Britney," he says, "doesn't carry it off as well as Paris." How about those other international party girls, the Bush twins?

"When you're a president who has destroyed the lives of probably a million people, our soldiers and Iraqis who are maimed and killed—you see children going into school in Baghdad with no arms and legs—I don't think Bush's kids should be having lots of fun in Argentina," he says.

Should viewers give Katie Couric another look?

If you can't get the ratings, he says, you're cooked: "I like Katie, but she's hit bottom and she'll stay there. She made a terrible, tragic mistake for her career. She looks extremely unhappy on the show. I watched her the other night, and she's not the same Katie."

Can Gwyneth rebound from her comments comparing Americans unfavorably with Brits? "Gwyneth Paltrow is a good actress with average looks," he says. "She likes to ride the high English horse. But when she puts down this country that gave her more than she should have had, it's disgusting."

Michael Richards and Judith Regan made irredeemable mistakes, in his view, as did Al Gore and John Kerry, when they couldn't win winnable elections, and W., Cheney and Rummy, when they invaded Iraq.

"No matter how long we stay in Iraq, no matter how many soldiers we send, the day we leave, the meanest, most vicious, most brilliant man in the country, a man who makes Saddam Hussein look like a baby, will take over and spit on the American flag," he says. "Bush will go down as the worst and by far the dumbest president in history."

Colin Powell, he considers irredeemable as well: "He's speaking up now, but he's no longer relevant. I call him a pathetic and sad figure."

He thinks John McCain has lost the 2008 election by pushing to send more troops to Iraq but that Hillary should be forgiven for her "horrendous" vote to authorize the war. "Don't forget that decision was based on lies given to her," he says. "She's very smart and has a major chance to be our next president."

He deems it "not a good sign" that Barack Obama got into a sketchy real estate deal with a sleazy Chicago political figure. "But he's got some wonderful qualities," Mr. Trump says, and deserves another chance.

And how about Monica Lewinsky, who just graduated from the London School of Economics? "It's good she graduated," he says. "She's been through a lot."

When it comes to having an opinion on everything, Trump towers.

# Interlude

## *The Escalator Down (the quotable DJT, part 2)*

**Maureen Dowd** @NYTimesDowd Jan 30

Asked if he would promise not to put Sarah Palin in his cabinet, Trump said "She's a great person."

**Maureen Dowd** @NYTimesDowd Jan 31

Trump on the charge that he's vituperative "I'm a great unifier and I always have been. Nobody knows it."

**Maureen Dowd** @NYTimesDowd Jan 31

Trump on Obama's climate fight "He flies a 25-year-old 747 spewing carbons to take a family golf vacation in Hawaii"

**Maureen Dowd** @NYTimesDowd Jan 31

Trump on his success winnowing the field: "The words 'Lindsey Graham' and 'army' don't work in the same sentence."

**Maureen Dowd** @NYTimesDowd Jan 31

On Fox's rejection of Trump's claim that Roger Ailes obsessively called to apologize "I could show you my phone. Roger called me many times"

**Maureen Dowd** @NYTimesDowd Mar 19

Attn @billmaher, Trump is not worried about being too authoritarian: "We need strength, that I will say."

**Maureen Dowd** @NYTimesDowd Mar 19

Trump is now warrin' with Warren: "She's got about as much Indian blood as I have."

**Maureen Dowd** @NYTimesDowd Mar 19

Despite record setting temperatures, Trump isn't sweating climate change: the temp. "Goes up a little, goes down a little." cc @billmaher

**Maureen Dowd** @NYTimesDowd Mar 20

Trump says rivals who think he's "nasty" about women say worse things when they're "drunk, standing in a corner."

**Maureen Dowd** @NYTimesDowd Mar 27

1/2 When I asked Trump about bullying other candidates and whether he had ever been bullied as a kid, he said: "No, um. no. I'm winning."

**Maureen Dowd @NYTimesDowd Mar 27**

2/2 "I have no great stories to tell you like all these guys who say, oh they were bullied, it probably never happened. I was never bullied"

**Maureen Dowd @NYTimesDowd Apr 5**

Trump dismissed contentions that he doesn't really want to be president: "Well, no. I'd like to win. Make American great again."

**Maureen Dowd @NYTimesDowd May 15**

Trump on Hillary's desire to open up gov UFO files: "They are talking about outer space I assume? I'm not a big fan"

**Maureen Dowd @NYTimesDowd May 15**

Trump on waiting for Megyn Kelly to call "I couldn't have made the call. I'm not saying that as a pos. about me, I think it's prob. a neg."

**Maureen Dowd @NYTimesDowd May 15**

(1/2) Trump on Obama's trip to Hiroshima: "he should never under any circumstance apologize…

**Maureen Dowd @NYTimesDowd May 15**

(2/2) "but anything to demonstrate the power of nuclear, so that people understand the threat, is a good thing"

**Maureen Dowd @NYTimesDowd May 15**

(1/2) Trump on Weekly Standard editor Bill Kristol recruiting a third-party candidate:

**Maureen Dowd** @NYTimesDowd May 15

(2/2) "He heads this magazine which is a loser, which is a dead magazine, it's called Death because it's so boring."

**Maureen Dowd** @NYTimesDowd May 15

Why Trump thinks it's OK to attack Hillary about Bill's affairs when he had one: "first of all, I wasn't president"

**Maureen Dowd** @NYTimesDowd May 15

(1/2) Trump on @Olivianuzzi story about @RogerJStoneJr book alleging, among many other things, that Bill isn't Chelsea's father:

**Maureen Dowd** @NYTimesDowd May 15

(2/2) "I have nothing to do with Roger Stone, he doesn't work for me. What did he do? He did a book?"

# 3

# Stacking the Deck with the Woman Card

# Can We Get Hillary Without the Foolery?

Please don't ask me this anymore.

It's such a silly question. Of course Hillary is running. I've never met a man who was told he could be president who didn't want to be president. So naturally, a woman who's told she can be the first commandress in chief wants to be.

"Running for president is like sex," James Carville told me. "No one ever did it once and forgot about it."

Joe Biden wants the job. He's human (very). But he's a realist. He knows the Democratic Party has a messianic urge to finish what it started so spectacularly with the election of Barack Obama—busting up the world's most exclusive white-bread old-boys' club. And he knows that women, both Democratic and Republican, want to see one of their own in the White House and became even more militant while listening to the GOP's retrogressive talk about contraception and vaginal probes last year.

Also, Joe genuinely likes Hillary. These two have no appetite for tearing each other apart.

As long as there are no more health scares—the thick glasses are gone—Hillary's age won't stop her. The Clinton scandals and dysfunction are in the rearview mirror at the moment, and the sluggish economy casts a halcyon glow on the Clinton era. Hillary is a symbol and a survivor, running on sainthood. Ronald Reagan, elected at 69, was seen as an "ancient king" gliding through life, as an aide put it. Hillary, who would be elected at 69, would be seen as an ancient queen striding through life.

She was supposed to go off to a spa, rest and get back in shape after her grueling laps around the world. But instead she's a tornado of activity, speaking at global women's conferences in DC and New York; starting to buckrake on the speaking circuit, putting out a video flipping her position to support gay marriage and signing a lucrative deal for a memoir on world affairs—all as PACs spring up around her, Bill Clinton and Carville begin to foment and Chelsea lands on the cover of this week's *Parade*, talking about how "unapologetically and unabashedly" biased she is about her mother's future.

"I can't see her taking it easy and sitting on the couch eating a bowl of popcorn," said Randall Johnston, a 25-year-old New York University Law School student who helped pass out "Ready for Hillary" signs on Friday outside Lincoln Center, while her icon was inside enthralling the crowd at Tina Brown's "Women in the World" conference.

Hillary jokes that people regard her hair as totemic, and just so, her new haircut sends a signal of shimmering intention: She has ditched the skinned-back bun that gave her the air of a KGB villainess in a Bond movie and has a sleek new layered cut that looks modern and glamorous.

In a hot-pink jacket and black slacks, she leaned in for a 2016 manifesto, telling the blissed-out crowd of women that America cannot truly lead in the world until women here at home are full partners with equal pay and benefits, careers in math and science and "no limit" on how big girls can dream.

"This truly is the unfinished business of the twenty-first century," she said. But everyone knew the truly "unfinished business" Hillary was referring to: herself.

"She's gone to hell and back trying to be president," Carville said. "She's paid her dues, to say the least. The old cliché is that Democrats fall in love and Republicans fall in line. But now Republicans want a lot of people to run and they want to fall in love. And Democrats don't want to fight; they just want to get behind Hillary and go on from there."

The real question is not whether but whither. Does Hillary have learning software? Did she learn, from her debacle with health care, to be more transparent and less my-way-or-the-highway? Did she learn, after voting to support W.'s nonsensical invasion of Iraq without even reading the intelligence estimate, that she doesn't need to overcompensate to show she's tough? (No one, even Fox News, thinks she's a Wellesley hippie anymore.)

Did she learn, from her viper's nest and money pit of a campaign in 2008, how to manage an enterprise rather than be swamped by rampant dysfunction? Did she learn, when she wrapped herself in an off-putting and opaque mantle of entitlement in the primary, that she's perfectly capable of charming reporters and voters if she wants to, without the obnoxious undertone of "I'm owed this"?

Even top Democrats who plan to support Hillary worry about her two sides. One side is the idealistic public servant who wants to make the world a better place. The other side is darker, stemming from old insecurities; this is the side that causes her to make decisions from a place of fear and to second-guess herself. It dulls her sense of ethics and leads to ends-justify-the-means wayward ways. This is the side that compels her to do anything to win, like hiring the scummy strategists Dick Morris and Mark Penn, and greedily grab for what she feels she deserves.

If Obama is the kid who studies only on the night before and gets an A, Hillary is the kid who studies all the time, stays up all night and does extra credit work to get the A. She doesn't know how not to drive herself into the ground.

As Carl Bernstein wrote in his Hillary biography, *A Woman in Charge*, her insecurities grew from her herculean effort to win paternal praise: "When Hillary came home with all A's except for one B on her report card, her father suggested that perhaps her school was too easy, and wondered half-seriously why she hadn't gotten straight A's. Hillary tried mightily to extract some unequivocal declaration of approval from her father, but he had tremendous difficulty in expressing pride or affection."

Hillary was an indefatigable secretary of state—she logged 956,733 diplomatic frequent-flier miles—and a star ambassador, especially on women's issues. But many experts feel, as John Cassidy wrote in *The New Yorker*, that, compared with the work of more geopolitical secretaries, her "signature achievements look like small beer."

Still, the job allowed her to get out of her husband's codependent shadow and develop a more authentic aura of inevitability. President Obama allowed his former rival to take Hillaryland into the State Department and then build it out, burnishing her own feminist brand around the world.

The idea of Hillary is winning, a grand historical gender bender: first lady upgrading to president. But is the reality winning? The Clintons have a rare talent for finding puddles to step in. Out of public life, can she adapt and make the leaps needed, in a world changing at a dizzying tempo, to keep herself on top?

Her challenge is to get into the future and stay there, adding fresh people and perspectives and leaving the Clinton mishegoss and cheesiness in the past.

The real question about Hillary is this: When people take a new look at her in the coming years, will they see the past or the future—Mrs. Clinton or Madam President?

# Brace Yourself for Hillary and Jeb

Oy. By the time the Bushes and Clintons are finished, they are going to make the Tudors and the Plantagenets look like pikers.

Before these two families release their death grip on the American electoral system, we're going to have to watch Chelsea's granddaughter try to knock off George P.'s grandson, Prescott Walker Bush II. Barack Obama, who once dreamed of being a transformational president, will turn out to be a mere hiccup in history, the interim guy who provided a tepid respite while Hillary and Jeb geared up to go at it.

Elections for president are supposed to make us feel young and excited, as if we're getting a fresh start. That's the way it was with JFK and Obama and, even though he was turning 70 when he got inaugurated, Ronald Reagan.

But, as the Clinton library tardily disgorged 3,546 pages of official papers Friday—dredging up memories of a presidency that was eight years of turbulence held steady by a roaring economy and an incompetent opposition, a reign roiled by Hillarycare, Vince Foster, Whitewater, Webb Hubbell, Travelgate, Monica, impeachment, Paula Jones, Kathleen Willey and Marc Rich—the looming prospect of another Clinton-Bush race makes us feel fatigued.

Our meritocratic society seems increasingly nepotistic and dynastic. There was a Bush or a Clinton in the White House and cabinet for 32 years straight. We're Bill Murray stuck at 6 a.m. in Harold Ramis's comic masterpiece *Groundhog Day*. As *Time*'s Michael Crowley tweeted on Friday, "Who else is looking forward to potentially TEN more years of obsessing about Hillary Clinton's past, present and future?"

The Clintons don't get defeated. They get postponed.

Just as Hillary clears the Democratic field if she is healthy and runs, a major Romney donor told the *Washington Post* that "if Jeb Bush is in the race, he clears the field." Jeb acknowledged in Long Island on Monday, referring to his mom's tart comment that "if we can't find more than two or three families to run for higher office, that's silly," that "it's an issue for sure." He added, "It's something that, if I run, I would have to overcome that. And so will Hillary, by the way. Let's keep the same standards for everybody."

We've arrived at the brave new world of 21st-century technology where robots are on track to be smarter than humans. Yet, politically, we keep traveling into the past. It won't be long before we'll turn on the TV and see Lanny Davis defending President Clinton (the next one) on some mishegoss or other.

When the Clintons lost to Obama, they simply turned Obama's presidency into their runway. Jim Messina, Obama's 2012 campaign manager, and a passel of other former Obama aides are now helping Hillary. And Bill is out being the campaigner in chief, keeping the Clinton allure on display in 2014.

The new cache of Clinton papers is benign—the press seems more enamored of speechwriters' doodles than substance—but just reading through them is draining. There are reams of advice on how to steer health care, which must have filled the briefing binders Hillary famously carried. But did she absorb the lessons, given that health care failed because she refused to be flexible and make the sensible compromises suggested by her husband and allies? She's always on listening tours, but is she hearing? As one White House health-care aide advised in the new document dump, "We need to be seen as listening."

Just as in the reminiscences compiled by Hillary's late friend Diane Blair, a political science professor at the University of Arkansas—some of which were printed in the *Washington Free Beacon* three weeks ago—the new papers reflect how entangled the Clintons' public and private lives were in the White House.

In a 1995 memo, Lisa Caputo, the first lady's press secretary, sees an opportunity for the upcoming reelection campaign by "throwing a big party" for the Clintons' 20th wedding anniversary.

"We could give a wonderful photo spread to *People* magazine of photos from the party coupled with old photos of their honeymoon and of special moments for them over the past 20 years," Caputo wrote, adding that they could turn it into "a nice mail piece later on."

Both sets of papers are revealing on the never-ending herculean struggle about how to present Hillary to the world, how to turn her shifting hairstyles and personas into one authentic image.

"Be careful to 'be real,'" media adviser Mandy Grunwald wrote to her before the launch of her listening tour at Daniel Patrick Moynihan's farm in upstate New York. "You did this well in the Rather interview where you acknowledged that of course last year was rough. Once you agree with the audience's/reporters' reality like that, it gives you a lot of latitude to then say whatever you want."

Grunwald advises the first lady to "look for opportunities for humor" and "Don't be defensive."

It's hard to understand why so many calculations are needed to seem "real," just as it's hard to understand how Hillary veers from feminist positions to unfeminist ones.

In the Blair papers, Hillary's private view of the Monica Lewinsky affair hewed closely to the lame rationales offered by Bill and his male friends.

"HRC insists, no matter what people say," Blair said, after

talking to Hillary on the phone, "it was gross inappropriate behavior but it was consensual (was not a power relationship) and was not sex within any real meaning (standup, liedown, oral, etc.) of the term." The president dallying with a 22-year-old intern was not "a power relationship" and certain kinds of sex don't count?

Like her allies Sidney Blumenthal and Charlie Rangel, Hillary paints her husband's mistress as an erotomaniac, just the way Clarence Thomas's allies painted Anita Hill. A little nutty and a little slutty.

"It was a lapse," Blair wrote, "but she says to his credit he tried to break it off, tried to pull away, tried to manage someone who was clearly a 'narcissistic loony toon'; but it was beyond control."

The cascade of papers evoke Hillary's stressful brawls—with her husband, the press, Congress and the Vast Right-Wing Conspiracy. And they evoke the issue about her that is so troubling and hard to fathom. She is an immensely complex woman with two sides. She is the tireless and talented public servant. And she is the tired warrior who can be insecure and defensive, someone who has cleaved to a bunker mentality when she would have been better served getting out of her defensive crouch.

Talking to her pal Blair, Hillary had a lot of severe words for her "adversaries" in the press and the GOP. Blair also said Hillary was "furious" at Bill for "ruining himself and the presidency" by 1994.

Hillary may have had a point when she said in 1993, after criticism of the maladroit firing of the veteran White House travel office staff, that the press "has big egos and no brains." But it speaks to her titanic battles and battle scars.

Hillary has spent so much time searching for the right identity, listening to others tell her who to be, resisting and following advice on being "real," that it leaves us with the same question we had when she first came on the stage in 1992.

Who is she?

# 42 and 45 Overpower 44

The first family is all over the news, discussing the management of the economy, income inequality, raising the minimum wage, the vicissitudes of press coverage and the benefits of healthy eating.

Everywhere you look, the Clintons rule.

Bill popped up on the front page of the *Times* giving a speech at his alma mater, Georgetown University, in which he defended his economic policies and chastised the press for its tendency to create a "story line" that doesn't match reality. (Sort of like the story line the Clintons created about Monica Lewinsky being a delusional stalker.)

Hillary's Apache dance with the press is detailed in the new issue of *Politico Magazine*, a piece that got a lot more buzz than the news the White House was excited about on Friday: a sharp drop in the unemployment rate.

Chelsea is serenely smiling from the cover of *Fast Company* for a story on how "the product of two of the most powerful brands in the world" is "carving out her own identity—by joining the family business" as vice chair in charge of shaping up the tangled finances of the Bill, Hillary & Chelsea Clinton Foundation. Her impending baby is being treated with enormous fanfare and exhaustive political analysis, like America's answer to Britain's bonny Prince George.

Obamaworld was even paranoid that Hillaryland would hijack the B-list festivities associated with the annual White House Correspondents' Dinner this weekend.

The former and future Democratic regime is clearly itching to get back in the saddle and relieve a president who is stalled on every front, and who never really got any joy from working the joystick of power or appreciated the value of the carrot/stick approach that helped Lincoln and LBJ bend history.

Both President Obama and Hillary have recently referred to leadership as a relay race. And if a fatigued and fed-up Obama looks ready to pass the baton early, the ravenous and relentless Clintons look ready to grab it—and maybe give him a few whacks over the head with it.

Obama's reign has become increasingly bloodless, and while the Clintons are not new blood, they do convey more vitality than the formerly electrifying politician in the White House.

Things have now reached the point where it feels as though 42 and 45 have already taken over the reins of Washington power from 44, who is fading Snapchat-fast.

The Clintons now have Obama, as one top Democrat said, "totally at their mercy" because they "take the oxygen out of the room."

Hillary's stock is so high—almost as high as her speaking fees— that in the *Daily Beast*, Tina Brown urged the front-runner to skip the campaign and simply go straight to becoming "post-President."

Just to make the Clintons feel completely at home as they ramp up to the restoration, there is even a congressional investigation spurred by the vast right-wing conspiracy.

House Speaker John Boehner announced Friday that he would call a vote to set up a select committee to look into the Benghazi debacle, and whether Congress was misled by former Secretary of State Hillary Clinton and others in the Obama administration.

As *Slate*'s Dave Weigel tweeted, "The nice thing about having a Benghazi select committee is you can roll it over into the Hillary presidency."

Many of those who aroused the Clintons' opprobrium and well-known taste for vengeance by supporting the rookie Barack Obama in 2008 thought they were headed to a fresh era in politics, moving past the gnarly braiding of the personal and political that led to chaos in the Clinton era.

But the Clinton machine, once described by David Geffen as "very unpleasant and unattractive and effective," has a Rasputin resilience. And now those who broke away are in the awkward position of having to make nice with the woman they helped vanquish.

Samantha Power recently said that she regretted calling Hillary a "monster" and offered her new view: "She just brings such rigor and conviction to everything she touches."

Claire McCaskill, who endorsed Obama in 2008 and said she didn't want her daughter near Bill Clinton and confided to a friend that she was nervous to be alone in an elevator with Hillary, announced in June that she is "Ready for Hillary."

Caroline Kennedy, whose endorsement in 2008 comparing Obama to her father was pivotal, told NBC's Chuck Todd: "I would like to see her run if that's what she wants to do. I think she would be great."

And Geffen, who gave Obama his first big Hollywood fund-raiser in 2008 and broke with the Clintons because he felt they lied "with such ease, it's troubling," now says he will "absolutely" support Hillary in 2016, calling her "an extraordinary, smart, accomplished woman."

Elizabeth Warren, who criticized Hillary in a 2003 book for an unprincipled stand on a bankruptcy bill, siding with the big banks she needed to bankroll her political career, lets Hillary off the hook in her new book.

Leon Panetta, who served as chief of staff for Bill Clinton and secretary of defense for Obama, told the *Times* that Obama had not yet defined America's 21st-century role in the world.

"Hopefully, he'll do it," Panetta said, "and certainly, she would."

The president who dreamed of being "transformative" seems bummed, and that's bumming out Americans.

But when you talk about batting singles, you're just asking to be overshadowed by the next big draft pick. If you're playing small ball and you're articulating your diminished expectations, it's only natural that someone is going to fill the void.

Some Obama aides get irritated when Hillary distances herself from Obama and when her advisers paint her as tougher than Obama, someone who wouldn't be afraid to drop the hammer and sickle on Vladimir Putin.

And some in Obamaworld think she could have skipped her $200,000-plus speeches to Goldman Sachs and helped the stumbling president make his push on health care, given that the push was focused on moms and kids, an area of interest for the woman who would be the first woman president.

But they were hoisted on their own petard. It was the lone-cat President Obama who ignored the usual practice in politics—dancin' with those who brung ya and dismantling your bitter rival's machine—and encouraged the view of Hillary as the presumptive nominee over his unfailingly loyal vice president, Joe Biden. Three of his key political advisers—Jim Messina, Jeremy Bird and Mitch Stewart—have gone to super PACs supporting Hillary.

David Plouffe, the president's former top political adviser, said Hillary could call him for advice and told Bloomberg's Al Hunt that "there's very little oxygen" for another Democrat to challenge her.

As Obama has learned, to his dismay, there's now very little oxygen for him, too.

*May 6, 2014*

# Burning the Beret

Monica Lewinsky says she would meet me for a drink.

I'm game.

In her new meditation in *Vanity Fair*, Monica mashes Hawthorne and Coleridge, proclaiming that she's ready to rip off her "scarlet-A albatross," "reimagine" her identity and reclaim her narrative.

At long last, she says, she wants to "burn the beret and bury the blue dress" and get unstuck from "the horrible image" of an intern who messed around with the president in the pantry off the Oval Office, spilled the details to the wrong girlfriend and sparked a crazy impeachment scandal.

I wish her luck. Though she's striking yet another come-hither pose in the magazine, there's something poignant about a 40-year-old frozen like a fly in amber for something reckless she did in her 20s, while the unbreakable Clintons bulldoze ahead. Besides, with the Clinton restoration barreling toward us and stretching as far as the eye can see to President Chelsea, we could all use a drink.

The last time I encountered Monica was at the Bombay Club, a restaurant nestled between my office and the White House. It was at the height of the impeachment madness and she was drinking a

Cosmo at a table with her family. After requesting that the piano player play "Send in the Clowns," she leaned in with me, demanding to know why I wrote such "scathing" pieces about her.

My columns targeted the panting Peeping Tom Ken Starr and the Clintons and their henchmen for their wicked attempt to protect the First Couple's political viability by smearing the intern as a nutty and slutty stalker. I did think Monica could skip posing for cheese-cake photos in *Vanity Fair* while in the middle of a plea bargain. But I felt sorry for her. She had propelled herself into that most loathed stereotype (except by Helen Gurley Brown): the overripe office vixen who seduces her married boss. Feminists turned on her to protect a president with progressive policies on women.

Monica bristled with confidence when she talked to me, but then she retreated to the ladies' room and had a meltdown on her cell phone with Judy Smith. Smith would go on to fame and fortune as a co-executive producer on Shonda Rhimes's *Scandal*, which focuses on Kerry Washington's Olivia Pope, a blend of Judy, who was an African American crisis manager, and her client Monica, who had an affair with the president.

Washington journalists fawned over the stars of *Scandal* last weekend at the White House Correspondents' Dinner festivities, which served mainly as a promotional vehicle for the ABC show and HBO's *Veep*.

The plot of *Scandal* is so luridly over-the-top, it makes the saga of the pizza-bearing intern who inspired it seem almost quaint. You'd think that the book *Monica's Story*, the HBO documentary, Barbara Walters's interview and the 1998 *Vanity Fair* spread would be enough about the most covered affair in history. Heck, the seamy Starr report was enough.

But she must feel that her reticence over the last 10 years of "self-searching and therapy" has led the public to hunger for her thoughts on the eve of Hillary's book rollout in June and at a moment when President Obama is struggling to pull focus back from the Clintons, whose past and future are more dominant than Obama's present. Monica is in danger of exploiting her own exploitation as she dishes about a couple whose erotic lives are of waning interest to the country.

But, clearly, she was stung and wanted to have her say about the revelation in February that Hillary had told her friend Diane Blair, knowing it would be made public eventually, that Bill was at fault for the affair but deserved props for trying to "manage someone who was clearly a narcissistic loony toon." Hillary also said she blamed herself for Bill's dalliance. Monica trenchantly notes about the feminist icon, who is playing the gender card on the trail this time around: "I find her impulse to blame the Woman—not only me, but herself—troubling."

Lewinsky said that Bill "took advantage" of her—in a consensual way. "Any 'abuse' came in the aftermath," she writes, "when I was made a scapegoat in order to protect his powerful position."

Disingenuously and pretentiously, Monica said that the tragedy of Tyler Clementi, the Rutgers freshman who committed suicide in 2010 after his roommate secretly streamed his liaison with another man over the Web, had wrought "a Prufrockian moment": Did she dare disturb the Clinton universe to become a spokeswoman against bullying?

Her bullies were crude strangers in person and online who reduced her to a dirty joke or verb. Monica corrects Beyoncé, who sings, "He Monica Lewinsky'd all on my gown," saying it should be "He Bill Clinton'd all on my gown." But her bullies were also the Clintons and their vicious attack dogs who worked so hard to turn "that woman," as Bill so coldly called her, into the scapegoat.

As Hillary gave a campaign-style speech in Maryland Tuesday, warning that economic inequality could lead to "social collapse," That Woman started her own campaign, keening about her own social collapse. It was like a Golden Oldie tour of a band you didn't want to hear in the first place.

# When Will Hillary Let It Go?

No one wrote about blondes like Raymond Chandler.

"There is the small cute blonde who cheeps and twitters and the big statuesque blonde who straight-arms you with an ice-blue glare," he wrote in *The Long Goodbye*. "There is the blonde who gives you the up-from-under look and smells lovely and shimmers and hangs on your arm and is always very, very tired when you take her home."

There's the pale, anemic, languid blonde with the soft voice. "You can't lay a finger on her," Chandler notes, "because in the first place you don't want to and in the second place she is reading 'The Waste Land' or Dante in the original." And when the New York Philharmonic is playing Hindemith, he writes dryly, "she can tell you which one of the six bass viols came in a quarter of a beat too late. I hear Toscanini can also. That makes two of them."

None of his descriptions, however, conjures the two regal blondes transfixing America at the moment: Hillary and Elsa.

Those close to them think that the queen of Hillaryland and the Snow Queen from Disney's *Frozen* have special magical powers, but worry about whether they can control those powers, show their humanity and stir real warmth in the public heart.

Just as Elsa's coronation suddenly became fraught, so has Hillary's. Like Arendelle, America is frozen: The war still rages in Iraq, the Clintons still dominate the political scene and Hillary still obsesses about money, a narrative thread that has existed since she was thwarted in her desire to build a pool at the governor's mansion in poor Arkansas and left the White House with a doggie bag full of sofas, rugs, lamps, TVs and china, some of which the Clintons later had to pay for or return. Even Chelsea was cashing in, getting a ridiculous $600,000-a-year scion salary from NBC, far greater than that of many of the network's correspondents.

As a Clinton White House aide once explained to me, "Hillary, though a Methodist, thinks of herself like an Episcopal bishop who deserves to live at the level of her wealthy parishioners, in return for devoting her life to God and good works."

After feeling stifled at times and misunderstood, after suffering painful setbacks, the powerful and polarizing Elsa and Hillary proclaim from their lofty height that they're going to "let it go" and go for it. (Although Elsa's wolves are not as fierce as the Fox predators after Hillary.)

"I don't care what they're going to say," Elsa sings at the climactic moment when she decides to let down her hair, ratchet up her star power and create her glittering ice palace. "Let the storm rage on. The cold never bothered me anyway!"

Hillary had a similar cri de coeur in her interview with Diane Sawyer. When Sawyer asked her about the focus on her appearance that has kept her so "scripted, cautious, safe," Hillary replied: "When you're in the spotlight as a woman, you know you're being judged constantly. I mean, it is just never-ending. And you get a little worried about, OK, you know, people over on this side are loving what I am wearing, looking like, saying. People over on this side aren't.

"You know, your natural tendency is how do you bring people together so that you can better communicate? I'm done with that. I mean, I'm just done." She continued: "I am over it, over it. I think I have changed; not worried so much about what other people are thinking." She vowed to now "say what I know, what I believe, and let the chips fall."

It would make a great Idina Menzel anthem, but it's not believable that Hillary Rodham Clinton will suddenly throw caution and calculation to the wind. Having market-tested the gender-neutral model in 2008, this time Hillary is presenting herself as a woman who has suffered the slings and arrows of sexism. Her apology for being "wrong" about voting to authorize W. to invade Iraq took 11 years to spit out, and she told the Council on Foreign Relations on Thursday that she "could not have predicted" the success of Al Qaeda–inspired insurgents in seizing control of Iraqi cities. If some bold voices had fought going into a patently unnecessary war against a country that had nothing to do with 9/11—a war, waged ignorantly for silly, macho reasons, that was never properly debated or planned in the White House—America would not be in a global crouch now, and Iraq would not be a killing field.

Hillary's new memoir, like her last one, is a testament to caution and calculation. It doesn't feel written so much as assembled by a "Hillary for President" algorithm. All this excitement is being ginned up, but nothing exciting is happening. There isn't one surprising or scintillating or provocative word in the whole book. *Hard Choices* is inert, a big yawn.

In her "If they'd listened to me" mode, she is distancing herself from the president on Syria, Russia and the Bergdahl trade because she does not, as the former Republican strategist Matthew Dowd puts it, want to be defeated by Obama twice.

The opening of her book tour/presidential campaign has featured some stumbles, causing some commentators to wonder if she has grown rusty and tone-deaf, isolated in the ice palace she erected to keep out the loathed press.

No one doubts that Hillary is tough and knowledgeable. But the question of how scarred and defensive she is, given all the fights and rough times she has gone through, and how that affects her judgment now, is a legitimate one.

Has she given up the my-way-or-the-highway imperiousness that doomed her health-care efforts? Has she toned down the defensiveness that exacerbated the Whitewater affair? Has she modified the ends-justify-the-means mind-set that allowed her to participate in the vivisection of young women she knew Bill had been involved with? Has she tempered the focus on political viability that led her to vote to allow W. to scamper into a vanity war? Has she learned not to surround herself with high-priced mercenaries like Mark Penn and Dick Morris?

In the last few days, two women interrogators have rattled Hillary's ice palace gates with questions that were obvious and reasonable.

With Sawyer, Clinton said she hadn't known enough to know the Benghazi outpost was unprotected, despite what Ambassador Chris Stevens had called "never-ending security threats."

On NPR's *Fresh Air*, Clinton grew testy when Terry Gross pressed her on whether the decision to finally publicly embrace gay marriage was a personal evolution or a political "calculus"—now that it's not as much of a political liability and now that the court has dismantled the dreadful Defense of Marriage Act, which her husband cravenly signed into law in 1996. Clinton said she couldn't do it as secretary of state. But the vice president was not constrained from saying what was in his heart and pushing the president in the right direction.

What Elsa discovers at the end of *Frozen* is that her powers can actually be used for good, once her heart is filled with love. She escapes from her prison, leaves behind the negative things that held her back and leads her kingdom to a happy and prosperous future.

Can Hillary?

# Isn't It Rich?

Chelsea Clinton never acted out during the eight years she came of age as America's first daughter.

No ditching of her Secret Service detail. No fake IDs for underage tippling. No drug scandal. No court appearance in tank top and toe ring. Not even any dirty dancing.

Despite a tough role as the go-between in the highly public and embarrassing marital contretemps of her parents, Chelsea stayed classy.

So it's strange to see her acting out in a sense now, joining her parents in cashing in to help feed the rapacious, gaping maw of Clinton Inc.

With her one percenter mother under fire for disingenuously calling herself "dead broke" when she left the White House, why would Chelsea want to open herself up to criticism that she is gobbling whopping paychecks not commensurate with her skills, experience or role in life?

As the 34-year-old tries to wean some of the cronies from the Clinton Foundation—which is, like the Clintons themselves, well-intended, wasteful and disorganized—Chelsea is making speeches that go into foundation coffers. She is commanding, as the *Times*'s Amy Chozick reported, up to $75,000 per appearance.

Chozick wrote: "Ms. Clinton's speeches focus on causes like eradicating waterborne diseases. ('I'm obsessed with diarrhea' is a favorite line.)"

There's something unseemly about it, making one wonder: Why on earth is she worth that much money? Why, given her dabbling in management consulting, hedge-funding and coattail-riding, is an hour of her time valued at an amount that most Americans her age don't make in a year? (Median household income in the United States is $53,046.)

If she really wants to be altruistic, let her contribute the money to some independent charity not designed to burnish the Clinton name as her mother ramps up to return to the White House and as she herself drops a handkerchief about getting into politics.

Or let her speak for free. After all, she is in effect going to candidate school. No need to get paid for it, too.

There was disgust over *Politico*'s revelation that before she switched to a month-to-month contract, Chelsea was getting wildly overpaid at $600,000 annually—or over $25,000 per minute on air—for a nepotistic job as a soft-focus correspondent for NBC News.

Chelsea is still learning the answer to a question she asked when she interviewed the Geico gecko: "Is there a downside to all this fame?"

The Clintons keep acting as though all they care about is selfless public service. So why does it keep coming back to gross money grabs? It's gone from two-for-the-price-of-one to three-for-the-price-of-20.

Hillary's book—which feels like something she got at Ikea and had someone put together—is drooping because it was more about the estimated $13 million advance and the campaign ramp-up than the sort of intriguing self-examination and political excavations found in the memoirs of Timothy Geithner and Bob Gates. If she had had something to say, the book might have been shorter.

Hillary doesn't see the disconnect between expressing grave concern about mounting student loan debt while scarfing six-figure sums from at least eight colleges, and counting. She says now that she's passing the university money to the foundation but, never Ms. Transparency, has refused to provide documentation of that. (She's still pocketing other huge fees for speeches like her April talk in Las Vegas to the Institute of Scrap Recycling Industries.)

Chozick estimated that the lucrative family speechmaking business has generated more than $100 million for the former president and first lady, whose fees range from $200,000 to $700,000 per appearance. Bill alone earned $17 million last year doing what he likes to do best—talking.

"The issue is that the philanthropic beneficiary of the speeches is a foundation, structured as a public foundation but clearly synonymous with and controlled by the Clinton family," Rick Cohen writes in *Nonprofit Quarterly*, adding: "Donors and institutions that are paying them and their daughter huge sums for their speeches may very well be buying recognition and face time with powerful political leaders who they hope will be able to deliver political favors in the future.

"It is troubling when corporate donors give to political charities with a more or less obvious expectation that softer and gentler treatment will ensue in the future. It is also troubling when some of the payers are public or nonprofit entities themselves such as colleges and universities, converting taxpayer funds and tax-exempt donations into signals that could end up in positive treatment when these institutions are themselves seeking access and favors, even if it is only a good word put in by one of the Clintons to a federal agency providing funding or to a regulator who might be taking a critical look at university tuitions and endowment payouts."

The Clintons were fiercely protective of Chelsea when she was a teenager, insisting on respect from the media and getting it. They need to protect their daughter again, this time from their wanton acquisitiveness.

# A Popular President

The thing about him is, he just keeps going.

At 67, he continues to be, as Anna Quindlen once wrote, like one of those inflatable toys with sand weighting the bottom—you knock him over and he pops back up.

As Hillary stumbles and President Obama slumps, Bill Clinton keeps getting more popular.

The women, the cheesy behavior, the fund-raising excesses, the self-pity, the adolescent narcissism, the impeachment, the charges of racially tinged insults against Obama in 2008, the foundation dishabille—all that percussive drama has faded to a mellow saxophone riff for many Americans.

A recent Wall Street Journal/NBC News/Annenberg center poll showed that Clinton was, by a long shot, the most admired president of the last quarter-century. A new YouGov poll finds that among the last eight elected presidents, Clinton is regarded as the most intelligent and W. the least.

(Clinton and W. both should have been more aggressive in catching Osama. But certainly, if Clinton had been president post-9/11, there would have been no phony invasion of Iraq, and Katrina would have elicited more empathy.)

A Washington Post/ABC News poll in May found Bill's approval ratings rebounding to the highest they had been since early in his presidency.

Even some who used to mock his lip-biting have decided that warmth, even if it's fake at times, beats real chilliness.

Speaking at the 92nd Street Y last month, Bill O'Reilly was asked by Geraldo Rivera whether the country would have been better off electing Hillary instead of Barack Obama.

"With Hillary you get Bill," O'Reilly replied. "And Bill knows what's going on. You may not like him but he knows what's going on. Hillary doesn't understand how the world works."

Except for LBJ and Nixon, ex-presidents tend to grow more popular. Yet Bill Clinton, wandering the global stage as a former president who may return to the White House as the husband of a president, plays a unique role in American history. (Newly released Clinton library documents revealed that Bill, believing it punchier, preferred to use "America" and "Americans" in speeches rather than "the United States" and "people of the United States.")

But why is he burning brighter now, when the spotlight should be on his successor and his wife?

Do we miss the days when the National Debt Clock was retired? Are we more accepting that politicians have feet of clay? Are we tired of leaders who act as burdened as Sisyphus? Do we miss having a showman and a show?

"Maybe they admire his vegan body," said David Axelrod impishly, before replying seriously: "He's the most seductive character that we've seen in American politics in our lifetime. He just has this unbelievably resilient and seductive personality."

James Carville noted dryly: "People are confused. They don't know which one they like more, the peace or the prosperity." He calls Clinton the "anti-Putin," someone who did not exercise power to harm people but to help them.

42 had greater strengths and greater weaknesses than the average pol.

Rand Paul accused Clinton of "predatory" behavior. Liz Cheney told *Politico*'s Mike Allen that she trusts Hillary more than she trusts Bill, implying that was because of Monica Lewinsky. And Todd "legitimate rape" Akin defended himself on Fox News this past week by hitting Clinton's "long history of sexual abuse and indecency."

But GOP pollster Kellyanne Conway said the words "Monica" and "liberal" rarely come up when she polls about Bill Clinton. The words "global" and "philanthropic" come up. She said that after Clinton, people "shrugged their shoulders at what had once made them raise their eyebrows."

"He was a good ambassador for the baby boomer generation," she said. "Who hasn't screwed up? Who hasn't had a third and fourth chance?"

Perhaps, given the tribal wars in Washington and dark tides loose in the world, there's a longing for Bill's better angels: the Happy Warrior desire to get up every day and go at it, no matter how difficult; the unfailing belief that in the future things will be better; the zest in the hand-to-hand combat of politics and policy, the reaching out to Newt Gingrich and other Republicans—even through government shutdowns and impeachment—and later teaming up with Bush senior. "There's a suspicion among a lot of people that Obama doesn't much care for politics," Carville said. "It's amazing that a man can be so successful at something he really doesn't like. It's like if you found out that Peyton Manning didn't like to play football."

Mike Murphy, the Republican strategist, said that Obama's fade has been "the best Clinton rehab."

Murphy noted the irony that first, Bill had to use his extroverted personality, his talent as Explainer in Chief and his "empathy ray gun" to help Obama get reelected, and now he will need to use those skills to push another clinical, cerebral candidate—his wife—up the hill.

"The one guy he can't help elect is himself because of that pesky Constitution," Murphy said. "But of course, that's what he'd love to do."

# Call Off the Dogs

I'll pay for this column.

The rottweilers will be unleashed.

Once the Clintons had a War Room. Now they have a Slime Room.

Once they had the sly James Carville, fondly known as "serpent-head." Now they have the slippery David Brock, accurately known as a snake.

Brock fits into the Clinton tradition of opportunistic knife-fighters like Dick Morris and Mark Penn.

The silver-haired 52-year-old, who sports colorful designer suits and, according to Roger Stone, once wore a monocle, brawled his way into a *Times* article about the uneasy marriage between Hillary Clinton's veteran attack dogs and the group of advisers who are moving over from Obamaland.

Hillary hasn't announced a 2016 campaign yet. She's busy polling more than 200 policy experts on how to show that she really cares about the poor while courting the banks. Yet her shadow campaign is already in a déjà-vu-all-over-again shark fight over control of the candidate and her money. It's the same old story: The killer organization that, even with all its ruthless hired guns, can't quite shoot straight.

Squabbling competing factions helped Hillary squander a quarter of a billion dollars in 2008.

As Nicholas Confessore and Amy Chozick chronicled, the nasty dispute spilled into public and Brock resigned last week from the board of a pro-Clinton super PAC called Priorities USA Action—whose cochairman is Jim Messina, Obama's 2012 campaign manager—accusing the political action committee of "an orchestrated political hit job" and "the kind of dirty trick I've witnessed in the right wing and would not tolerate then."

He should know.

The former "right-wing hit man" and impresario of "dirty tricks," as Brock has said of himself, made his living in the '90s sliming Anita Hill as "a little bit nutty and a little bit slutty" and breaking the Troopergate story, which accused Arkansas state troopers of setting up liaisons for Bill Clinton and spurred Paula Jones's 1994 sexual harassment lawsuit.

He has tried to discredit anyone who disagreed with his ideological hits (myself and reporters I know included). And that's still the business he's in, simply on the other side as a Hillary zealot. (His conversion began in 1996 when he published a biography of Hillary that was not a total hit job and that began the thaw.)

Just as Bill Clinton was able to forgive another architect of the vast right-wing conspiracy, Richard Mellon Scaife, once Scaife was charmed by Hillary in person and began giving money to the Clinton Foundation, so, too, was Bill won over by Brock's book, *Blinded by the Right: The Conscience of an Ex-Conservative*, and Brock's *Media Matters* and Correct the Record websites, which ferociously push back against any Hillary coverage that isn't fawning.

With the understood blessing of the Clintons, Brock runs a $28 million cluster of media monitoring groups and oppo research organizations that are vehicles to rebut and at times discredit and threaten anyone who casts a gimlet eye at Clinton Inc.

As Confessore and Chozick wrote, he uses a fund-raiser named Mary Pat Bonner, whose firm has collected millions of dollars in commissions—a practice many fund-raising experts consider unethical.

Everyone wants to be at the trough for this one because Hillary is likely to raise, and more important, spend more than $1 billion on her campaign.

The Clinton crowd is trying to woo Brock back into the fold because he's good at getting money and knows how their enemies think. The Clintons appreciate the fact that Brock, like Morris, is a take-no-prisoners type with the ethical compass of a jackal. Baked in the tactics of the right, Brock will never believe that negative coverage results from legitimate shortcomings. Instead, it's all personal, all false and all a war.

This is a bad harbinger for those who had hoped that Hillary would "kill off the wild dogs," as one Obama loyalist put it, and Bill would leave behind the sketchy hangers-on in the mold of Ron Burkle and Jeffrey Epstein.

Hillary's inability to dispense with brass-knuckle, fanatical acolytes like Brock shows that she still has an insecure streak that requires Borgia-like blind loyalty, and can't distinguish between the real vast right-wing conspiracy and the voices of legitimate concern.

Moneygrubbing is always the ugly place with the Clintons, who have devoured $2.1 billion in contributions since 1992 to their political campaigns, family foundation and philanthropies, according to the Old (Good) *New Republic*.

David Axelrod, the author of a new memoir, *Believer*, wrote that Hillary's past gurus, Morris and Penn, were nonbelievers—mercenary, manipulative and avaricious. He told *Politico*'s Glenn

Thrush that he would have advised Hillary not to cash in with her book and six-figure speeches.

Axelrod reiterated to me that Hillary's designated campaign chairman, John Podesta, Bill Clinton's last chief of staff who left his post as an Obama counselor on Friday, "has the strength and standing to enforce a kind of campaign discipline that hasn't existed before."

But, for now, what Republicans say about government is true of the Clintons: They really do believe that your money belongs to them.

Someday, they should give their tin cup to the Smithsonian. It's one of the wonders of the world.

# With the Clintons, Only the Shadow Knows

Somewhere in Smithsonian storage sits a portrait of Bill Clinton with two odd features: He is standing next to a shadow meant to conjure Monica Lewinsky's blue dress, and he is not wearing his gold wedding ring.

As we have been reminded by a recent wild cascade of stories, everything about the Clintons is convoluted. Nothing is simple, even a celebratory portrait.

Nelson Shanks, picked by Clinton to do his portrait for the National Portrait Gallery, revealed to the *Philadelphia Daily News* that he had used a blue dress on a mannequin to evoke the shadow of the Lewinsky scandal in the portrait.

I called the 77-year-old artist to ask about his devilish punking.

"It's an extra little kick going on in the painting," he said. "It was a bit humorous, but there was also a sort of authenticity to it. To do a Pollyanna, basically meaningless, symbolically neutral painting of somebody that has had a powerful influence on society is really copping out." He said that Clinton's lack of a wedding band has no ulterior meaning, noting: "I just forgot the ring." But Clinton aides weren't buying it.

He said when the omission first made news after the portrait was unveiled in 2006, Hillary Clinton sent him "a lovely little note saying don't worry about it, this is just a tempest in a teapot."

In an op-ed article last week, Eugénie Bisulco, a Clinton administration staffer who led the search team for a White House portrait artist, said it wasn't Shanks's attempt to put in "a moral compass" that grated. (The Clintons didn't even know about that.) Bisulco said that it was that the portrait made Clinton look like "a disheveled Ted Koppel."

Other Clintonistas dismissed the allegorical shadow as "put-a-bunny-in-the-pot crazy."

Shanks said it was "like an ice pick going through my back" when he learned that his portrait was "exiled to the dark recesses" in 2009. On a visit to the museum a year and a half ago, he heard a docent telling a tour group that the Clintons put the kibosh on the painting.

He asked Kim Sajet, now director of the National Portrait Gallery, and she confirmed his darkest fears in an email, saying that they took it down because the Clintons disliked it. But, in response to a query, Sajet admitted that she was "repeating unfounded gossip," according to a spokeswoman, and insisted that the painting is merely in rotation.

Shortly after the art imbroglio broke, an email imbroglio broke. The *Times*'s Michael Schmidt reported that, as secretary of state, Hillary did not preserve her official correspondence on a government server and exclusively used a private email account. She used a private server linked to her Chappaqua home, only turning over cherry-picked messages in December at the State Department's request.

Given the paranoid/legalese perspective that permeates Clinton-land, this made sense: It's hard to request emails from an account you don't know exists. And your own server can shield you from subpoenas and other requests. If you want records from the Clinton server, you have to fight for them. Clinton Inc. can tough it out and even make stuff disappear. Instead of warning the secretary that she could be violating regulations, her aides fetishized her clintonemail.com account as a status symbol. Chelsea took on the pseudonym Diane Reynolds.

Near midnight on Wednesday, Hillary tweeted that she had asked the State Department to release the emails she had coughed up when pressed, noting: "I want the public to see my email."

Less true words were never spoken.

Schmidt's scoop followed the *Wall Street Journal* revelation that at least 60 companies that lobbied the State Department when Hillary was in charge had funneled more than $26 million to the Clinton Foundation.

Certainly, Hillary wants a lot of control. She has spent a lifetime cleaning up messes sparked by her overweening desire for control and her often out-of-control mate. She always feared that her emails could become fodder for critics, and now they have.

Everyone is looking for signs in how Hillary approaches 2016 to see if she's learned lessons from past trouble. But the minute this story broke, she went back to the bunker, even though she had known for months that the Republicans knew about the account. The usual hatchets—Philippe Reines, David Brock, Lanny Davis and Sidney Blumenthal—got busy.

The Clintons don't sparkle with honesty and openness. Between his lordly appetites and her queenly prerogatives, you always feel as if there's something afoot.

Everything needs to be a secret, from the Rose Law Firm records that popped up in a White House closet two years after they were subpoenaed to the formulation of her health-care plan.

Yet the Clintons always act as though it's bad form when you bring up their rule-bending. They want us to compartmentalize, just as they do, to connect the dots that form a pretty picture and leave the other dots alone.

If you're aspiring to be the second president in the family, why is it so hard to be straight and direct and stand for something? Why can't you just be upright and steady and good?

Given all the mistakes they've made, why do they keep making them? Why do they somehow never do anything that doesn't involve shadows?

*March 14, 2015*

# An Open Letter to
# hdr22@clintonemail.com

*(This column was inspired by an explosive open letter written by Republican Senator Tom Cotton addressed to "Leaders of the Islamic Republic of Iran" warning that the president's pact on nuclear enrichment could be reversed.)*

Since open letters to secretive and duplicitous regimes are in fashion, we would like to post an Open Letter to the Leaders of the Clinton Republic of Chappaqua:

It has come to our attention while observing your machinations during your attempted restoration that you may not fully understand our constitutional system. Thus, we are writing to bring to your attention two features of our democracy: the importance of preserving historical records and the ill-advised gluttony of an American feminist icon wallowing in regressive Middle Eastern states' payola.

You should seriously consider these characteristics of our nation as the Campaign-That-Must-Not-Be-Named progresses.

If you, Hillary Rodham Clinton, are willing to cite your mother's funeral to get sympathy for ill-advisedly deleting 30,000 emails, it just makes us want to sigh: OK, just take it. If you want it that bad, go ahead and be president and leave us in peace. (Or war, if you have your hawkish way.) You're still idling on the runway, but we're already jet-lagged. It's all so drearily familiar that I know we're only moments away from James Carville writing a column in David Brock's *Media Matters*, headlined, "In Private, Hillary's Really a Hoot."

When you grin and call out to your supporters, like at the Emily's List anniversary gala, "Don't you someday want to see a woman president of the United States of America?" the answer is: Yes, it would be thrilling.

But therein lies the rub.

What is the trade-off that will be exacted by the Chappaqua Republic for that yearned-for moment? When the Rogue State of Bill began demonizing Monica Lewinsky as a troubled stalker, you knew you could count on the complicity of feminists and Democratic women in Congress. Bill's female cabinet members and feminist supporters had no choice but to accept the unappetizing quid pro quo: The Clintons would give women progressive public policies as long as the women didn't assail Bill for his regressive private behavior with women.

Now you, Hillary, are following the same disheartening "We'll make you an offer you can't refuse" pattern. You started the *Guernica* press conference defending your indefensible droit du seigneur over your State Department emails by referring to women's rights and denouncing the letter to Iran from Republican senators as "out of step with the best traditions of American leadership."

None of what you said made any sense. Keeping a single account mingling business and personal with your own server wasn't about "convenience." It was about expedience. You became judge and jury on what's relevant because you didn't want to leave digital fingerprints for others to retrace. You could have had Huma carry two devices if you really couldn't hoist an extra few ounces. You insisted on piggybacking on Bill's server, even though *The Wall Street Journal* reported his aides were worried about hackers, because you were gaming the system for 2016. (Or even 2012.)

Suffused with paranoia and preemptive defensiveness, you shrugged off The One's high-minded call for the Most Transparent Administration in History.

It depends upon what the meaning of @ is.

The subtext of your news conference cut through the flimsy rationales like a dagger: "You can have the first woman president. You can get rid of those epically awful Republicans who have vandalized Congress, marginalized the president and jeopardized our Iran policy. You can get a more progressive American society. But, in return, you must accept our foibles and protect us."

You exploit our better angels and our desire for a finer country and our fear of the anarchists and haters in Congress.

Because you assume that if it's good for the Clintons, it's good for the world, you're always tangling up government policy with your own needs, desires, deceptions, marital bargains and gremlins.

Instead of raising us up by behaving like exemplary, sterling people, you bring us down to your own level, a place of blurred lines and fungible ethics and sleazy associates. Your family's foundation gobbles tens of millions from Saudi Arabia and other repressive regimes whose unspoken message is: "We're going to give you money to go improve the world. Now leave us alone to go persecute women."

That's an uncomfortable echo of a Clintonian trade-off, which goes: "We're going to give you the first woman president, who will improve the country. Now leave us alone to break any rules we please."

Bill, your pathology is more human and interesting. It's almost like you need to create messes to see if your extraordinary political gifts can get you out of them. It's a fatherless boy's "How Much Do

You Love Me?" syndrome. Do you love me enough to let me get away with *this*?

Hillary, your syndrome is less mortal, more regal, a matter of "What Is Hillary Owed?" Ronald Reagan seemed like an ancient king, as one aide put it, gliding across the landscape. You seem like an annoyed queen, radiating irritation at anyone who tries to hold you accountable. You're less rhetorically talented than Bill but more controlling, so it's harder for you to navigate out of tough spots.

No Drama Obama and his advisers are clearly appalled to be drawn into your shadowy shenanigans, just as Al Gore once was. Whatever else you say about this president, he has no shadows.

We hope this letter enriches your knowledge of our constitutional system and promotes mutual understanding and clarity as the campaign progresses.

Sincerely,
America

# Grandmama Mia!

When my brother Michael was a Senate page, he delivered mail to John F. Kennedy and Richard Nixon, who had offices across the hall from each other. (As vice president, Nixon served as president of the Senate.)

Michael recalled that Kennedy never looked up or acknowledged his presence, but Nixon would greet him with a huge smile. "Hi, Mike," he'd say. "How are you doing? How's the family?"

It seemed a bit counterintuitive, especially since my dad, a DC police inspector in charge of Senate security, was a huge Kennedy booster. (The two prominent pictures in our house were of the Mona Lisa and JFK.) But after puzzling over it, I finally decided that JFK had the sort of magnetism that could ensorcell big crowds, so he did not need to squander it on mail boys. Nixon, on the other hand, lacked large-scale magnetism, so he needed to work hard to charm people one by one, even mail boys.

Hillary Clinton has always tried to be more like the Democratic president she lived with in the White House, to figure out how he spins the magic. "I never realized how good Bill was at this until I tried to do it," she once told her adviser Harold Ickes. But she ends up being compared with the Republican president she investigated as a young lawyer for the House Judiciary's Watergate investigation.

Her paranoia, secrecy, scandals and disappearing act with emails from her time as secretary of state have inspired a cascade of comparisons with Nixon.

Pat Buchanan, a former Nixon adviser, bluntly told Jason Zengerle recently in *New York* magazine: "She reminds me of Nixon," another pol who's more comfortable behind the scenes than grinding it out in the arena.

As Hillary finally admits the axiomatic—she wants to be president—she will take the Nixon approach, trying to charm people one by one in the early states for 2016, an acknowledgment that she cannot emulate the wholesale allure of Bill Clinton or Barack Obama.

That reality hit her in 2008, when throngs waited hours to get in to hear The One. "Enough with the speeches and the big rallies," a frustrated Hillary cried out to a Cincinnati crowd.

She wants to avoid the coronation vibe this time, a member of her orbit told *Politico*'s Glenn Thrush, even though Martin O'Malley, a potential rival, objected that "the presidency of the United States is not some crown to be passed between two families" and the *Onion* reported her campaign slogan is "I deserve this."

Hillary's team plans to schedule low-key events where she can mingle with actual voters. "I think it's important, and Hillary does, too, that she go out there as if she's never run for anything before and establish her connection with the voters," Bill Clinton told *Town & Country* for a cover story.

The Big Dog, who got off his leash last time in South Carolina, said he will start small as well, noting: "My role should primarily be as a backstage adviser to her until we get much, much closer to the election."

Democratic strategists and advisers told the *Washington Post*'s Anne Gearan and Dan Balz that "the go-slow, go-small strategy" plays to her strengths, "allowing her to meet voters in intimate settings where her humor, humility and policy expertise can show through."

As the old maxim goes, if you can fake humility, you've got it made. But seeing Rahm and Hillary do it in the same season might be too much to take.

President Obama has said: "If she's her wonderful self, I'm sure she's going to do great." But which self is that?

Instead of a chilly, scripted, entitled policy wonk, as in 2008, Hillary plans to be a warm, spontaneous, scrappy fighter for average Americans. Instead of a woman campaigning like a man, as in 2008, she will try to stir crowds with the idea of being the first woman president. Instead of haughtily blowing off the press, as in 2008, she will make an effort to play nice.

It's a do-or-die remodeling, like when you put a new stainless steel kitchen in a house that doesn't sell.

In 1992, Clinton strategists wrote a memo aiming to recast Hillary in a skeptical public's mind as a warm, loving mother. They even suggested an event where Bill and Chelsea would surprise Hillary on Mother's Day.

Now, after 25 years on the national stage, Hillary is still hitting the reset button on her image, this time projecting herself as a warm, loving grandmother.

On the eve of her campaign launch, she released an updated epilogue to her banal second memoir, *Hard Choices*, highlighting her role as a grandmother.

"I'm more convinced than ever that our future in the 21st century depends on our ability to ensure that a child born in the hills of Appalachia or the Mississippi Delta or the Rio Grande Valley grows up with the same shot at success that Charlotte will," she wrote, referring to her granddaughter.

This was designed to rebut critics who say she's too close to Wall Street and too grabby with speech money and foundation donations from Arab autocrats to wage a sincere fight against income inequality.

But if Hillary really wants to help those children, maybe she should give them some of the ostensible and obscene billion dollars that she is planning to spend to persuade us to make her grandmother of our country.

# Granny Get Your Gun

The most famous woman on the planet has a confounding problem. She can't figure out how to campaign as a woman.

In 2008, Hillary Clinton took advice from two men—Bill Clinton and Mark Penn—and campaigned like a man. Worried about proving she could be commander in chief, Hillary scrubbed out the femininity, vulnerability and heart, in image and issues, that were anathema to Penn. Consciously tamping down the humor and warmth in Hillary and playing up the muscularity and bellicosity, her strategist modeled Hillary on Iron Lady Margaret Thatcher.

"In analyzing the current situation, regardless of the sex of the candidates, most voters in essence see the presidents as the 'father' of the country," Penn wrote in a memo. "They do not want someone who would be the first mama, especially in this kind of world."

Trying to project swagger, she followed her husband's advice and voted to authorize the Iraq war without bothering to read the unpersuasive National Intelligence Estimate—a move that she now surely knows helped cost her the election. Bill Clinton's philosophy after 9/11, as Jeff Gerth and Don Van Natta Jr. reported in their book,

*Her Way*, was encapsulated in what he told a group of Democrats in 2003: "When people feel uncertain, they'd rather have someone who's strong and wrong than somebody who's weak and right."

Hillary followed this maxim on the day of the war vote in the Senate when, as Gerth wrote last year in *ProPublica*, she "went further than any other Democratic senator—and aligned herself with President Bush—by accusing Saddam Hussein of giving 'aid, comfort and sanctuary to terrorists, including Al Qaeda.'" Gerth asserts that Clinton's aversion to the subject of Iraq kept her from engaging fully as the nation's top diplomat during the period when Iraq was crumbling and the Islamic State was rising.

Hillary saw the foolishness of acting like a masculine woman defending the Iraq invasion after she fell behind to a feminized man denouncing it. After losing Iowa and watching New Hampshire slip away to the tyro, Barack Obama, Hillary cracked. She misted up, talking to a group of voters in New Hampshire when a woman asked her how she kept going, while staying "upbeat and so wonderful."

Her aides thought the flash of tears would be a disaster, that she would seem weak. But it was a triumph because she seemed real. As the *Washington Post*'s Dan Balz wrote in his campaign book, it "let a glimmer of her humanity peek through."

Hillary always overcorrects. Now she has zagged too far in the opposite direction, presenting herself as a sweet, docile granny in a Scooby van, so self-effacing she made only a cameo in her own gauzy, demographically pandering presidential campaign announcement video and mentioned no issues on her campaign's website.

In her Iowa roundtables, she acted as though she were following dating tips from 1950s advice columnists to women trying to "trap" a husband: listen a lot, nod a lot, widen your eyes, and act fascinated with everything that's said. A clip posted on her campaign Facebook page showed her sharing the story of the day her granddaughter was born with some Iowa voters, basking in estrogen as she emoted about the need for longer paid leave for new mothers: "You've got to *bond* with your baby. You've got to learn how to take *care* of the baby."

She and her fresh team of No-Drama ex-Obama advisers think that this humility tour will move her past the hilarious caricature by Kate McKinnon on *Saturday Night Live* of Hillary as a manipulative, clawing robot who has coveted the role as leader of the free world for decades. But isn't there a more authentic way for Hillary to campaign as a woman—something between an overdose of testosterone and an overdose of estrogen, something between Macho Man and Humble Granny?

Tina Fey and Amy Poehler showed the way in 2008, deploring the sexism against Hillary and hailing her as the unapologetically tough chick. It was a precursor to her cool "Don't mess with me" Tumblr meme, showing her with dark glasses serenely checking her BlackBerry on a military plane.

"Bitches get stuff done," Fey proclaimed in a Weekend Update segment on *Saturday Night Live* that ended with, "Bitch is the new black."

In one skit, Amy as Hillary described how she would battle Big Oil: "It's going to take a fighter, not a talker, someone who is aggressive enough and relentless enough and demanding enough to take them on. Someone so annoying, so pushy, so grating, so bossy and shrill, with a personality so unpleasant, that at the end of the day the special interests will have to go 'Enough! We give up! Life is too short to deal with this awful woman! Just give her what she wants so she'll shut up and leave us in peace.' And I think the American people will agree, that someone is me."

As she hits the trail again, Hillary is a blur of competing images, a paean to the calibrated, artful and generic, a low-key lady who doesn't stand for anything except low-keyness. She has seen, over and over, that overcorrecting can be self-defeating for her and parlous to the nation, but she keeps doing it.

Let's hope that the hokey Chipotle Granny will give way to the cool Tumblr Chick in time to teach her Republican rivals—who are coming after her with every condescending, misogynist, distorted thing they've got—that bitch is still the new black.

*May 30, 2015*

# Hooray for Hillarywood?

Is Hollywood really ready to give a 67-year-old woman a leading role in a big-budget production?

Hillary Clinton's campaign has echoes of various classic movies: *Single White Female*, with Hillary creepily co-opting the identity of the more trendy Elizabeth Warren; *My Fair Lady*, with Hillary sitting meekly and being schooled on how to behave by tyrannical Pygmalions (Iowa voters); *The Usual Suspects*, with Hillary's hoodlums, Sidney Blumenthal and David Brock, vying to be Keyser Söze; and, of course, *How to Steal a Million*, a caper about a heist plotted by a couple that doesn't need the money.

From a narrative point of view, Hollywood is more intrigued with the scenario of their old raffish Southern favorite, Bill Clinton, as the first First Lad than the earnest Midwestern Hillary as the first female POTUS.

On TV, after all, women presidents are old hat.

I recently interviewed several dozen Hollywood players, mostly on background because of fears about the famed Clinton vindictive streak.

They aren't over the moon about Barack Obama anymore, and

even feel burned. He was like a razzle-dazzle trailer that turned out to be a disappointing movie with mediocre box office.

You hear plenty of complaints about the president's mingy care and feeding of donors.

"It's not unheard-of to think that liking people is part of the job," one political consultant to the stars said tartly.

Hollywood is mostly united behind Hillary, with a few Bernie outliers and Elizabeth dreamers. But it's a forced march.

"There's this feeling like, 'Oh, damn! Now we're all going to have to show up to Jeffrey's event,'" said one studio big shot.

Drinking wine at his glamorous house, an Obama bundler who is trying to work up some Hillary enthusiasm agreed: "'Jeffrey Katzenberg is calling' is a call that you avoid in a way that you couldn't before."

Because the Clintons have been in politics for decades, there is a throng at the teat, making donors, bundlers and retainers fret that the rewards and appointments will be spread thin.

"Hollywood needs perpetual attention from its presidents, from filming bar mitzvah congratulations to stays in the Lincoln Bedroom," said one Obama associate in Hollywood.

The sheer size of the Clinton universe has caused, as a political consultant to bold-faced names says, "a palpable lack of energy amongst the people who have been insiders for years." Not to mention a huge management challenge.

"Money in this town is value driven, ego driven," one major fund-raiser said. "It's not about tracking legislation as it affects our own interests."

Hollywood helped create Clinton Inc., finding an early pop-culture affinity with the young governor of Arkansas and jumping in to be his ATM.

The symbiotic attraction between the two capitals of illusion peaked—and even got a little overripe—during Bill's reign, when he acted like a Hollywood groupie, hanging with the moguls and stars under the palms into the wee hours. Even some in Hollywood thought it unseemly when he began flying around with highfliers Ron Burkle and Steve Bing.

Bill and Hillary were stunned and furious when David Geffen, Steven Spielberg and Katzenberg held a fund-raising reception at the Beverly Hilton and a dinner at Geffen's home for Obama—a knife in the heart of Clinton Inc. Now Hollywood must kiss the ring to fund the restoration and counteract conservative dark money, ponying up a chunk of the billion-plus Hillary plans to spend on her campaign.

Katzenberg made his peace with Hillary and is helping spearhead her super PAC. Geffen, who has not talked to the Clintons, gave her primary campaign the maximum of $2,700. Bill Maher, who sent Obama's super PAC a check for a million (and never got a thank-you note) says he will vote for her but won't fork over another mill.

Haim Saban, the Mighty Morphin Power Rangers billionaire who describes himself as "a former cartoon schlepper," never deserted Hillary and this month hosted a $1.9 million fund-raiser for her at his Beverly Hills mansion.

Recalling the bitter 2008 civil war as we nibbled biscotti in his LA office, he waved off those who yearn for fresh and new.

"When I go to buy potatoes and tomatoes, I look for fresh and new," he said. "We're talking about electing the leader of the free world."

But his childlike excitement is less common than the jaded attitude of a Hillary supporter who sighed: "Nobody wants to go to a fund-raiser and get another picture with her. But we have to figure out how to get her there," for the sake of their issues.

The joke circulates in Hollywood that Hillary is like Coca-Cola's Dasani water: She's got a great distribution system, but nobody likes the taste.

Fortunately for her, there's no difference between an enthusiastic check for $250,000 and an unenthusiastic check.

The prevailing mood in this faltering Dream Factory is cynical. Some worry about the drip, drip of revelations about the Clintons. "It's like that Dorothy Parker line, 'What fresh hell is this?'" said one top Hollywood Democrat.

Said another: "It sits badly when something drops and it's, here they go again, thinking they can write their own rules, be cute by half."

Some still worry, as Geffen did in 2008, that Bill shenanigans will get Hillary into trouble.

Sipping vodka at the Chateau Marmont, Bill Maher said he was not concerned, noting: "Who could have less to do with Bill Clinton's sex life than Hillary?"

# Trade Winds Blow Ill for Hillary

It's hard being Elizabeth Warren.

Especially when you're not Elizabeth Warren.

Hillary Clinton had an awkward collision last week juggling her past role as President Obama's secretary of state, her current role as Democratic front-runner and her coveted future role as president.

As secretary of state, she helped Obama push the Trans-Pacific Partnership that is at the center of the current trade fight. In Australia in 2012, she was effusive, saying that the trade pact "sets the gold standard in trade agreements to open free, transparent, fair trade, the kind of environment that has the rule of law and a level playing field. And when negotiated, this agreement will cover 40 percent of the world's total trade and build in strong protections for workers and the environment."

Now Hillary says she is unsure about the pact and would likely oppose giving President Obama the special authority to negotiate trade deals for an up-or-down vote in Congress. As a future president, of course, she would want the same authority to negotiate trade deals that Obama is seeking in the messy Capitol Hill donnybrook.

But as a candidate pressured by progressives like Warren and

Bernie Sanders and by labor unions, she turned to Jell-O, shimmying around an issue she had once owned and offering an unpleasant reminder of why "Clintonian" became a synonym for skirting the truth.

It depends on what your definition of trade is—and trade-off.

Hillary has vowed to be more straightforward this time about running as a woman, her position on immigration and her relations with the press (which are still imperious). The heartbreaking mass shooting in a black church in Charleston, SC, Hillary said, should force the country to face up to "hard truths" about race, violence and guns.

But even after all her seasoning as a senator and secretary of state, even after all her enthusiastic suasion on the president's trade bill, she can't face up to hard truths on trade.

And we have to play this silly game with her, as she dances and ducks, undermining President Obama by siding with Nancy Pelosi after Pelosi filleted the trade deal on the House floor.

"The president should listen to and work with his allies in Congress, starting with Nancy Pelosi," Hillary said in Iowa last weekend, torpedoing White House efforts to lure Democrats back on board.

In an interview with the Nevada journalist Jon Ralston on Thursday, Hillary slid around her previous support of the Pacific trade pact and said that if she were still in the Senate, she would "probably" vote no on the trade promotion authority bill.

Obama loyalists were quick to note the irony that Hillary did not help Obama, even though he is working to combat the deep Democratic resistance spawned by the North American Free Trade Agreement that President Bill Clinton signed.

The White House is certainly irritated with Hillary. Perhaps it will spur Obama to wonder why he pulled the rug out from under poor old Joe, his own vice president, to lay out the red carpet for his former rival.

As David Axelrod told the *Times*'s Michael Shear and Amy Chozick:

"The fact is, she was there when this thing was launched and she was extolling it when she left. She's in an obvious vise, between the work that she endorsed and was part of and the exigencies of a campaign. Obviously, her comments plainly weren't helpful to moving this forward."

CNN reported that Hillary had enthusiastically promoted the trade pact 45 times as secretary of state.

Aside from the fact that Hillary should be able to take a deep breath and stick with something she's already argued for, it plays into voters' doubts about her trustworthiness.

If you want to be president and you shape your principles to suit the shifting winds—as Hillary did when she voted to authorize W.'s Iraq invasion—then how can people on either side of an issue trust you?

Since she hasn't sparked much passion herself yet, she may be frightened by the passionate acolytes of Warren and Sanders—whose uncombed authenticity is buoying him in New Hampshire.

And, given her own unseemly money grabs, she may not be willing to push back on primal forces swirling around the trade issue about unbridled corporatism in an era of stagnant wages.

But the greater danger for her is in looking disingenuous.

At the end of the day, leaders have to sometimes step up on some issues that are not 80 percent issues. Unfortunately for her, Hillary is not as artful a dodger as her husband.

Trade is a sticky wicket for her. But the path to the presidency is full of sticky wickets. And being president is full of sticky wickets. So you have to try to say what's true and what you actually believe, not just what's tactical.

Surprisingly, I received a fund-raising letter recently. "Hillary Rodham Clinton" was in large letters on the upper left-hand side of the envelope and above my address was the typed message: "Maureen, this is our moment . . . are you with me?"

Not at the moment.

*October 17, 2015*

# Will Hillary Clinton Be Pilloried?

Hillary Clinton is wrong about the Benghazi committee.

It's not the longest-running special congressional investigation ever, as the Hillary campaign tweeted. According to PolitiFact, other congressional probes have lasted a lot longer than 17 months, including hearings on the conduct of the Civil War (40 months) and the assassinations of JFK and Martin Luther King Jr. (30 months).

But Hillary Clinton is also right about the Benghazi committee. It has nullified itself.

The Republicans created the committee in 2014, but it soon became clear it was going to stretch into 2016 as a way to torment Hillary during campaign season and keep her back on her heels after the Republicans had picked a candidate.

Then House Majority Leader Kevin McCarthy went on Sean Hannity's Fox News show, spilling and crowing about how the Republicans had put together the Benghazi committee to tar the Democratic front-runner as "untrustable" and drag down her numbers.

In that moment, Hillary shook off her bad juju and McCarthy got it, losing his shot at being speaker.

The questions the panel initially planned to look into were legitimate, even though there were cascading inquiries.

It remains hard to believe that Ambassador Christopher Stevens and other personnel could have been under attack at different facilities in Benghazi, Libya, over a span of seven and a half hours without any nearby military bases ready and able to provide air cover.

As Senator John McCain once put it on ABC, why didn't Hillary see the cable that came to her office three weeks before the murderous siege that said the consulate in Benghazi could not withstand a coordinated attack, and where were the Department of Defense assets?

It is still painful to contemplate that the four deaths came after repeated requests from Stevens's team for many more security agents for the embassy in Tripoli and mission in Benghazi had been unceremoniously rebuffed by the State Department.

On Friday, CNN's Jake Tapper pressed Clinton about why the State Department rejected those increasingly jittery requests.

"That was left to the security professionals," she replied, adding that reports had concluded that "the security professionals in the State Department had to look worldwide and had to make some tough decisions."

She said it wasn't the job of a secretary of state to "be reaching down" and making those decisions. But, as the main proponent of getting rid of Muammar el-Qaddafi, which led to Libya deteriorating into violence and chaos, Clinton should have been more vigilant about the safety of the intrepid ambassador whose death, she said, was "a great personal loss."

Trey Gowdy's Benghazi committee was initially set up to investigate issues such as: How did the Defense Department deal with security at American embassies and other overseas facilities? How does the government respond when its employees abroad are in trouble? How much did administration officials, thinking about the president's looming re-election, try to spin the explanation of the attack on the Benghazi compound?

But as the *Times*'s Eric Lipton, Noam Scheiber and Michael Schmidt reported in a front-page story last week, the committee fell into disarray.

Bradley Podliska, an Air Force Reserve officer and Republican staffer fired from the committee, told the *Times* that things degenerated to the point where members formed a wine club and staffers started a gun club, discussing buying monogrammed 9-millimeter Glock handguns in the committee conference room. So at least something was accomplished.

The committee came to life only when it stumbled into the fact that Clinton had used a private email server while secretary of state to keep some of her communications off the books.

Gowdy told Speaker John Boehner that looking into the emails could be a distraction from the Benghazi investigation. But the committee couldn't resist, becoming more and more obsessed with the scintillating email trail.

Hillary's decision to circumvent the State Department email system showed bad and paranoid judgment, and left her official emails as secretary vulnerable to hacking. And all her tap dancing that other secretaries did it and that none of the emails were marked classified at the time she sent or received them doesn't get her off the hook.

As enjoyable as it is seeing Sidney Blumenthal on the hot seat, Gowdy and Company should have left the email matter to another congressional committee and the Justice Department. They just couldn't stop themselves, any more than they could stop themselves from cutting Democrats out of witness interviews or from trumpeting that Clinton's aide Huma Abedin was going to testify on Friday.

Clinton told Tapper she didn't know what to expect from the grilling this coming Thursday by her Republican inquisitors. It has been touted as a huge moment that could determine whether she can survive in a campaign already clouded with all the usual Clinton rule-breaking and conflicts of interest. Would she be so wounded that Joe Biden would have to jump in and rescue the party?

Republicans are still savoring the idea of getting Hillary to raise her hand to take the oath.

"They do seem to enjoy coming after me," Hillary told Tapper with a smile.

But it's going to be less a showdown than a show trial. The verdict is already in. The Republicans are guilty.

It's not that Hillary has gotten so much more trustable. It's just that the Republicans are so much less credible.

# The Empire Strikes Back

Nobody plays the victim like Hillary.

She can wield that label like a wrecking ball.

If her husband humiliates her with a girlfriend in the Oval Office, Hillary turns around and uses the sympathy engendered to launch a political career. If her Republican opponent gets in her space in an overbearing way during a debate, she turns around and uses the sympathy engendered to win a Senate seat. If conservatives hold a Salem witch trial under the guise of a House select committee hearing, she turns around and uses the sympathy engendered to slip into the HOV lane of a superhighway to the presidency.

Hillary Clinton is never more alluring than when a bunch of pasty-faced, nasty-tongued white men bully her.

And she was plenty alluring during her marathon session on Thursday with Republican Lilliputians, who were completely oblivious to the fact that Hillary is always at her most potent when some Teanderthal is trying to put her in her place.

Trey Gowdy and his blithering band of Tea Partiers went on a fishing expedition, but they forgot to bring their rods—or any fresh facts.

It was a revealing display of hard-core conservatives in their parallel universe, where all their biases are validated by conservative media. They crawled out of the ooze into the sea of cameras, blinking and obtuse. Ohio's Jim Jordan, bellowing. South Carolina's Gowdy, sweating. Alabama's Martha Roby, not getting the joke. And Indiana's Susan Brooks, allowing that "most of us really don't know much about Libya."

Hillary acted bemused, barely masking her contempt at their condescension. She was no doubt amazed at what an amateur job they were doing at character assassination.

The Republicans came across as even more conspiratorial than their other target, Sidney Blumenthal, and his nickname is G.K., for grassy knoll. One conservative on the panel, trying to paint Clinton as an addled 68-year-old, as of Monday, kept snidely offering to pause while she read the notes her posse was passing her.

They must have been mistaking her for W., who always looked as if he wouldn't know what to say if his notes blew away in the wind.

It is not the terrain of Gowdy's lame committee, but it is legitimate to examine Clinton's record in the Middle East.

As a senator, she made a political vote to let W. invade Iraq. As much homework as she did to get ready for the Libya committee, she chose not to do her homework on Iraq in 2002—neglecting to read the sketchy National Intelligence Estimate. She didn't want to seem like a hippie flower girl flashing a peace sign after 9/11.

Then she urged President Obama to help topple Muammar el-Qaddafi without heeding the painful lesson of Iraq—that if America went into another nebulously defined mission, there would have to be a good plan to prevent the vacuum of power being filled by militant Islamic terrorists.

Since she was, as her aide Jake Sullivan put it, "the public face of the US effort in Libya," one of the Furies, along with Samantha Power and Susan Rice, who had pushed for a military intervention on humanitarian grounds, Hillary needed to stay on top of it.

She had to be tenacious in figuring out when Libya had deteriorated into such a cauldron of jihadis that our ambassador should either be pulled out or backed up. In June 2012, the British closed their consulate in Benghazi after their ambassador's convoy was hit by a grenade. A memo she received that August described the security situation in Libya as "a mess."

When you are the Valkyrie who engineers the intervention, you can't then say it is beneath you to pay attention to the ludicrously negligent security for your handpicked choice for ambassador in a lawless country full of assassinations and jihadist training camps.

According to Republicans on the committee, there were 600 requests from J. Christopher Stevens's team to upgrade security in Benghazi in 2012 and 20 attacks on the mission compound in the months before the September 11 siege.

In a rare moment of lucidity, Representative Mike Pompeo of Kansas said to Clinton: "You described Mr. Stevens as having the best knowledge of Libya of anyone," but "when he asked for increased security, he didn't get it."

As Hillary kept explaining, that job was the province of the "security professionals," four of whom were later criticized for providing "grossly inadequate" security at the Benghazi compound and removed from their posts.

The 11-hour hearing showcased the good Hillary, but there were occasional flashes of the bad. She still doesn't believe that setting up her own server was so wrong. Even though the inspector general of government intelligence said that there was top secret information in her emails, she sticks with her parsing. "There was nothing marked classified on my emails, either sent or received," she told Jordan.

She seemed oddly detached about Stevens, testifying that he didn't have her personal email or cell number, "but he had the 24-hour number of the State Operations in the State Department that can reach me 24/7."

There were no call logs of talks between Stevens and Clinton, and she said she could not remember if she ever spoke to him again after she swore him in in May. "I was the boss of ambassadors in 270 countries," she explained.

But Libya was the country where she was the midwife to chaos. And she should have watched that baby like the Lady Hawk she is.

# Leo, Hillary and Their Bears

It's hard to say which of the three monomaniacal, monumentally grueling quests is the most riveting.

There's the torturous trek portrayed in *The Revenant* of Hugh Glass, a 19th-century trapper who, inflamed by revenge, dragged his bloody body 200 miles through the Western wilderness after being gnawed by a grizzly and deserted by fellow trappers.

Then there's the hunt by Leonardo DiCaprio for his first Oscar, for portraying Glass. He has been on the press circuit dramatizing the agonizing shoot, bragging about his verisimilitude in eating raw bison liver. The director, Alejandro Iñárritu, told *Variety* he had to fly ants twice, first class, to Calgary so they could crawl over Leo's fractured frontiersman.

Some wags suggested Leo was so eager to inhabit the solitary Glass's misery that he broke up with Kelly Rohrbach, his latest supermodel girlfriend, because she was bringing a frivolity to the saturnine mood of the promotional effort by taking the bouncy Pamela Anderson role in the new *Baywatch* movie.

And finally, of course, there's the politician most like Glass in her willingness to crawl through glass, flip her positions and persona and even bear up under a mauling by a merciless, manic bear to reach that goal most yearned for. In Hillary Clinton's grimly relentless trudge toward the White House, the part of the bear is played by Donald Trump. (The bear in the movie is also a counterpuncher; when Leo tries to shoot the animal in the face, the grizzly races back to molest him again.)

Trump is like a CGI Rathtar or Indominus Rex, a larger-than-life, fight-to-the-death animated creature who improbably pops up in the ordinarily staid presidential campaign and stomps around, devouring attention and sinking his Twitter teeth into rivals. With his muddle of charm, humor, zest, vulgarity, bigotry, opportunistic flexibility, brutal candor, breathtaking boorishness and outrageous opening bids on volatile issues, he has now leapt into that most sensitive area: the Clintons' tangled conjugal life.

Hillary was asked by the *Des Moines Register* about Trump's crude comments that she had been "schlonged" by Barack Obama in 2008 and that her prolonged debate bathroom break was "disgusting." She replied that Trump had a "penchant for sexism."

That spurred him to declare "open season" on the Clintons' seraglio imbroglios. On Thursday, he put out an Instagram ad showing the *Daily News* cover about Bill, after he admitted the affair with Monica Lewinsky, blaring "Liar, Liar."

The ad goes straight at what Hillary sees as her strengths: Bill, and running as a woman. Playing her famous line in Beijing in 1995 that "women's rights are human rights," it features pictures of the Clintons with "friends" who have been ensnared in seamy scandals—Bill Cosby and Anthony Weiner, the husband of Hillary's close aide Huma Abedin.

In 1999, when I interviewed him, Trump said of Bill: "He handled the Monica situation disgracefully. It's sad because he would go down as a great president if he had not had this scandal. People would have been more forgiving if he'd had an affair with a really beautiful woman of sophistication. Kennedy and Marilyn Monroe were on a different level. Now Clinton can't get into golf clubs in Westchester. A former president begging to get into a golf club. It's unthinkable."

Ignoring our more gender-fluid society, the skyscraper-obsessed Trump has hectored male rivals for being girlie men. But he knows Hillary is tough. So he's wielding his knife on her most sensitive pressure point: her hypocrisy in running as a feminist icon when she was part of political operations that smeared women who told the truth about Bill's transgressions. Hillary told friends that Monica was a "troubled young person" getting ministered to by Bill and a "narcissistic loony toon." Hillary's henchman Sidney Blumenthal spread around the story that Monica was a stalker and Charlie Rangel publicly slandered the intern as a fantasist who wasn't playing with "a full deck."

Trump may be a politically incorrect Frank Sinatra ring-a-ding type with cascading marriages to hot babes, but he knows that a retrospective of the Clintons' cynical campaigns against "bimbo eruptions" will not play well in a politically correct society sensitized by epidemics of rape in colleges and the military and by the Cosby effect.

Bill hid behind the skirts of feminists—including his wife and esteemed women in his cabinet—when he got caught playing around. And feminists, eager to protect his progressive agenda on women, allowed the women swirling around Bill to become collateral damage, torched as trailer trash or erotomaniacs.

In Iowa last fall, Hillary promised to fight sexual assault on campuses, saying that survivors had "the right to be heard" and "the right to be believed." But when a woman last month asked if the women who claimed they were sexually harassed by Bill Clinton should be believed, Hillary faltered, replying lamely: "I would say that everybody should be believed at first until they are disbelieved based on evidence." She's in a dicey spot on this, as Trump well knows.

Hillary reacted to his ad by tweeting, "It's important to stand up to bullies."

Trump can be a bully. But Hillary was a bully, too, in the way she dealt with her husband's paramours. Her impulse, as Lewinsky wrote in *Vanity Fair*, was to blame the woman—even herself. Hillary was not going to be hurt twice by Those Women, letting them damage her marriage and her political future. If someone had to be collateral damage, it was not going to be Hillary. For now, she will have to deal with that old show business saw: Exit, pursued by a bear.

# Hillary Battles Bernie Sanders, Chick Magnet

Hillary Clinton first grabbed the national spotlight 47 years ago as an idealistic young feminist, chiding the paternalistic establishment in her Wellesley commencement speech.

So it's passing strange to watch her here in Manchester, New Hampshire, getting rebuffed by young women who believe that she lacks idealism, that she overplays her feminist hand and that she is the paternalistic establishment.

Bernie Sanders may be a dead ringer for Larry David, but Hillary is running the *Curb Your Enthusiasm* campaign. She can't fire up young voters by dwelling on what can't be done in Washington and by explaining that she's more prose than poetry.

She's traveling around New Hampshire with a former president who could easily layer in some poetry, and a handful of specific snappy plans for the future, to her thicket of substance and stack of white papers. But somehow, Hill and Bill campaign side by side without achieving synergy.

Is it that he's as tired as he looks or does she feel too competitive with him to ask for that kind of help?

As one Hillary booster in Hollywood marveled: "There's no chance her husband doesn't understand the problem. The look on his face during her speeches evokes a retired major league All Star watching his son strike out in a Little League game. This is so fixable."

Hillary is like a veteran actor who doesn't audition well. Bill could tell her not to shout her way through rallies, that it doesn't convey passion but just seems forced, adding to her authenticity problem. Her allies think mentioning her shouting is sexist, and sexism does swirl around Hillary, but her campaign cries sexism too often. In 2008, Barack Obama used race sparingly.

Even after all this time watching Bill and Barry, she still has not learned the art of seduction on stage. She's surrounded by former Obama and Bill Clinton strategists, but they are not helping her achieve "the goose bump experience," as Lily Tomlin called it. Hillary has ceded the inspirational lane to the slick Marco Rubio, who's more like the new John Edwards than the new Obama.

In the MSNBC debate on Thursday night, Hillary huffily said she could not be an exemplar of the establishment, as Sanders suggested, because she's "a woman running to be the first woman president."

But she is establishment. So is Nancy Pelosi. So was Eleanor Roosevelt. Hillary must learn to embrace that and make it work for her, not deny it. As a woman, as a former first lady, senator and secretary of state, she's uniquely equipped to deliver a big, inspiring message with a showstopping speech that goes beyond income inequality, that sweeps up broader themes of intolerance, fusing the economic, cultural and international issues at stake.

She could, as one talented political speechwriter riffed, say something like this: "We're a stronger country when more people have higher incomes; when women get paid the same as men; when we draw on the diverse talents of immigrants; when we show the world that America is a place that embraces all religions, that offers refuge to the persecuted and the terrorized. When a few old rich white men are the only ones who succeed, that's not just unfair, it's untenable."

Hillary's most poignant moment came during the CNN town hall on Wednesday night when she said that, as a young woman, she had never expected to run for president herself, given that her husband was "a natural." It was her misfortune in 2008 to run into another natural. She was not "likable enough" that year.

But it was at least fathomable. She was running against the Tulip Craze Barack Obama. Now she's running against a grumpy gramps, a stooped socialist with a narrow message, brusque manner and shaky grasp of world affairs. But the Clintons are still leveling the same charges, that her opponent's stances are fairy tales and that his idealism masks tough tactics.

And she's still not likable enough for the young women who were supposed to carry her forward as a Joan of Arc. According to an NBC News/Wall Street Journal/Marist poll, Sanders won among young men and women in Iowa by 70 points. And in New Hampshire, going into the weekend, polls showed him leading with women, racking up yawning margins with women under 45 and with both sexes under 30.

Lyndon Johnson said that the two things that make politicians more stupid than anything else are sex and envy. With Hillary, there are three things: sex, money and the need for secrecy.

She was in on sliming her husband's ex-girlfriends who told the truth about liaisons. She has long been driven by a fear of being "dead broke," as she put it—and a conviction that she deserved the life and perks she would have had if she had gone into the private sector. That led her to do her suspiciously lucrative commodity trades while Bill was Arkansas attorney general and to make Wall Street speeches on the cusp of her 2016 campaign, even though she and Bill had already made more than $139 million between 2007 and 2014.

The Nixonian obsession with secrecy by the woman who was

once an idealistic lawyer on the Watergate committee staff—on Whitewater, health care and her State Department emails—caused her to unnecessarily damage herself and leave Democrats perennially spooked.

While she was giving three speeches to Goldman Sachs for $675,000, her party was changing. As the economy slowly healed, Democrats were seething with anger over the big banks that never got punished for wrecking the economy and the reckless billionaires who are still living large. A tone-deaf Hillary was there sucking at the teat and that rubs people the wrong way.

Sanders noted in Thursday's debate that Hillary's super PAC had raised $15 million in the last quarter from Wall Street. *The Wall Street Journal* calculates that since the Clintons first entered national politics in the early '90s, Wall Street has given more than $100 million to their campaigns, foundation and personal finances.

When Anderson Cooper asked why Hillary had taken the obscene Goldman Sachs windfall, she gave a stupefyingly bad answer to a predictable question. "Well, I don't know," she said, throwing up her hands and shrugging. "That's what they offered." She was reluctant to release the texts of her "Don't worry, I'm one of you" speeches.

As with the Chappaqua email server, Hillary is not sorry she did it. She's only sorry people are making a fuss about it.

Typical of the Clintons, she tried to drag in others to excuse her own ethically lax behavior, noting that "every secretary of state that I know has done that." After the Monica scandal broke, Clinton aides cited Thomas Jefferson, FDR and JFK to justify Bill's Oval Office cavorting.

But the other secretaries of state were not running for office, Cooper pointed out.

"To be honest I wasn't—I wasn't committed to running," Hillary said.

It's that sort of disingenuous answer that has spurred so many

Democrats to turn to the straight-shooting, Wall Street–bashing Sanders.

When Hillary accused Sanders during the debate of doing an "artful smear" on her, charging him with insinuating that she engaged in pay-for-play with Wall Street, drug companies and other special interests, some Republicans predicted that the moment would go down as a Gary Hart–style challenge that would come back to haunt her.

They said that surely Matt Rhoades, the Hillary oppo-research expert at America Rising, must already be plotting ads slamming the disturbing cat's cradle of foreign money that came into the Clinton Foundation while Hillary was at State, and the unseemly tentacles of Teneo, the global firm run by Bill Clinton's former body man, Doug Band, where Huma Abedin, Hillary's closest aide, worked while she was at State.

Sanders's populist surge—he raised $20 million last month, $5 million more than Hillary—has led some top Democrats to wonder if President Obama will have to step in and endorse her.

Wouldn't that be rich? The Wellesley idealist-turned-realist needs the Chicago idealist-turned-realist who beat her last time to save her from the Vermont idealist clinging to a simple reality: Wall Street fleeced America and none of the big shots got punished.

# Sarah Palin Saves Feminism

It's a tough call to figure out which place is more benighted: Hollywood or Saudi Arabia.

Saudi Arabia was pulling ahead with all its beheadings and its top cleric's fatwa on chess as "the work of Satan."

But then Hollywood took the lead with its Jim Crow Oscars, Scully being offered half of Mulder's pay for the *X-Files* reboot, and its second-class treatment of Rey—the scrappy heroine of *Star Wars: The Force Awakens*. Rey, played by Daisy Ridley, embodies the awakening Force. Yet even the director, J. J. Abrams, called it "preposterous and wrong" that Rey's action figure was missing in action from some game and toy tie-ins—a traditionally male realm.

And Lucasfilm is run by a girl action figure, Kathleen Kennedy, so go figure.

That is why it's so inspiring to see a woman out on the campaign trail who has had such a historic impact on feminism, helping to recast outmoded assumptions about women.

Yes, Sarah Palin, I'm giving you a shout-out.

Before Palin, if a woman flamed out in a spectacular fashion, it was considered an X through the X chromosome. If Billie Jean King lost to Bobby Riggs, women would be seen as second-class athletes. If Geraldine Ferraro seemed unfit for the White House, all women might be judged incapable.

But when Palin turned out to be utterly unqualified and unintelligible, spouting her own special Yoda-like language, it did not reflect poorly on women as a whole—only on her and John McCain. What the hell were you thinking, Senator?

Ordinarily, it's considered sexist to call a woman shrill. But Palin liberated us on that score. She really is shrill.

Ordinarily, it's dicey to focus on what a woman in politics is wearing. But again, Palin has freed us up. She sported a cardigan so gaudy and rogue at her Iowa endorsement of Donald Trump (the man who viciously mocked her former running mate's war record) that we would be remiss not to mention that it was the sartorial reflection of Palin and Trump themselves.

Ordinarily, you have to tread gingerly in critiquing a working woman on her mothering skills. But Palin's brawling brood runs so wild around the state she once governed, in a way that is so contrary to her evangelistic, sanctimonious homilies on family values, that it seems only Christian to advise her to study the Obamas to see what exceptional parenting looks like.

With Palin and Trump, a failed reality star and a successful one, gall is divided into two parts. There has been a lot of talk this campaign season about how women pols bring superior qualities to the table: collegiality and listening skills. But Sarahcuda shows that we are truly the equals of men, capable of narcissistic explosions, brazen hypocrisy and unapologetic greed. She had barely finished the endorsement Tuesday when she began using it to raise money for SarahPAC, so she can take her show on the road.

Her oldest son, Track, was a kid with a temper before he served in Iraq for a year, conveniently shipping off in the fall of 2008 as his mother began her hockey-mom spiel. The 26-year-old was arrested

Monday on an assault charge, accused of punching his girlfriend in the face and kicking her during an alcohol-fueled argument at the Palins' home in Wasilla, Alaska. His girlfriend told the police that he was also waving around an AR-15 assault rifle.

Instead of just admitting that her family is a mess, Palin exhibited Trumplike swagger, conjuring a story in an attempt to gin up the crowd and occlude her son's behavior.

She used the last refuge of scoundrels in Tulsa, Oklahoma, Wednesday, wrapping herself in patriotism. In her convoluted, disingenuous way, she charged President Obama with a lack of "respect" for veterans and suggested that Track had post-traumatic stress disorder and became "hardened," implying this is what led to the incident prompting his arrest. This from the archconservative who presents herself as a model of personal responsibility and scourge of victimhood?

Outraged vets urged Palin not to reduce PTSD to a political "chew toy," as one put it, or to excuse domestic violence by citing the disorder.

The rattlebrained Palin has reversed her Iraq position, so that now her stance somehow matches Trump's consistent and prescient one against the Iraq invasion.

When she saw Track off to Iraq in 2008, she echoed W.'s specious argument, calling the war a "righteous cause" to avenge "the enemies who planned and carried out" 9/11. But in her endorsement of Trump, she praised Rand Paul, who thinks we should have left Saddam Hussein in place, and argued that America should stop "footin' the bill" for oil-rich nations and "their squirmishes that have been going on for centuries, where they're fightin' each other and yellin' *Allah akbar*, calling jihad on each other's heads forever and ever."

Hillary Clinton is presenting herself as the embodiment of women, an American Marianne, pushing her gender in an all-for-one-one-for-all, now-or-never way. She's even campaigning this week in Iowa with Billie Jean King. Women should support her because if she founders, it will be bad for women. One Democratic senator said privately that many Democrats believe that Hillary is still the presumed nominee only because she is a woman.

But Palin has done us a favor by proving that a woman can stumble, babble incoherently on stage and spew snide garbage, and it isn't a blot on the female copybook.

It's all on her. Can I get a hallelujah?

# When Hillary Clinton Killed Feminism

The Clinton campaign is shell-shocked over the wholesale rejection of Hillary by young women, younger versions of herself who do not relate to her.

Hillary's coronation was predicated on a conviction that has just gone up in smoke. The Clintons felt that Barack Obama had presumptuously snatched what was rightfully hers in 2008, gliding past her with his pretty words to make history before she could.

So this time, the Clintons assumed, the women who had deserted Hillary for Barack, in Congress and in the country, owed her. Democrats would want to knock down that second barrier.

Hillary believed that there was an implicit understanding with the sisters of the world that now was the time to come back home and vote for a woman. (The Clintons seem to have conveniently forgotten how outraged they were by identity politics when black leaders deserted them in 2008 to support Obama.)

This attitude intensified the unappetizing solipsistic subtext of her campaign, which is "What is Hillary owed?" It turned out that female voters seem to be looking at Hillary as a candidate rather than as a historical imperative. And she's coming up drastically short on trustworthiness.

As Olivia Sauer, an 18-year-old college freshman who caucused for Bernie Sanders in Ames, Iowa, told a *Times* reporter: "It seems like he is at the point in his life when he is really saying what he is thinking. With Hillary, sometimes you get this feeling that all of her sentences are owned by someone."

Hillary started, both last time and this, from a place of entitlement, as though if she reads her résumé long enough people will surrender. And now she's even angrier that she has been shown up by someone she considers even less qualified than Obama was when he usurped her place.

Bernie has a clear, concise "we" message, even if it's pie-in-the-sky: The game is rigged and we have to take the country back from the privileged few and make it work for everyone. Hillary has an "I" message: I have been abused and misunderstood and it's my turn.

It's a victim mind-set that is exhausting, especially because the Clintons' messes are of their own making.

On the trail in New Hampshire, Madeleine Albright made the case that it was a betrayal of feminist ideals to support Bernie against Hillary, noting that "there's a special place in hell for women who don't help each other." When Sanders handily won the women's vote on Tuesday, David Axelrod noted dryly that they were going to need to clear out a lot of space in hell.

And in a misstep for the feminist leader who got famous by going undercover as a *Playboy* bunny, Gloria Steinem told Bill Maher that young women were flocking to Bernie to be where the boys are. Blaming it on hormones was odd, given the fact that for centuries, it was widely believed that women's biology made them emotionally unfit to be leaders.

What the three older women seemed to miss was that the young women supporting Sanders are living the feminist dream, where gender no longer restricts and defines your choices, where girls grow up knowing they can be anything they want. The aspirations of '70s feminism are now baked into the culture.

The interesting thing about the spectacle of older women trying to shame younger ones on behalf of Hillary is that Hillary and Bill killed the integrity of institutional feminism back in the '90s—with the help of Albright and Steinem.

Instead of just admitting that he had had an affair with Monica Lewinsky and taking his lumps, Bill lied and hid behind the skirts of his wife and female cabinet members, who had to go out before the cameras and vouch for his veracity, even when it was apparent he was lying.

Seeing Albright, the first female secretary of state, give cover to President Clinton was a low point in women's rights. As was the *New York Times* op-ed by Steinem, arguing that Lewinsky's will was not violated, so no feminist principles were violated. What about Clinton humiliating his wife and daughter and female cabinet members? What about a president taking advantage of a gargantuan power imbalance with a 22-year-old intern? What about imperiling his party with reckless behavior that put their feminist agenda at risk?

It rang hollow after the Anita Hill–Clarence Thomas hearings. When it was politically beneficial, the feminists went after Thomas for bad behavior and painted Hill as a victim. And later, when it was politically beneficial, they defended Bill's bad behavior and stayed mute as Clinton allies mauled his dalliances as trailer trash and stalkers.

The same feminists who were outraged at the portrayal of Hill by David Brock—then a Clinton foe but now bizarrely head of one of her super PACs—as "a little bit nutty and a little bit slutty," hypocritically went along when Hillary and other defenders of Bill used that same aspersion against Lewinsky.

Hillary knew that she could count on the complicity of feminist leaders and Democratic women in Congress who liked Bill's progressive policies on women. And that's always the ugly Faustian bargain with the Clintons, not only on the sex cover-ups but the money grabs: You can have our bright public service side as long as you accept our dark sketchy side.

Young women today, though, are playing by a different set of rules. And they don't like the Clintons setting themselves above the rules.

# Hillary Is Not Sorry

It's hard not to feel sorry for Hillary Clinton. She is hearing ghostly footsteps.

She's having her inevitability challenged a second time by a moralizing senator with few accomplishments who chides her on her bad judgment on Iraq and special-interest money, breezily rakes in millions in small donations online, draws tens of thousands to rock-star rallies and gets more votes from young women.

But at least last time, it was a dazzling newcomer who also offered the chance to break a barrier. This time, Hillary is trying to fend off a choleric 74-year-old Democratic socialist.

Some close to the campaign say that those ghostly footsteps have made Hillary restive. The déjà vu has exasperated Bill Clinton, who griped to an audience in New York on Friday that young supporters of Bernie Sanders get excited because it sounds good to say, "Just shoot every third person on Wall Street and everything will be fine."

At the Brooklyn debate, there was acrimony, cacophony, sanctimony and, naturally, baloney.

Hillary gazed at Bernie as though she could hypnotize him into skedaddling. And Bernie waved his index finger and flapped his hands, miming that he won't budge, no matter how aggravating it is for Clinton Inc.

Sanders flew to the Vatican that night to underscore his vision of himself as the moral candidate. And Hillary headed to California, underscoring Bernie's portrayal of her as the mercenary candidate. She attended fund-raisers headlined by George and Amal Clooney in San Francisco and at the Clooneys' LA mansion that cost $33,400 per person and $353,400 for two seats at the head table in San Francisco—an *Ocean's Eleven* safecracking that Sanders labeled "obscene."

Clinton sowed suspicion again, refusing to cough up her Wall Street speech transcripts. And Sanders faltered on guns, fracking and releasing his tax returns. But he was gutsy, in a New York primary, to say he'd be more evenhanded with Israel and the Palestinians. As my colleague Tom Friedman has warned, we can hurt Israel by loving Israel to death.

Hillary alternately tried to blame and hug the men in her life, divvying up credit in a self-serving way.

After showing some remorse for the 1994 crime bill, saying it had had "unintended" consequences, she stressed that her husband "was the president who actually signed it." On Libya, she noted that "the decision was the president's." And on her desire to train and arm Syrian rebels, she recalled, "The president said no."

But she wrapped herself in President Obama's record on climate change and, when criticized on her super PACs, said, well, Obama did it, too.

Sanders accused her of pandering to Israel after she said that "if Yasir Arafat had agreed with my husband at Camp David," there would have been a Palestinian state for 15 years.

Hillary may be right that Bernie is building socialist castles in the sky. But Bernie is right that Hillary's judgment has often been faulty.

She has shown an unwillingness to be introspective and learn from her mistakes. From health care to Iraq to the email server, she only apologizes at the point of a gun. And even then, she leaves the impression that she is merely sorry to be facing criticism, not that she miscalculated in the first place.

On the server, she told Andrea Mitchell of NBC News that she was sorry it had been "confusing to people and raised a lot of questions." She has never acknowledged, maybe even to herself, that routing diplomatic emails with classified information through a home-brew server was an outrageous, reckless and foolish thing to do, and disloyal to Obama, whose administration put in place rules for record-keeping that she flouted.

Wouldn't it be a relief to people if Hillary just acknowledged some mistakes? If she said that her intentions on Libya were good but that she got distracted by other global issues and took her eye off the ball? That the questions that should have been asked about Libya were not asked and knowing this now would make her a better chief executive?

Obama, introspective to a fault, told Chris Wallace of Fox News that not having a better plan after Muammar el-Qaddafi was overthrown was the worst mistake of his presidency. But as usual, Clinton, who talked Obama into it, is defiantly doubling down. As her national security advisers told Kim Ghattas for a piece in *Foreign Policy*, Clinton "does not see the Libya intervention as a failure, but as a work in progress."

Clinton accused Sanders of not doing his homework on how he would break up the banks. And she is the queen of homework, always impressively well versed in meetings. But that is what makes her failure to read the National Intelligence Estimate that raised doubts about whether Iraq posed a threat to the US so egregious.

Like other decisions, it was put through a political filter and a paranoid mind-set. She did not want to be seen, in that blindingly patriotic time, as the bohemian woman standing to the left of the military.

When Barack Obama was warned by some supporters in 2002 not to make a speech against the Iraq invasion because it might hurt his political future, he said he was going to do it anyhow because the war was a really terrible idea.

What worries me is whether Hillary has the confidence to make decisions contrary to her political interests. Can she say, "But it's a really terrible idea"?

# Weakend at Bernie's

Hillary Clinton is the Democratic nominee.

Really.

Just ask her.

She should have been able to finally savor shattering that "highest, hardest glass ceiling"—the one she gloried in putting 18 million cracks in last time around—when she attends her convention in Philadelphia in July.

Instead, she is reduced to stomping her feet on CNN, asserting her dominance in a contest that has left her looking anything but dominant. Once more attempting to shake off the old socialist dude hammering her with a sickle, Clinton insisted to Chris Cuomo on Thursday: "I will be the nominee for my party, Chris. That is already done, in effect. There is no way that I won't be."

It's a vexing time for the Clintons. As Bill told a crowd in Fargo, North Dakota, on Friday, it's been an "interesting" year: "That's the most neutral word I can think of."

After all, why should Bernie Sanders get to be the Democratic nominee when he isn't even a Democrat? And how is Donald Trump going to be the Republican nominee when he considers being a Republican merely a starting bid?

It must be hard for Hillary to look at all the pictures of young women swooning over Bernie as though he were Bieber.

She assumed that the fix was in, that she and the DNC had arranged for the coronation that she felt she was robbed of in the Obamamania of 2008.

Everyone just laughed when Sanders, a cranky loner from Vermont with a nondescript Senate record, decided to challenge Queen Hillary. Clinton and her aides intoned—wink, wink—that it would be healthy to have a primary fight with Sanders and Martin O'Malley.

But Bernie became the surprise belle of his side's revolutionary ball. And now he has gotten a taste of it and he likes it and he won't let it go. He's bedeviling the daylights out of Hillary.

Hillary and her allies are spinning a narrative that Bernie is less loyal to the Democratic cause than she was with Obama. And Trump does delight in quoting Bernie's contention that Hillary lacks the judgment to be president. On Friday, when he accepted the endorsement of the NRA at its convention, Trump mischievously urged Sanders to run as a third-party candidate and said he would love to have a debate with both Hillary and Bernie on stage.

Hillary says Sanders needs to "do his part" to unify the party, as she did in 2008. But even on the day of the last primaries in that race, when she was the one who was mathematically eliminated unless the superdelegates turned, she came on stage to Terry McAuliffe heralding her as "the next president of the United States." She then touted having more votes than any primary candidate in history as her fans cheered, "Yes, she will!" and "Denver!"

Seeing Trump's soaring negatives, Sanders thinks, if he could just get past Hillary, he could actually be president.

The Bernie bro violence—chair throwing, sexist name-calling,

and feral threats—at the Nevada state party convention last weekend was denounced as "a scary situation" by his Senate colleague
Barbara Boxer.

Sanders condemned the violence while stoking the outrage, urging the Democratic Party to "open the doors, let the people in." He
flashed a bit of Trump, so sure in his belief that the system is rigged
that he fed off the nasty energy.

Boxer had to call Sanders several times before he called back.
She and other Democratic Senate women are fed up with his cru-
sade, feeling enough is enough.

I've talked to several former Clinton and Obama White House
aides who don't enjoy checking in with the joyless Clinton campaign
in Brooklyn. "It's the Bataan Death March," one says.

Hopeful acceptance of Hillary has shifted to amazed disbelief
that she can't put away Bernie. Given dynasty fatigue and Hillary's
age, many Democrats assumed that their front-runner would come
out of the gate with a vision for the future that gave her campaign
a fresh hue, instead of white papers tinkering around the edges. She
should have been far over her husband's bridge to the 21st century
and way down the highway by now.

Instead, her big new idea is to put Bill in charge of the economy
again (hopefully, with less Wall Street deregulation). Again with the
two for the price of one. And please don't deny us the pleasure of seeing Bill choose the china patterns.

Hillary's Bataan Death March is making Republicans reconsider their own suicide mission with Trump. More are looking at
Clinton's inability to get the flashing lights going like her husband,
and thinking: Huh, maybe we're not dead here. Maybe Teflon Don
could pull this off.

The 2016 race is transcendentally bizarre. We have two near-
nominees with the highest unfavorables at this point in the race of
any in modern history. We seem to have a majority of voters in both

parties who are driven by the desire to vote against the other candidate, rather than for their own.

Debbie Wasserman Schultz tries to herd young women to Hillary by raising the specter of *Roe v. Wade* being overturned. And former Pennsylvania Governor Ed Rendell said Trump's obsession with 10s and D-cups would "come back to haunt him" and give Democrats wins because "there are probably more ugly women in America than attractive women."

Hillary can't generate excitement on her own so she is relying on fear of Trump to get her into the White House. And Trump is relying on fear of everything to get him into the White House.

So voters are stuck in the muck of the negative: What are you most afraid of?

# John Adams Was a Hermaphrodite?

This is a town where scripts routinely come back to writers from entertainment executives with the same scrawled command about a female character: "Make her more likable."

As Hillary Clinton fights up and down California to fend off Bernie Sanders and clinch the nomination, Democrats watch with clenched teeth. Sure, the Republicans are engaged in a hilarious performance of *The Taming of the Shrew* with their tart-tongued presumptive nominee.

But can plodding Hillary be, as Barack Obama famously put it, likable enough?

Or does it even matter?

Hollywood's most famous icon of likability thinks not.

"Over the past months, I have heard the word 'likability' used so frequently," Sally Field said Friday at a Hillary rally here in Los Angeles at a community college. "How Hillary Clinton is not likable. How she's cold or shrill or an opportunist or just not someone you'd like to have a beer with. What is this? A high school popularity contest?"

Actually, it kind of is.

This was, funnily enough, the actress who had one of the most memorably needy moments in Oscar history in 1985, when she won her second statuette for *Places in the Heart* and marveled to the audience: "I can't deny the fact that you like me right now. You like me!"

But Field, one of several actresses and women pols warming up the crowd for Hillary, was determined to make the case that unpopularity shouldn't be disqualifying—especially for a woman.

"We don't need someone who is nice," she said. "And c'mon. Honestly. Women have spent the last hundred years trying to get out from under the expectation that they had to be sugar and spice and everything nice. We don't need sugar and spice and everything nice."

This is not an election where anyone needs to worry about an overdose of sugar and spice and everything nice. This is an election of vinegar and venom and endless nests of vipers.

You would think that Hillary Clinton would be used to maneuvering in a political landscape where the mud is flying. But it took her a year, several speechwriters and the example of Elizabeth Warren to figure out how to riposte Donald Trump's peculiar combination of viciousness and playfulness.

You can't do it the way Marco Rubio did, where you end up mired in absurd and self-defeating anatomical one-upmanship. And you can't do it as Jeb Bush did, where you assume for too long that people will see Trump as a vainglorious vulgarian without you pointing it out.

You have to lob his own jejunosity back at him.

In a Trump takedown billed as a foreign policy address in San Diego on Thursday, Hillary scored several points.

Noting that he picked fights with everyone from the British prime minister to the pope, she mocked: "He says he doesn't need to listen to our generals or our admirals or our ambassadors and other high officials because he has, quote, 'a very good brain.'"

After floundering, her campaign has now settled on a strategy of painting the mogul as unhinged and thin-skinned, which always really gets under his thin skin.

"It's no small thing," Hillary said, "when he suggests that America should withdraw our military support for Japan, encourage them to get nuclear weapons, and said this about a war between Japan and North Korea—and I quote: 'If they do, they do. Good luck. Enjoy yourself, folks.' I wonder if he even realizes he's talking about nuclear war."

With its typical arrogance, Clintonworld can go too far.

Madeleine Albright, who specializes in being unhelpfully helpful to Hillary, dismissed the email controversy on CNN: "She has said she made a mistake and nobody is going to die as a result of anything that happened on emails."

That, of course, is an open invitation for Trump to recall that many did die in the Iraq war Clinton voted for and that the email imbroglio represented reckless judgment on her part. (Or, as Trump spells it in his tweets, "judgement.")

She has not forthrightly taken responsibility or explained how she could stonewall the State Department inspector general. She's still acting as though what she did was acceptable—"Well, it was allowed," she says—even though the inspector general has made it clear that it wasn't and that she never bothered to ask for permission to use a private email server. It was a request that would have been rejected had she made it, he said.

As usual with Hillary, she clearly feels the only problem was that people found out. It undercuts her claims that Trump is reckless when she can't fathom how reckless she was.

She made a really good speech in San Diego. But even if she dispatches Sanders on Tuesday, Trump isn't going to be easy. Given the slurs and punches and eggs and salacious, hellacious stuff flying around, this could be the wildest, meanest election in modern history.

Just look at Friday alone.

Trump was on a tarmac in Redding, California, recounting a story about a black "great guy" who slugged a protester at a prior rally. He interrupted himself to point at a random black supporter in the crowd, saying: "Oh, look at my African American over here. Look at him."

This followed an interview with CNN's Jake Tapper in which Trump was unyielding in his insistence that he was not being racist when he said that the judge presiding in a lawsuit over Trump University was biased because "he's a Mexican" and "we're building a wall between here and Mexico."

Tapper gamely tried to point out, more than once, that the judge, Gonzalo Curiel, was born and raised in Indiana. But Trump held his ground: "He's proud of his heritage. I respect him for that."

The latest installment in a nutty attack on the judge—coming more than a week after a nutty attack on New Mexico's Republican governor, Susana Martinez—forced Paul Ryan, who had finally dragged himself over to Trump a day earlier, to start skittering away again.

Trump speculated at his rally that Hillary might share sensitive information with her aide Huma Abedin, who might share it with her husband, saying: "I know Anthony Weiner. I don't want him knowing anything. And I never, ever want him to tweet me."

So, of course, Weiner tweeted immediately and incoherently: "Wait, is he talking to me. I'll hit that guy with so many rights, he'll be begging for a left."

Naturally, Lin-Manuel Miranda of *Hamilton* fame provided the perfect kicker for the week in a new *Rolling Stone* interview, saying that this election is "no more bizarre than the election in 1800 wherein Jefferson accused Adams of being a hermaphrodite and Adams responded" by spreading rumors "that Jefferson died so that Adams would be the only viable candidate. He was counting on news to travel slow! That, weirdly, gives me hope."

# Girl Squad: Imagining the Superpower Summit between Hill and Liz

Hillary Clinton greets Elizabeth Warren in the cream-and-coral sunroom of her home on Embassy Row in Washington.

"Elizabeth, welcome," Clinton says, smiling stiffly. "I was worried that you were lost since it was taking you so-o-o-o long to finally get here."

"Ha-ha-ha," Warren replies. "I've always heard you're a hoot in private. I know I was the last Democratic woman in the Senate to endorse you, but Bernie and I have more in common. We don't buckrake on Wall Street. People are enthusiastic about us and believe what we say. We're pure."

"Pure scolds," Hillary sniffs. "I guess it hit you, when you saw me fighting for my life against a dyspeptic seventy-four-year-old socialist with one suit, that if you had jumped in, you could have been the first woman president."

"Yes," Warren muses. "I only loaned Bernie my progressive hordes. I'm the real leader of that movement."

"Not anymore," Hillary says.

Warren sighs. "True, my faithful are peeved at me for not running and for endorsing you instead of Bernie."

Hillary pours herself some coffee. "I know you're intrigued by the idea of being my vice president," she says. "I heard you tell our gal Rachel Maddow that you're prepared to be commander in chief. But you know I can't put you on the ticket, don't you?"

"Because the country isn't ready for two wonky women for the price of one?" Warren asks dryly.

"No," Hillary says, biting her biscotti, "I'm not ready. You, the so-called Sheriff of Wall Street, attacked me as the Shill of Wall Street. Why should you get the glass slipper when you were foot-dragging on my glass-shattering moment?"

Warren protests, "I went up against that loud, nasty, thin-skinned, mud-flinging, money-grubbing, racist, sexist, reckless, pathetic loser Trump. You were flailing around, not knowing how to take on that repugnant bully until I showed you the way on Twitter."

"Yeah," Hillary says sarcastically, "you're a big help on Twitter. Trump is tweeting out video from 2004 where you're trashing me as 'the scary part about democracy' for taking campaign donations from the banking industry and then voting for an anti-consumer bankruptcy bill that would have helped the credit card companies."

Warren smiles primly, sipping her Pellegrino. "Speaking of credit, you have to give me some for this: In my last book, I left out the stuff I had in my previous one about you being an unprincipled sellout. By 2014, when that one came out, it looked like you were going to go the distance. My purity sometimes gives way to expediency.

"You know all the Democrats want me on the ticket to add some sizzle since the crowds you draw wouldn't even fill this couch. I know you are afraid I will overshadow you and I will. But I can help you reel in all the young women who find you more shifty than nifty. And the Bernie Bros dig me."

"Thanks, Pocahontas," Hillary replies, looking steely. "I can do some things on my own. I did manage to secure a spot in the Ivy League without pretending to be Native American. I hope you noticed that I've decorated my house in all the colors of the wind."

Warren bristles, Church Lady–style: "You have done a fine job here, except that one painting looks crooked, Hillary. I'm surprised you don't have oil portraits of Goldman and Sachs. And let me give you some free advice: Now that Bernie and I have forced you to address income inequality, you might want to hide that $12,495 tweed Armani jacket you wore on the trail in the back of your closet."

The senator from Massachusetts stands up. "Where's the bathroom?" she asks. "Can I squeeze in there with the server?"

Hillary gives that big laugh that indicates she is not amused. "No need to go on the warpath," she says in her best Cersei manner. "Let's bury the hatchet—in The Donald."

Warren exhales and sits back down: "You're right. The sisterhood has to be united in supporting the first woman leading a major ticket against the worst misogynist leading a major ticket. Can you believe Trump said *he* broke the glass ceiling by promoting women in construction? The only glass he knows is the mirror. And the thrice-married huckster had the nerve to tell evangelicals here Friday that marriage and family are the building blocks for success. That dog gets my blood boiling!

"He calls me Goofy? Picture America under this Mad Man. He'd want us gussied up in gingham aprons, baking casseroles. Remember that horrible crack he made about Ivana? 'I think that putting a wife to work is a very dangerous thing,' he said. 'The softness disappeared.' I'll show him softness disappearing. He also said, 'When I come home and dinner's not ready, I go through the roof.' A Trump Supreme Court would take away abortion rights and bring back those hideous vaginal probes. Hillary, think about it—they might even outlaw pantsuits. That tyrant would drag women away from their desks and exile them to the kitchen and the nursery."

Hillary nods rhythmically: "Trump's the one who belongs in the nursery. He's so needy, he even needs to talk to those scorpions in the press."

Warren agrees, "That's the craziest thing he does. Nuts."

Hillary ushers her guest to the door. "We're going to be a great girl squad," she says, squeezing Warren's hand. "It will be so easy to beat this airhead. I bet he doesn't even know what Cafta is. Sorry to cut this short. I need to call Tim Kaine. But I will dictate a nice tweet about you."

# Interlude

## *Living History (one email at a time)*

*Top aide Huma Abedin tries to help Hillary with the fax machine.*

From: Abedin, Huma <AbedinH@state.gov>
To: H
Cc: Oscar Flores
Sent: Wed Dec 23 14:38:52 2009
Subject: can you hang up the fax line, they will call again and try fax

From: H <HDR22@clintonemail.com>
To: Abedin, Huma
Sent: Wed Dec 23 14:39:39 2009

I thought it was supposed to be off hook to work?

From: Abedin, Huma <AbedinH@state.gov>
To: H
Sent: Wed Dec 23 14:43:02 2009

Yes but hang up one more time. So they can reestablish the line.

From: H <hrod17@clintonemail.com>
Sent: Wednesday, December 23, 2009 2:50 PM
To: 'abedinh@state.gov'

I did.

From: Abedin, Huma <AbedinH@state.gov>
To: H
Sent: Wed Dec 23 14:53:30 2009

Just pick up phone and hang it up. And leave it hung up.

From: H <hrod17@clintonemail.com>
Sent: Wednesday, December 23, 2009 3:02 PM
To: 'abedinh@state.gov'

I've done it twice now.

From: H <HDR22@clintonemail.com>
To: Abedin, Huma
Sent: Wed, Dec 23, 15:13:34 2009

Still nothing. Call Oscar if they need help. I'll be out of pocket for an hour or so.


Hillary has FOMO

From: H <HDR22@clintonemail.com>
To: Valmoro, Lona J; Huma Abedin
<Huma@clintonemail.com>
Sent: Mon Jun 08 05:52:59 2009
Subject: Cabinet mtg

I heard on the radio that there is a Cabinet mtg this am. Is there? Can I go? If not, who are we sending?

From: Valmoro, Lona J <ValmoroU@state.gov>
To: H; Huma Abedin; Mills, Cheryl D
<MillsCD@state.gov>
Sent: Mon Jun 08 06:04:08 2009

It is actually not a full cabinet meeting today—those agencies that received recovery money were invited to attend/participate. We were welcome to send a representative though, not sure if we have anyone going.

*Hillary arrives at the White House only to realize that her meeting has been canceled. She emails four of her top aides.*

From: H [mailto:HDR22@clintonemail.com]
Sent: Friday, June 12, 2009 10:22 AM
To: Valmoro, Lona J; Abedin, Huma; Sullivan, Jacob J
Cc: 'cheryl.mills'
Subject: No WH mtg

I arrived for the 10:15 mtg and was told there was no mtg. Matt said they had "released" the time. This is the second time this has happened. What's up???

From: Sullivan, Jacob J
Sent: Friday, June 12, 2009 10:56 AM
To: Abedin, Huma; 'H'; Valmoro, Lona J

Cc: 'cheryl.mills'

I will start calling Matt before small groups to confirm.

*Nora Toiv, Cheryl Mills's assistant, gives Hillary her personal gmail address, but Hillary is confused.*

From: Nora Toiv
Sent: Tuesday, July 26, 2011 09:58 AM
To: H; Huma Abedin
Subject: My gmail

For future reference, this is my gmail. Thanks.

From: H <HDR22@clintonemail.com>
Sent: Tuesday, July 26, 2011 10:01 AM
To: Nora Toiv
Subject: Re: My gmail

That's all I have—pls send me your state address. Thx.

From: Nora Toiv
Sent: Tuesday, July 26, 2011 10:03 AM
To: H

You've always emailed me on my State email which is toivnf@
state.gov

From: H <HDR22@clintonemail.com>
Sent: Tuesday, July 26, 2011 10:11 AM
To: Nora Toiv

Even weirder—I just checked and I do have your state but not your gmail—so how did that happen. Must be the Chinese!

From: Nora Toiv
Sent: Tuesday, July 26, 2011 10:15 AM
To:

Agreed!

*Hillary's Senior Adviser Philippe Reines devises a rudimen-*
*tary flowchart to determine the pecking order of who rides*
*in the car with Secretary Clinton.*

To: Monica Hanley
To: SXP
Cc: Huma Abedin
Cc: Jake Sullivan
Cc: CPM
Subject: Riding w/HRC
Sent: Jul 12, 2012 11:40 AM

Monica & Shilpa -

With Jake coming and going, CPM doing the same, and Huma
rejoining the roadshow after all this time of defaulting to Jake,
we know it's tough to figure out who should jump in the car with
the Secretary. So I've created this flowchart to help you make
that determination:

```
                    Huma Here? YES
                      |        |
                      |   Huma in Limo
                      |        |
                     NO    SUV? YES
                      |        |
                      |   +Jake in Limo
                      |
                      |
                    Jake Here? YES
                      |        |
                      |    Jake in Limo
                      |        |
                      |     SUV? YES
                      |        |
                     NO     So What
                      |
                      |
                    Capricia Here? YES
                      |        |
                     NO   CPM in Limo
                      |
                      |
                    Ambassador Tolerable?
                      |        |
                      |       YES
                      |        |
                     NO   Ambo in Limo
                      |
                      |
                    Drive 10 Mins Or More?
                       / \
                      /   \
                    YES   NO
                    /      \
                   /    Time in US?
                  /         |
              Ride Solo     |
                            |
                            |

                    Too Early/Late to Call CDM?
                       / \
                      /   \
                    NO    YES
                    /       \
                   /         \
              Ride Solo;       |
              Call CDM         |
                               |
                               |
                    Philippe Should Jump In
                             /


                           /
                          /
                    He Presumptuously Already In?
                       /    \
                      /      \
                    NO       YES
                     |        |
               Invite Him In  |
                              |
                              |
                          Chutzpah!
```

From: Philippe Reines
To: Huma Abedin
To: Jake Sullivan
To: Shilpa Pesaru
To: Mon new
Cc: CPM
Sent: Jul 15, 2012 3:20 AM

Can't for the life of me figure out what just made me think of this....

But I did NOT/NOT receive sufficient appreciation for the below. Only Jake reacted. It took HOURS to get the formatting right. Literally hours to ensure it would work on every size font.

Without positive reinforcement I'm not sure I can continue to really invest myself in these missives/diatribes.

From: Sullivan, Jacob J [mailto:SullivanJ.J@state.gov]
Sent: Sunday, July 15, 2012 03:23 AM
To: H

See below

From: H <hrod17@clintonemail.com>
Sent: Sunday, July 15, 2012 4:54 PM
To: 'Russorv@state.gov'

Pls print.

*Hillary emails her aide Monica Hanley Sunday evening to discuss important things for the new year.*

From: H <hrod17@clintonemail.com>
Sent: Sunday, January 3, 2010 6:20 PM
To: 'hanleymr@state.gov'
Subject: Happy New Year!

Monica—I hope you had a wonderful holiday season and
thank you for all of your help this past year. You've been a
life saver. I'm looking forward to 2010 being even
better.

Here are a few things as we start the year—

I'd like to work w you to prepare a menu for Jason. Also does
he give me a monthly bill for the food he buys and prepares for
me?

Could you or he buy skim milk for me to have for my tea? Also,
pls remind me to bring more tea cups from home.

Also, pls try to get me a copy of the Human Rights Watch
report titled "We Have the Promises of the World: Women's
Rights in Afghanistan."

Can you give me times for two TV shows: Parks and
Recreation and The Good Wife?

*Hillary emails longtime ally John Podesta about the
United Nations and his sleepwear.*

From: H <hrod17@clintonemail.com>
Sent: Sunday, September 20, 2009 10:28 PM
To: 'jpodesta'
Subject: Re: When could we talk?

I'm on endless calls about the UN. Could I call you early
tomorrow? Would btw 6:30 and 8:00 be too early?

Please wear socks to bed to keep your feet warm.

*Hillary is trying to call her office but the White House
operator doesn't believe it's really her.*

From: H <hrod17@clintonemail.com>
To: 'abedin@state.gov'
Sent: Wednesday, February 10, 2010 3:19 PM
Subject: Re: Diane Watson to retire

I'd like to call her.

But right now I'm fighting w the WH operator who doesn't
believe I am who I say and wants my direct office line even
tho I'm not there and I just have him my home # and the State
Dept # and I told him I had no idea what my direct office # was
since I didn't call myself and I just hung up and am calling thru
Ops like a proper and properly dependent Secretary of State—
no independent dialing allowed.

*Hillary loses the signal to NPR and asks her aides to look
up the right radio station.*

From: H
To: 'JilotyLC@state.gov' <JilotyLC@state.gov>;
'Russorv@state.gov' <Russorv@state.gov>;
'ValmoroLJ@state.gov' <ValmoroLJ@state.gov>
Sent: Fri Aug 20 15:45:04 2010
Subject: Question

Can you find out for me what the NPR stations I can hear on Long
Island are? I lost the WNYC signal half way down the island and
can't figure out from Google what the next stations are.

From: H <hrod17@clintonemail.com>
Sent: Saturday, August 21, 2010 6:41 PM
To: 'JilotyLC@state.gov'; 'Russorv@state.gov';
'ValmoroLJ@state.gov'

Did any of you get this?

# 4

# Hillary's Long Trudge Up—and On—the Hill

*May 18, 1992*

# The 1992 Campaign Hillary Clinton as Aspiring First Lady: Role Model, or a "Hall Monitor" Type?

*I covered Hillary from 1992 to 1995 as a news reporter before I became a columnist.*

After chatting sympathetically with Hillary Clinton for a moment about the silliness of judging a woman by her hairdo, a television reporter from Columbus, Ohio, zeroed in for the sound bite.

"You know, some people think of you as an inspiring female attorney mother, and other people think of you as the overbearing yuppie wife from hell," the reporter said. "How would you describe yourself?"

A look of annoyance glittered through Mrs. Clinton's blue eyes, but she was on a mission to soften her image and show that she has a sense of humor. So she smiled and described herself as a wife, a mother and an activist. Later, on her small campaign plane traveling in Kentucky, she took a bite of an apple and said, "I'm too old to be a yuppie."

Mrs. Clinton has stepped into the eye of the stormy debate about the role of women in society and in politics, and about the image of feminism. And the 44-year-old lawyer seems a bit at a loss over how to deal with all the powerful negative and positive reactions she has unleashed as her husband, Governor Bill Clinton of Arkansas, campaigns for the Democratic presidential nomination.

## The Two Extremes

One night, eating dinner and sipping a glass of white wine at a revolving restaurant atop a hotel in Covington, Kentucky, where she was staying, Mrs. Clinton talked about the two extremes: She is moved by the women of all ages who approach her to tell her that she is a role model, but she is dismayed by the resistance to the idea of a first lady openly engaged in the affairs of state.

"I saw Rosalynn Carter in Little Rock and we talked about this," Mrs. Clinton said. "She got all this criticism for sitting in on Cabinet meetings. Well, so what if she did?"

Republicans now regard the outspoken wife of the Arkansas governor as one more vulnerability in an already vulnerable Clinton campaign. Even though it is now clear that Nancy Reagan helped run the country, with astrological charts and her own political agenda, and even though it is apparent that Barbara Bush is a significant voice on politics, the Republicans are busy mining fears as old as Adam and Eve about the dangers of an assertive, ambitious woman speaking into the ear of her man.

"Hillary Clinton is exceedingly polarizing," said Roger Stone, a Republican consultant. "It's not that she's an accomplished modern woman. It's just that she's grating, abrasive and boastful. There's a certain familiar order of things, and the notion of a coequal couple in the White House is a little offensive to men and women."

She has become a paradigm of the overstructured supermom. A recent *New Yorker* cartoon showed a woman asking a salesclerk for a jacket and saying, "Nothing too Hillary."

## Unprecedented Partnership

Even among women who are Mrs. Clinton's natural constituents, there is criticism about what they call "the Hillary situation." Some leading Democratic women privately worry that, while Mrs. Bush may be the last of the first ladies who have never worked outside the home, the public is still skittish about the idea of a first lady who is more involved in substance than ceremony.

These critics say that the Clintons may have pushed too hard on the concept of an unprecedented partnership in the White House, and suggest that they should wait until after the election to break precedents.

There was Mr. Clinton's suggestion, since revoked, that he might give his wife a Cabinet job. And there was Mrs. Clinton's petulant defense on conflict-of-interest questions about her legal career in Arkansas, when she said she could have "stayed home, baked cookies and had teas."

One Republican campaign official suggests that it is less her sex than her demeanor, noting that Mrs. Clinton is "a hall monitor" type whose drive and earnestness are off-putting: "She doesn't complement Clinton because she appears to be another liberal policy wonk. It doesn't seem like a family—more like a merger."

Mrs. Clinton is far more articulate than the two men on the Republican ticket, but she lacks her husband's ability to stir emotions with speeches. She can be an amiable companion, but she has a studious turn of mind. Even when chatting with the television reporter about hair and perceptions, she asked, "Has anybody done a survey or study about that?"

## Walking a Narrow Line

Ruth Mandel, the director of the Center for Women and Politics at the Eagleton Institute at Rutgers, is sympathetic to women in politics who must walk a narrow line to avoid offending various constituencies.

"Hillary Clinton's life and behavior represent the changes that have taken place in women's lives and marriages, and yet she is faced with the dilemma of not confronting the public with the extent of those changes," Ms. Mandel said. "When it comes to women, people are not ready to take more than a teaspoonful of change at a time."

Now the campaign is keeping Mrs. Clinton on a low-key schedule while strategists try to figure out a way to mend her image problems.

"The public is looking at a new kind of political spouse through a Mamie Eisenhower lens," complained Linda Bloodworth-Thomason, the producer of the television shows *Designing Women* and *Evening Shade*, who is a friend of the Clintons. "The Republicans are constantly ready to take any idea that's new or progressive in terms of men and women and turn it into a negative."

Susan Thomases, a New York lawyer who is an adviser to Mrs. Clinton, agrees that she has been "pigeonholed" and that she has to show herself as a more rounded person. "The public needs to see her not just as a career woman but as a mother, a daughter, a friend, a member of her church," Ms. Thomases said. "There are parts of her personality that are more conservative and traditional than a lot of people project onto her."

## Trying to Reassure Doubters

Everywhere Mrs. Clinton went last week, the high-powered litigator who brought home more than five times the salary her husband did last year tried to reassure doubters that she is not Lady Macbeth in a black preppy headband.

She told reporters again and again that she did not dominate her husband—"He has a real core of toughness"; that her husband would not offer her a Cabinet post—"That's not going to happen, and I wouldn't take it if it did"; that she would not sit in on Cabinet meetings—"I never did that in Arkansas and I'm not going to start now"; and that she would not be a pioneer first lady making radical changes—"I don't think so; I hope I'm going to be myself."

Mrs. Clinton is circumspect on the subject of feminism, saying she believes in equality but rejects some of what the term "has come to mean today."

"I don't think feminism, as I understand the definition, implies the rejection of maternal values, nurturing children, caring about the men in your life," she said. "That is just nonsense to me."

And she even tried to point out the similarities between herself and Mrs. Bush, who identifies herself on her tax returns as "housewife." "Barbara Bush and I have a lot in common," Mrs. Clinton said. "We're both very committed women. We care very deeply about our families, and we're supportive of our husbands."

Mrs. Clinton is intimately involved in strategy and policy planning and, even in a rush, she still includes her family name when she signs autographs, Hillary Rodham Clinton. Yet last week her campaign schedule was traditional enough to have pleased Mrs. Bush, consisting mostly of cutting ribbons to open new campaign headquarters and reading stories like *Chicka Chicka Boom Boom* to children in preschool classes littered with plastic ironing boards and stoves.

Just as President Bush uses his Texas twang on occasion for politicking, dropping *g*'s and substituting "git" for "get," so Mrs. Clinton sometimes falls into some of the folksier twang of Arkansas. She talked a lot about her 12-year-old daughter, Chelsea, her interest in educational programs and her desire to be "a voice for children" in the White House.

## Two for the Price of One

But the difficulty of her situation was underscored as she left a school in Newport, Kentucky. She was surrounded by dozens of children in a warm, fuzzy and maternal photo session. But Ruth Ezell, the reporter for the local CBS affiliate, offered this commentary to her viewers: "When Bill and Hillary Clinton were students at Yale Law School, they were moot court partners. Ever since, they have been a personal and professional team. If Hillary Clinton becomes first lady, you can expect she will reinvent the role and America will get two in the White House for the price of one."

Mrs. Clinton's friends say that while she may be willing to compromise on smaller things for political expediency, as she did when she changed her name to that of her husband to help him in a quest for a second term as governor, she will never compromise on big things. And, indeed, a story she tells over dinner in the hotel in Covington illustrates that strong will.

She is talking about the summer during law school when she went to Alaska and got a job in a fish-processing plant. She was supposed to scoop out the entrails, but she began to get worried about the state of the fish.

"They were purple and black and yucky looking," she recalled. She questioned the owner about how long the fish had been dead, and he warned her to stop asking questions. But she continued asking questions and was fired within a week.

She didn't care. "I found another job," she said coolly.

# Clinton's Health Plan
# First Lady Takes Stage: Ending
# Era on the Hill

Tim Crippen, a member of the House Ways and Means Committee staff, stood in the deserted hearing room, peering at the two mugs in his hand.

"This one has a better lipstick print on it," he said, holding one up and grinning. "Maybe I'll auction it off."

Everything about Hillary Rodham Clinton—what she said, how she said it, how she sat and even what sort of feminine imprint she left drinking tea out of the blue-and-gold Ways and Means Committee china—caused a great stir on Capitol Hill today.

This historic moment may not have been as stunning as the Palestinian-Israeli handshake that shook the capital two weeks ago, but it was remarkable in its own soft-spoken, fact-laden way. It was, in a way, the official end of the era in which presidential wives pretended to know less than they did and to be advising less than they were.

Mrs. Clinton has often been on the Hill in recent months, lobbying and briefing lawmakers on the Administration's emerging health-care proposal. But her bravura in back-to-back appearances today before two House committees carried a sense of wonder.

As oil portraits of the fraternity of past committee chairmen stared down benevolently—men with curling mustaches, men with white hair parted in the middle and men holding important papers and wearing conservative dark suits—Mrs. Clinton testified in an emerald suit with crystal clarity, becoming the first First Lady to appear before Congress defending major legislation which she is helping to draft.

"This is as big as it comes," said an aide to Mrs. Clinton. "This is Eleanor Roosevelt time."

She called her husband "the president," and some lawmakers called her "Madame First Lady."

She is, like her husband, a skilled debater. She did not refer to notes or confer on answers with her health-care aides. Indeed, she left her chief adviser, Ira C. Magaziner, at the White House. She sat at the witness tables by herself, a technique often used by lawyers who do not want to look overwhelming by showing up with a squadron of high-priced talent.

"Hillary for the defense," one White House official proudly called her.

Her polished appearance, following her husband's well-received speech to Congress on health care and his national teach-in on ABC News's town hall program last week, helps give the administration the lift that it has been seeking to help erase the memory of an amateurish debut in Washington.

"Health care shows both the Clintons at their best in a way that no other issue has," said Geoffrey Garin, a Democratic political consultant. "Mrs. Clinton looks good in terms of a mastery of a very complicated matter, and President Clinton looks good in terms of his compassion and willingness to take on hard issues of change."

Both Clintons have made occasional political blunders—like the week they both chose to get their hair cut by the most expensive hairdressers the East and West Coasts have to offer—but they also proved during the campaign that they are fast learners and determined politicians.

It is early yet, and the debate is still in a gentle stage. But, at the start at least, taking a lesson from the White House's errors in selling the budget, the president and first lady are doing an elegant tango on health care, keeping control of the debate and defining the details before opponents can.

## Experience Shows

Mrs. Clinton has conceded that she went through a tough period of adjustment as the wife of the governor of Arkansas.

She was shaped by that experience. But by the time she left Arkansas, she was more popular than her husband with many lawmakers.

Her arc in Arkansas showed today, as she expertly plied the elaborate flattery and back-scratching so cherished in Congress.

When she talked to Dan Rostenkowski, the Illinois Democrat who is the chairman of the Ways and Means Committee, she mentioned that her hometown was Chicago. When she talked to Blanche Lambert, the freshman Congresswoman from Little Rock, she spoke about her home as Arkansas.

She nodded and smiled and gave the impression that much was still negotiable, if she could get proper guidance from these kind and sagacious lawmakers. And she filigreed her answers with those ingratiating clauses that members of Congress hold dear. "Which you know better than I," she would say, or "as you have pointed out."

Her true talent and thorough preparation could be seen in an answer to Representative Bill Brewster, an Oklahoma Democrat who, in a rare show of Congressional modesty, had neglected to mention that he was a pharmacist.

"As a pharmacist," she said to him, "you know that one of the problems is getting affordable drugs to everybody."

When she spoke in the afternoon to the Energy and Commerce Committee, she began with a paean to the father of Representative John D. Dingell, who as a member of Congress in 1943 was an author of the first attempt to pass national health-care legislation.

"The Chairman's father understood the importance of health care," she said. "You both proved to be men ahead of your time." With Mr. Dingell looking moved, she added that Congress had "yet to fulfill your father's dream."

When Representative Fred Grandy, the Republican from Iowa who was in the popular television situation comedy *The Love Boat*, asked her a tough question about breaks for unions and corporations, she gave him a detailed answer with no bite at all. Mr. Grandy is among the Republicans she still hopes to woo.

During the campaign, Mrs. Clinton was surprised to learn from polls that many Americans did not picture her in a maternal way and did not even know that she had a daughter. Today, she was careful to lace her testimony with personal references, beginning in the morning by telling the Ways and Means Committee that she was "here as a mother, a wife, a daughter, a sister, a woman."

She mentioned her mother several times, the last in an exchange with Representative Lynn Schenk, a freshman Democrat from California on the Energy and Commerce Committee.

Ms. Schenk told Mrs. Clinton she had a message for the first lady from her own mother.

"She said to tell you that not since Eleanor Roosevelt has she so admired a woman in public life—and my mother is not a woman who admires easily," Ms. Schenk said, to laughter from the audience.

Representative John Lewis, a Georgia Democrat, gave Mrs. Clinton her most eloquent tribute. "I really believe," he told her, "when historians pick up their pen and write about this period, they will say that you were largely responsible for health-care reform in America."

And Mr. Rostenkowski gave her the one that caused her smile to freeze a bit, perhaps thinking of how her husband would react: "I think in the very near future the president will be known as your husband. 'Who's that fella? That's Hillary's husband.'"

At the end of her testimony, Mrs. Clinton left as formally as she had come, thanking Mr. Dingell for his "courtesy."

Her aides said that throughout the day, on her way to the Hill, when she took a lunch break to eat a turkey club, potato chips and tomato soup in a windowless room in the Rayburn Building, off the Energy and Commerce hearing room, Mrs. Clinton did not show any exultation at the reception she was given on her big day.

# Hillary's Stocking Stuffer

Poor little Hillary.

She's the most famous face in the Senate. She just got $8 million for her story. She has a huge house in Chappaqua and is shopping for another huge house in DC. Her husband is set to make a fortune writing his own memoir and pocketing six figures a pop to do what he loves to do: talk.

And yet, something is missing.

A $2,340 Spode soup tureen, with stand, for starters.

Some of the first lady's wealthy friends and contributors have been fretting that Hillary has never had a chance to accumulate the sort of elegant appurtenances that they have, that the poor girl is starting her grand new life with nothing.

So they decided it would be nice to treat her like a bride—building a nest from scratch—and send her housewarming presents from one of her favorite stores, Borsheims Fine Jewelry and Gifts, the Omaha emporium and subsidiary of Berkshire Hathaway, owned by Hillary admirer and donor Warren Buffett.

Attention, Hillary shoppers! Only nine more days before that pesky Senate gift ban goes into effect!

The Clintons have spent most of their adult lives enjoying affordable public housing. They had scant furniture stored to decorate the Chappaqua manse—probably precious period pieces such as Marimekko wall hangings and bookcases made of cinder blocks and plywood—much less a Washington manse.

Sure, Bill wouldn't care. He looks as if he'd be completely at home with shag rugs, lava lamps and Styrofoam coffee cups.

Some lawmakers think of their Washington digs as temporary and live like college students. Two years ago, millionaire Senator Sam Brownback of Kansas rented the cramped two-bedroom Capitol Hill apartment that Marc Santora, my 26-year-old assistant, was leaving. Mr. Brownback bunked in with Representative Jim DeMint of South Carolina, keeping Marc's exquisite white plastic trash can, bamboo shades and whiffle bat, until the property was condemned a year later.

But Mrs. Clinton is no longer a Crate & Barrel liberal. She's a populist with a sweet tooth for the perquisites of arriviste life. She'll need something to suit her new station, and her new airs.

Lissa Muscatine, Mrs. Clinton's spokeswoman, says that the first lady's silver and china patterns can be found at Borsheims. Hillary shopped there when she was in Omaha last March to raise campaign money, with Mr. Buffett's help.

I clicked onto Borsheims' bridal registry on the Web to sample the merchandise. What would Mrs. Clinton like? Just some basics to get her started. Place settings for 40, including oyster forks and marmalade spoons?

Supporters have suggested the Faberge Sterling Imperial Court silverware for the former czarina of health care. The website describes this as "a magnificent neo-Classical style pattern that was originally produced for the Grand Palace, Peterhof . . . intricate detailing with a laurel wreath on the tip."

The vegetable serving spoon is a bargain at $510 and an iced-tea spoon goes for only $240. Asparagus tongs are a mere $535.

For china, some of her friends give the nod to the Spode Stafford Flowers china pattern, described on the website as "a breathtaking pattern. Stafford Flowers has a scalloped shape with generous gold trim in a raised design. Twenty-two different flowers in vivid purples, pinks, blues and yellows are featured...."

It's easy to picture Bill tossing leftover pizza onto a $980 vegetable dish or spearing some fries with a $284 lobster fork.

But Hillary will need the booty—the $716 teapot, the $476 sauceboat, the $792 punch ladle—to entertain a parade of possible contributors for her next political adventure.

As a senator, Mrs. Clinton won't be able to accept gifts worth more than $100. But as first lady, she can take gifts as long as she discloses those over $250. So we have a nice window of opportunity before January 3.

Ms. Muscatine said of the first couple that "people have routinely gotten them gifts, especially around the holidays. This year, because of the holidays and because it is their last year in the White House, there have been more inquiries."

So don't miss your chance to influence a future senator or president. Call 1-800-642-GIFT to be part of Hillary's holiday haul.

Fork over a fork today.

# Weird Psychic Lock

First there was that woman.

Now there is that person.

As in Hillary telling a group of us huddled around her in the Russell Senate Office Building on Thursday that we should go hunt down "the person" or "people" who issued those sulfurous pardons, because she was plum shocked about the whole thing.

"With respect to any of these decisions, you'll have to talk with people who were involved in making them," she said. "And that leaves me out."

Again and again, she alluded to her husband without using his name.

No matter what bad, bad thing her bad, bad boy did in the past, Hillary never before shoved him into traffic, saying: "You'll have to ask him."

It was the first shot in the War of the Roses. The dame has decided to ice the dude.

Bill has been chained in Chappaqua, while Hillary reigns on Embassy Row. But they know they're bad for each other, so they won't be able to stay apart. Soon they'll be hanging from that pricey

Walter Kaye chandelier and screaming about who owes what to whom. We have reached ground zero of America's most byzantine marriage. The Clintons have run out of aides to blame, friends to ruin, Republicans to decry, conspiracies to denounce and hearts to break.

Now they are turning on each other.

Hillary can't put her political career back on track unless she makes Bill take the fall. And Bill can't put his post-presidential career back on track unless he stops Hillary from forcing him to take the fall.

It's reminiscent of *Prizzi's Honor* when Kathleen Turner and Jack Nicholson, married hit men for the Mob, suddenly turn on each other.

She takes a pistol out of her makeup drawer. He removes a dagger taped to his shin. She shoots. He throws. She gets it in the throat.

So place your bets, mesdames et messieurs.

The cagey senator known as "the Warrior"? Or the cunning ex-president known as "the Survivor"?

Despite the bitter betrayals involved, they never turned on each other during earlier cataclysms because they shared a political goal: to make Bill president, to keep Bill president, to do Great Things.

But now their ambitions are on different tracks.

"This is the first time their political self-interest has diverged," says Dee Dee Myers, Mr. Clinton's former press secretary who is now a *West Wing* consultant. "Before, they were all wound up together on the national stage. Now she has hung out her own shingle and Senator Clinton is not dependent for success or failure on the ex-president."

Ms. Myers is often asked: Will they stay married? She always said yes, "because they have this weird, magnetic, psychic lock between them. And I think she's hot for him. But this is the first time in their married life when she is not the caboose or sidecar connected to his career. Maybe she will want to split off."

When Hillary tried to send the hounds chasing off after her husband, she was feeling the heat from revelations about her brother Hugh taking "a success fee" of $400,000 for helping secure a pardon for a Miami vitamin charlatan and a commutation for an LA drug kingpin. And for the cat's cradle of her intimates—old friend Harry Thomason, campaign guru Harold Ickes and her former campaign treasurer, William Cunningham—involved in the pardons of two Little Rock restaurateurs convicted of tax evasion.

But the pack was not so easily diverted. By Friday, we learned that Mary Jo White, nicknamed Sid Vicious by tennis partners familiar with her ferocity, was not only investigating the pardon of Marc Rich, but also the decision to commute the sentences of four Hasidic New Yorkers whose clemency was championed at a White House meeting that Mrs. Clinton attended. In her Senate race, Hillary got an outlandishly large margin of the vote in the Hasidic community where the four men resided.

There's always the chance, with this pair, that Bill is strategically instructing Hillary to distance herself from him, as some Democrats said he did during her Senate campaign. Sid Vicious needs to get these two into separate interrogation rooms.

If this really is marital mutually assured destruction, which half will prevail? Will Bill talk to Tom Brokaw, and "accidentally" drop something devastating about Hill?

On the one hand, Senator Hillary now has the power. On the other hand, he is Bill Clinton.

*June 29, 2003*

# The Real Hillary

*My review of Hillary Clinton's memoir for the Sunday* New York Times Book Review

*Living History* is neither living nor history. But like Hillary Rodham Clinton, the book is relentless, a phenomenon that's impossible to ignore and impossible to explain.

Her memoir does not fascinate with its dubious Monica revelations. Hillary was a college intern in Washington herself, under much less erotically charged circumstances, working for Representatives Gerald Ford and Melvin Laird. She dispatches the pesky Monica as quickly from her story as Bill should have from his study. It's far more interesting to know that Hillary Rodham was president of her high school's Fabian fan club. That explains a lot.

Poor Bill Clinton. He's trying to deal with Osama bin Laden and he's got a bunch of angry women on his case and a sex-obsessed special prosecutor. He's like Ethan Frome, a guy who just wants to take a joy ride on a sled, and ends up getting stuck for life in a cramped cabin with the wife he betrayed and his now irritating and ubiquitous former dalliance.

Bill is bookended in history by Monica's plea to him in a note:

"I need you right now not as president, but as a man" and Hillary's explanation of why she stuck with him: "As his wife, I wanted to wring Bill's neck. But he was not only my husband, he was also my president." It makes you wonder whether Hillary would have forgiven Bill if he were merely her United States trade representative.

This book is important not because of the history Senator Clinton records but because of the history she doesn't record, and what that airbrushing tells us about the history she aspires to shape. In her coda, she notes that she cannot give undisputed facts, only her own Rashomon tact: "I am responsible for the opinions and interpretations expressed in this memoir. These pages reflect how I experienced the events I describe. I'm sure there are many other—even competing—views of the events and people I describe. That's someone else's story to tell." Like the dutiful student she is, Hillary, assisted by a team of helpers, has finished up her book first, so dawdling Bill will have to fit his "competing views" of events into his wife's "interpretations," rather than vice versa.

Hers is not history in the Churchillian sense, but in the Carvillean sense—campaign literature for the 2008 HILLARY! presidential campaign, with an "acknowledgments" section to hundreds of Ellen Jamesians from "Hillaryland," as they called their cult-like universe, who are determined to see their warrior queen take back the White House from the hypermasculine and domestically Dickensian reign of the Bushies. She wows some people and others, as Ben Bradlee puts it, "she bugs."

When the graduating Hillary took a final swim in Lake Waban at Wellesley, the college's president, apparently still irritated over Hillary's fiery commencement speech, directed a security officer to confiscate the clothes and glasses she had left on the shore.

As a successful alpha female in an era when women are doing a lot of retro-cooing and clawing on *The Bachelor*, and when rampant "blondenfreude," as the *New York Times*'s Alessandra Stanley calls it, makes it treacherous for brainy, blond, controlling women to fly

Icarus-high, Hillary followed a trajectory—from being tormented by Al D'Amato to becoming Al D'Amato—that is compelling.

But anyone who had hoped to gain greater insight into the weird codependent Clinton marriage or the sphinxlike senator may be disappointed. The language of the book is more dead than living, press-release soul-searching, not matching the poignant and painfully candid Katharine Graham memoir Senator Clinton said she was using as her model. Much of it is a travelogue, ranging from the puckish, when Boris Yeltsin serves Hillary soup with gelatinous moose lips floating on top, to the pedantic—"Bangladesh, the most densely populated country on earth, presented the starkest contrast of wealth and poverty I saw in South Asia." *Living History* aims to bury questions, not raise hackles. Unlike Dan Quayle, Nancy Reagan and Barbara Bush in their memoirs, Hillary Clinton does not emphasize tartly settling scores with rivals or the press—except for smacking Kenneth Starr, the *Wall Street Journal* over its "spiteful" editorials on Vince Foster that preceded his suicide and William Rehnquist for not curbing his "ideological…partisan zeal" with the Clintons and in the case of *Bush v. Gore*.

Her frictions with the Secret Service and the chief White House usher are glancingly mentioned. She notes that she knew she was not in totally friendly territory the night of the Inaugural when her pals, the Thomasons, found a black-humor note tucked under a pillow in the Lincoln Bedroom: "Dear Linda, I was here first, and I'll be back," the note said, and was signed Rush Limbaugh. When the first lady came home after her father's funeral to find items in the bedroom askew, the chief usher informed her "that a security team had searched all of our possessions to check for bugging devices and other breaches of security." (That's scary, but it's scarier when the Little Rock decorator Kaki Hockersmith and the television guru Tony Robbins show up as advisers.)

The revelations are so calculated and calibrated they might have been vetted by the pollster Dick Morris. She leaves out almost all mention of her husband's history of messing about (which, as David Maraniss writes in his biography of Bill Clinton, she worried about even before they were married, sending her father and brother to Arkansas to check up on him), so that her scene of being stunned over Monica plays more convincingly. By ignoring the trail of infidelities, she can ignore the marital dynamic caused by those infidelities, which ended up having seismic consequences for the Democrats in the 1994 election and the country.

Bill Clinton handed over huge chunks of responsibility to his wife on policy and appointments not only because he thought she was brilliant, but because he felt he owed her—for giving up the career she could have had to become a "lady lawyer" in a place she didn't want to go (Arkansas), for taking a name she didn't want to take (Clinton), for assuming a title she didn't like (first lady) and for putting up with humiliation she didn't deserve (Gennifer, Paula et al.).

When I asked one of Hillary's top health-care deputies once why Bill hadn't insisted that his wife scale down the size of her health-care plan, and warned her that the tactics of speed and secrecy might backfire, he replied the president felt too beholden to intervene: "She has a hundred-pound fishing wire around" a delicate part of her husband's anatomy. In his book, the former presidential aide David Gergen said that he believed that President Clinton did not step in on health care because he did not dare to challenge Hillary after news reports that Arkansas state troopers fetched women for him.

What we cannot know from this book (since events are given other "interpretations" in other White House books) is whether Hillary was a gulping-for-air victim of her husband's affairs—miserable, she is happy to include herself in the company of history's A-list victims, Elie Wiesel, the Dalai Lama and Nelson Mandela—or an unflinching partner in combating the damage of such escapades, even the efforts by Clinton strategists to smear the women as "cash-for-trash" bimbos or delusional erotomaniacs.

When the Monica story broke, the president told Sidney Blumenthal That Woman was nicknamed "the Stalker." Hillary told

Sidney, as he later testified, that "she was distressed that the president was being attacked, in her view, for political motives, for his ministry of a troubled person." Hillary's good friend Charlie Rangel told reporters that Monica had "serious emotional problems" and was "fantasizing."

If Hillary participated in the vivisection of young women she knew Bill had been involved with, it doesn't add luster to her portfolio, lavishly documented throughout this book, as someone who protects women and the vulnerable in society. It would mean she cares about women unless they get in the way of the Clintons' mission to help humanity, in which case they're expendable.

Hillary chafed at what she calls "derivative" power. During her husband's first presidential campaign, the uneasy realization hit her, when she got some stationery delivered with the Rodham dropped out of her name: "Now I was solely 'the wife of,' an odd experience for me." She sent the stationery back, stat.

She acts willfully naïve about her outsize influence over the president, as though she were just another West Wing official on the domestic side. She dismisses her role in the destruction of the veteran travel office staff members as an example of people trying too hard to please her after an offhand comment, like the time she said she liked Diet Dr Pepper and was deluged with it for years. "I said to Chief of Staff Mack McLarty that if there were such problems" with the travel office finances, "I hoped he would 'look into it.'"

I had dinner with her once during the 1992 campaign, in a revolving restaurant in Kentucky. She had a sly sense of humor, which she has never been able to incorporate into her public persona. In the book, she writes that she inherited her great laugh—"the same big rolling guffaw that can…send cats running from the room"—from her gruff, right-wing and loving dad, Hugh Rodham, who owned a drapery fabric business in Illinois. Her remarkable mother, deserted as a child, instilled in her the chutzpah that would allow her to triumph over feral assaults from the right, including a trifecta of attack books by blond conservative pundettes.

At our dinner, sipping white wine, Hillary talked about a job she had one summer sliming fish in a makeshift salmon factory in Valdez, Alaska. When she complained that some of the fish looked bad, the manager fired her. As she writes: "Of all the jobs I've had, sliming fish was pretty good preparation for life in Washington."

In her book, she drolly describes technicians setting up an interview at the White House with Barbara Walters; they "bathed the room in a golden light so gentle and flattering that even the powdered-wig portrait of Benjamin Franklin above the fireplace seemed to glow with youth."

At her best, she seems like Sarah Brown, the mission doll in *Guys and Dolls*, taken with a charming rake and trying to save the world, but fun if you'd get her out for a night in Cuba. (She tells a hilarious story about the State Department warning her to hide from Castro, who wanted to meet her, at Nelson Mandela's inauguration. "I'd suddenly spot Castro moving toward me, and I'd hightail it to a far corner of the room," she writes.)

But Senator Clinton is also maddening. She will say she learned lessons from bad decisions but then often circle back to insist she was right all along. She resents the St. Hillary image (even as she talks often about the importance of prayer and Scripture in her life), but she can't confess to having a materialistic side that sometimes led her into inexplicably tacky choices, from her dealings with a dubious savings and loan operator in Arkansas to her $100,000 windfall in commodities to her attempts to avoid Senate ethics rules by negotiating an $8 million book advance and her agreeing at the end of her first ladydom to accept largesse from wealthy benefactors so she could buy china and silver for her post–White House life in an Embassy Row home.

"Hillary, though a Methodist," a top Clinton aide once explained to me, "thinks of herself like an Episcopal bishop who deserves to live at the level of her wealthy parishioners, in return for devoting her life to God and good works."

# Obama's Big Screen Test

Hillary is not David Geffen's dreamgirl.

"Whoever is the nominee is going to win, so the stakes are very high," says Mr. Geffen, the Hollywood mogul and sultan of *Dreamgirls*, as he sits by a crackling fire beneath a Jasper Johns flag and a matched pair of de Koonings in the Beverly Hills house that Jack Warner built (which old-time Hollywood stars joked was the house that God would have built). "Not since the Vietnam War has there been this level of disappointment in the behavior of America throughout the world, and I don't think that another incredibly polarizing figure, no matter how smart she is and no matter how ambitious she is—and God knows, is there anybody more ambitious than Hillary Clinton?—can bring the country together.

"Obama is inspirational, and he's not from the Bush royal family or the Clinton royal family. Americans are dying every day in Iraq. And I'm tired of hearing James Carville on television."

Barack Obama has made an entrance in Hollywood unmatched since Scarlett O'Hara swept into the Twelve Oaks barbecue. Instead of the Tarleton twins, the Illinois senator is flirting with the Dream-Works trio: Mr. Geffen, Steven Spielberg and Jeffrey Katzenberg, who gave him a party last night that raised $1.3 million and Hillary's hackles.

She didn't stand outside the gates to the Geffen mansion, where glitterati wolfed down Wolfgang Puck savories, singing the Jennifer Hudson protest anthem "And I Am Telling You I'm Not Going." But she's not exactly Little Miss Sunshine, either. Hillary loyalists have hissed at defecting donors to remember the good old days of jumping on the Lincoln Bedroom bed.

"Hillary is livid that Obama's getting the first big fund-raiser here," one friend of hers said.

Who can pay attention to the Oscar battle between *The Queen* and *Dreamgirls* when you've got a political battle between a Queen and a Dreamboy?

Terry McAuliffe and First Groupie Bill have tried to hoard the best ATM machine in politics for the Missus, but there's some Clinton fatigue among fatigued Clinton donors, who fret that Bill will "pull the focus" and shelve his wife's campaign.

"I don't think anybody believes that in the last six years, all of a sudden Bill Clinton has become a different person," Mr. Geffen says, adding that if Republicans are digging up dirt, they'll wait until Hillary's the nominee to use it. "I think they believe she's the easiest to defeat."

She is overproduced and overscripted. "It's not a very big thing to say, 'I made a mistake' on the war, and typical of Hillary Clinton that she can't," Mr. Geffen says. "She's so advised by so many smart advisers who are covering every base. I think that America was better served when the candidates were chosen in smoke-filled rooms."

The babble here is not about *Babel*; it's about the battle of the billionaires. Not only have Ron Burkle and David Geffen been vying to buy the *Los Angeles Times*—they have been vying to raise money for competing candidates. Mr. Burkle, a supermarket magnate, is close to the Clintons, and is helping Hillary parry Barry Obama by arranging a fund-raiser for her in March, with a contribution from Mr. Spielberg.

Did Mr. Spielberg get in trouble with the Clintons for helping Senator Obama? "Yes," Mr. Geffen replies, slyly. Can Obambi stand up to Clinton Inc.? "I hope so," he says, "because that machine is going to be very unpleasant and unattractive and effective."

Once, David Geffen and Bill Clinton were tight as ticks. Mr. Geffen helped raise some $18 million for Bill and slept in the Lincoln Bedroom twice. Bill chilled at Chateau Geffen. Now, the DreamWorks cochairman calls the former president "a reckless guy" who "gave his enemies a lot of ammunition to hurt him and to distract the country."

They fell out in 2001, when Mr. Clinton gave a pardon to Marc Rich after rebuffing Mr. Geffen's request for one for Leonard Peltier. "Marc Rich getting pardoned? An oil-profiteer expatriate who left the country rather than pay taxes or face justice?" Mr. Geffen says. "Yet another time when the Clintons were unwilling to stand for the things that they genuinely believe in. Everybody in politics lies, but they do it with such ease, it's troubling."

The mogul knows it's easy to mock Hollywood—"people with Priuses and private planes"—and agrees with George Clooney that it's probably not helpful for stars to campaign for candidates, given the caricatures of Hollywood.

I ask what he will say if he ever runs into Bill Clinton again. "Hi," he replies. And will he be upset if Hillary wins and he never gets to sleep in the Lincoln Bedroom again?

"No," he says with a puckish smile. "It's not as nice as my bedroom."

# Gift of Gall

Girlfriend had a rough week.

First Hillary got brushed back by the boys in the debate. Then some women bemoaned Hillaryland's "Don't hit me, I'm a girl" strategy.

The *Washington Post*'s Ruth Marcus deplored the "antifeminist subtext" of Hillary's campaign playing the woman-as-victim card. "Using gender this way," she said, "is a setback."

I must rush to a sister's defense.

Women need to rally to support Hillary and send her money because there are men, men like Tim Russert, who have the temerity to ask her questions during a debate. If there are six male rivals on stage and two male moderators and heaven knows how many men manning lights and boom mikes, the one woman should have the right to have it two ways.

It's simple math, really, an estrogen equation.

If she wants to run on her record as first lady while keeping the lid on her first lady record, that's only fair for the fairer sex. And if she wants to have it both ways on illegal immigrants getting driver's licenses, then she should, especially if those illegal immigrants are men, or if Lou Dobbs is ranting on the issue, because he's not only a man, he's a grumpy, cranky, border-crazed man.

She should certainly be allowed to play the gender card two ways, or even triangulate it. As her campaign manager, Patti Solis Doyle, said after the debate, she is "one strong woman," who has dwarfed male rivals and shown she's tough enough to deal with terrorism and play on the world stage. But she can break, just like a little girl, when male chauvinists are rude enough to catch her red-handed being slippery and opportunistic.

If the gender game worked when Rick Lazio muscled into her space, why shouldn't it work when Barack Obama and John Edwards muster some mettle? If she could become a senator by playing the victim after Monica, surely she can become president by playing the victim now.

Sometimes when Hillary takes heat, she gets paranoid and controlling. But this time she took the heat by getting into the kitchen. After trying to have it both ways during the debate, she tried to have it both ways after the debate.

In New Hampshire on Friday, she stayed above the fray, saying that her male rivals are not "piling on" because she's a woman but because she's "winning." Meanwhile, she let her aides below the fray stir up fem-outrage by putting a video on the campaign website called "The Politics of Pile On," edited to highlight men ganging up on her to the tune of Mozart's *Marriage of Figaro*.

Mark Penn presided over a conference call on Wednesday to rally supporters to the idea of a fem-backlash, during which one devoted Ellen Jamesian suggested that Tim Russert "should be shot." The woman quickly repented, not the sentiment, but the fact that she shouldn't have said it on a conference call. (NBC security remained on high alert.)

Nothing should be sacred when it comes to rousing the women's vote, especially the working-class women Hillary needs to carry her back to the White House. That may be why she recently blew off a *Vogue* photo shoot with Annie Leibovitz at the last minute, according to Liz Smith: to show solidarity with supporters who can't afford *Vogue* frocks.

And remember the time Hillville used a *Washington Post* story about a sighting of the senator's cleavage in the Senate to spearhead a fund-raising drive with women? Dollars for décolletage. Genius!

When pundettes tut-tut that playing the victim is not what a feminist should do, they forget that Hillary is not a feminist. If she were merely some clichéd version of a women's rights advocate, she never could have so effortlessly blown off Marian Wright Edelman and Lani Guinier when Bill first got in, or played the Fury with Bill's cupcakes during the campaign.

She was always kind enough to let Bill hide behind her skirts when he got in trouble with women. Now she deserves to hide behind her own pantsuits when men cause her trouble.

We underestimate Hillary if we cast her as Eleanor Roosevelt. She's really Alfonse D'Amato. Not just the Senator Pothole role, but the talent for playing the aggrieved victim.

D'Amato pulled off a dramatic upset in '92 against Robert Abrams, the New York attorney general, by pouncing when Abrams slipped one night and called D'Amato a "fascist." Though never a sensitive soul about insulting other ethnic groups, D'Amato quickly cast "fascist" as an insult to Italian Americans, producing an ad with scenes of Mussolini.

"It was sheer gall," Anthony Marsh, D'Amato's media consultant, proudly told the *Times*'s Alessandra Stanley.

Like Alfonse, Hillary has the gift of gall. She can be righteous while playing brass-knuckle politics. She will cozy up to former enemies she can use, like Matt Drudge and David Brock, and back W.'s bellicosity if it helps banish her old image as anti-military.

There is nowhere she won't go, so long as it gets her where she wants to be.

That's the beauty of Hillary.

# Duel of Historical Guilts

Some women in their 30s, 40s and early 50s who favor Barack Obama have a phrase to describe what they don't like about Hillary Clinton: shoulder-pad feminism.

They feel that women have moved past that men-are-pigs, woe-is-me, sisters-must-stick-together, pantsuits-are-powerful era that Hillary's campaign has lately revived with a vengeance.

And they don't like Gloria Steinem and other old-school feminists trying to impose gender discipline and a call to order on the sisters.

As a woman I know put it: "Hillary doesn't make it look like fun to be a woman. And her 'I-have-been-victimized' campaign is depressing."

But Hillary—carried on the padded shoulders of the older women in Texas, Ohio and Rhode Island who loved her "I Will Survive" rallying cry that "I am a little older and I have earned every wrinkle on my face"—has been saved to fight another day.

Exit polls have showed that fans of Hillary—who once said they would be happy with Obama if Hillary dropped out—were hardening in their opposition to him, while Obama voters were not so harsh about her.

Three Hillary volunteers from Boston talked to a *New York Times* reporter in an Austin, Texas, parking lot on Tuesday, venting that Hillary hasn't gotten a fair shake from the press. They said that they used to like Obama but now can't stand him because they think he has been cocky and disrespectful to Hillary.

As Hillary, remarkably and cleverly, put Obama on the defensive about a real estate deal, health care and NAFTA, her campaign ratcheted up the retro battle of the sexes when they sent Dianne Feinstein onto the Fox News Sunday morning show to promote the idea that Hillary should not be forced out, regardless of the results of Tuesday's primaries, simply because she's a woman.

"For those of us that are part of 'a woman need not apply' generation that goes back to the time I went out to get my first job following college and a year of graduate work, this is an extraordinarily critical race," the senator said.

With Obama saying the hour is upon us to elect a black man and Hillary saying the hour is upon us to elect a woman, the Democratic primary has become the ultimate nightmare of liberal identity politics. All the victimizations go tripping over each other and colliding, a competition of historical guilts.

People will have to choose which of America's sins are greater, and which stain will have to be removed first. Is misogyny worse than racism, or is racism worse than misogyny?

As it turns out, making history is actually a way of being imprisoned by history. It's all about the past. Will America's racial past be expunged or America's sexist past be expunged?

As Ali Gallagher, a white Hillary volunteer in Austin, told the *Washington Post*'s Krissah Williams: "A friend of mine, a black man, said to me, 'My ancestors came to this country in chains; I'm voting for Barack.' I told him, 'Well, my sisters came here in chains and on their periods; I'm voting for Hillary.' "

And meanwhile, the conventional white man sits on the

Republican side and enjoys the spectacle of the Democrats' identity pileup and victim lock.

Just as Michelle Obama urged blacks to support her husband, many shoulder-pad feminists are growing more fierce in charging that women who let Obama leapfrog over Hillary are traitors.

Julie Acevedo, a precinct captain for Obama in Austin, noticed that things were getting uglier on Friday, during the early voting, when she "saw some very angry women just stomping by us to go vote for Hillary. They cut us off when we tried to talk about Barack.

"I'm forty-six," Ms. Acevedo, a fund-raiser for state politicians, said Tuesday night. "Maybe I missed it by a few years, but I don't know why these women are so fueled by such hostility and think other women are misogynists if they don't vote for Hillary. It's insulting and disturbing."

She said that if Obama definitively outpaces Hillary, she will work to "heal the wounds" and woo back women who are now angry at him.

Watching Bill Clinton greet but not address—the Big Dog has been muzzled—an excited group of students at Texas State University in San Marcos on Tuesday, 19-year-old Allison Krolczyk said she was leaning toward Obama and felt no gender guilt about voting for him. "Not at all," she said. "I think they're both pretty amazing."

The crowd held up their camera phones to capture the former president, in his bright orange tie and orange-brown ostrich cowboy boots.

"We love you, Bill!" yelled one boy. "You did a good job, except for Monica."

# Butterflies Aren't Free

In his memoir, the legendary Elia Kazan wrote about directing Vivien Leigh in *A Streetcar Named Desire*. While he did not think that Leigh was a great natural actress, he was impressed that she would crawl through glass to get the role right.

Hillary Clinton may not be a great natural politician, but traveling across the country on her own Bus Named Desire, she has crawled through glass to get the role right.

She showed again with her squeaker win in Indiana that for many white working-class men, she is The Man—more tenacious and less concerned with the judgments of the tony set, economists and editorial writers. Talking up guns, going to the Auto Racing Hall of Fame, speaking from the back of pickup trucks and doing shots of populism with a cynicism chaser, Hillary emerged from a lifetime of government limos to bask as queen of the blue-collar prom.

Nobility is for losers.

Just as Obama spent his youth trying not to be threatening, so as not to unnerve whites, Hillary spent her life learning to be threatening so she could beat back challenges to her and her husband—from

Republicans and from "bimbo eruptions" and now from a charmed younger rival.

As Obama learned to accommodate, the accommodating Hillary learned to triangulate and lacerate. As he learned that following the rules could get you far with adoring mentors, she learned from Bill and Dick Morris and Mark Penn that following the rules was for saps.

Hillary is less Blanche than Scarlett. "Heaven help the Yankees if they capture you," Rhett told the willful belle at the start of her rugged odyssey.

And heaven help the Democrats as they try to shake off Hillary. On top of her inane vows to obliterate Iran, OPEC and the summer gas tax, she plans "a nuclear option" during her Shermanesque march to Denver. Tom Edsall reported in the *Huffington Post* that the Hillaryites will try, at a May 31 meeting of the Democratic Rules and Bylaws Committee, to renege on their word and get the Michigan and Florida delegations seated. As she addressed supporters here, she urged the counting of the Florida and Michigan votes, noting "it would be a little strange to have a nominee chosen by forty-eight states."

"It's full speed on to the White House," she said.

Fox News reports that the Clintons are planning a summer campaign with TV appearances, fliers and rallies, between the end of the primary and the convention, to drag back superdelegates trying to flock to Obama. The Democratic race has been a scorpion and a butterfly in a bottle. Hillary tore Barry's wings off, and so psyched him out with her silly goading—"Enough about the speeches and the big rallies!" she cried—that he gave up his magical trump cards.

Wandering around Indiana, appearing in neighborhoods and at diners without any advance notice, talking to handfuls of people, Obama strived to seem less lofty and more mortal. Hounded by Hillary, Bill and Reverend Wright, he just looked sort of numb. When Obama went to an 11:30 p.m. shift change at an auto components plant here in Indianapolis, a *Newsday* reporter on the scene noted that many of the white men "were less likely to smile or look him in the eye or seem impressed with him."

In a restaurant in Greenwood on Tuesday, Obama approached an older white guy who waved him off, muttering afterward to a reporter: "I can't stand him. He's a Muslim. He's not even pro-American as far as I'm concerned."

Even though people at diners kept trying to fatten up Obama, he drew the line at gravy—he looked increasingly diaphanous, like antimatter to Hillary's matter. She's more appealing when she's beaten down; he's less imposing. Even his strategists admit that he will now need to "step it up," as one said. And he did that with his victory speech in Raleigh, NC, with a vivid paean to patriotism and "telling the truth forcefully, repeatedly, confidently." As one aide crowed, "He's back!"

It's hard to believe that this Hillary is the same Wellesley girl who said she yearned for a more "ecstatic and penetrating mode of living." What would that young Hillary—who volunteered on Gene McCarthy's antiwar campaign; who cried the day Martin Luther King Jr. was killed; who referred to some of her "smorgasbord of personalities" in a 1967 letter to a friend as an "alienated academic," and an "involved pseudo-hippie"; who once returned a bottle of perfume after feeling guilty about the poverty around her—think of this shape-shifting, cynical Hillary?

She's so at odds with who she used to be, even in the Senate, that if she were to get elected, who would voters be electing?

Obama is like her idealistic, somewhat naïve self before the world launched 1,000 attacks against her, turning her into the hard-bitten, driven politician who has launched 1,000 attacks against Obama.

As she makes a last frenzied and likely futile attempt to crush the butterfly, it's as though she's crushing the remnants of her own girlish innocence.

# Watch Out, Meryl Streep! She's a Master Thespian

How much Hillary Clinton can help Barack Obama will depend on how good an actress she is.

And I bet she is a very good actress indeed.

Not only because, as first lady, she played the diverse roles of someone interested in China and someone interested in china. Not only because, as a presidential candidate, she morphed from Queen Elizabeth I to Norma Rae, as *Newsweek* put it.

But because, through humiliation and pain, she has shown herself to be a skilled survivor. She said she embraces the old saying, "Fake it till you make it."

After the roiling rollout of the Clinton administration, a sad and unnerved Hillary sought answers from self-help gurus like Jean Houston.

"Houston felt at one point that being Hillary was like being Mozart with his hands cut off, unable to play," Bob Woodward wrote. "She felt that the first lady was going through a female crucifixion."

At critical junctures of her life, Hillary makes the same mistake.

She comes on strong, showing an arrogant, abrasive side, gets brushed back and then repackages herself in a more appealing way.

It happened when she began as Arkansas's first lady; when she campaigned with Bill in '92; when she started as a "two for the price of one" first lady; when she did health care and when she started her presidential campaign wearing an off-putting ermine robe of entitlement and presumption. And it happened when she lost the nomination, refused to admit it and, instead of congratulating Obama, wielded her female fan base as a bludgeon over him so she could once more share a presidency.

Now, as she transforms herself into a team player, she must again fake it till she makes it. She still doesn't believe Obama can win, but she knows she can move ahead only as a beguiler, not a begrudger.

Meanwhile, she wants another power-sharing arrangement. She will help Obama be king, if he lets her be queen of the women.

As the *Times*'s Jodi Kantor wrote Saturday, Hillary's "grieving" voters "say that she will remain their leader, that she has created a lasting female constituency, a women's electoral movement unlike any other."

So, you may wonder: Will Hillary's historic bid turn out to be good or bad for women?

*The Wall Street Journal* reported back in March that some women were worried that "the resistance to Senator Clinton may embolden some men to resist women's efforts to share power with them in business, politics and elsewhere."

It's a reasonable fear. Every fizzy triumph of feminism I have covered—Geraldine Ferraro's selection, the Anita Hill hearings, Hillary's copresidency—ended up triggering awful backlashes. In the end, feminism sputtered out as a force.

Hillary has brought back that old feminist religion, at least for now.

She should not have pitted the women against the men. She

did it to her detriment within her own campaign, where Patti Solis Doyle, the tyro campaign manager and self-styled "queen bee" of Hillaryland, battled with Bill's "White Boys," as they were known, and often left Bill feeling dissed.

And Hillary did it to Obama's detriment with her female fan base, stirring up such fury that some women are still vowing to jump to John McCain, even if it means voting against their self-interest.

She should not have repeated the mistake she made after her health-care plan failed. Instead of simply admitting her own mistakes in judgment, she played the victim and blamed sexism.

Of course, powerful women evoke sexism, and the attacks are more personal and slights can be grating. But it's counterproductive to dwell on it, magnify it and exploit it during a campaign—especially when you're getting all that love from Joe Sixpack.

I don't believe Hillary's campaign will cause a backlash. As long as her Denver Liberation Army doesn't cause Obama to lose, it may well be good for women.

When I interviewed scores of women after Ronald Reagan won the women's vote in '84, I was stunned at what I heard. Many working-class women said they didn't vote for Ferraro because they didn't feel capable of running the country, so how could she?

Maybe women have seen enough male boo-boos in the last eight years to give them more confidence. Or maybe Hillary's grit and gall allowed them to easily envision her cuffing generals and dictators.

While studies continue to say that being taller and having a deeper voice can make you seem like a more credible leader, Hillary thrillingly proved herself the best debater and the toughest candidate while being shorter and having the higher voice.

She didn't lose because she was a woman. She didn't lose because America isn't ready for a woman as president. She lost because of her own—and her husband's and Mark Penn's—fatal missteps.

# Interlude

## *Parodying an Election beyond Parody:* SNL's *Lorne Michaels and Kate Mckinnon Dish on Political Humor*

*February 9, 2016*

Bernie Sanders was a no-show at the *Saturday Night Live* after-party in the Flatiron district. It may be one of the coolest parties in town, but Sanders didn't care. The improbably hip 74-year-old candidate didn't need any validation; he felt pret-ty, pret-ty, pret-ty good about his performance.

He was relaxed on the show, wearing his usual baggy gray suit pants. Some were shocked to see something on Sanders's face they had never spied before: a smile. The avatar of voter anger even gamely did a bit with the host, Larry David, about the semantic parsing of socialism and Democratic socialism, which some *SNL* folks were pleasantly surprised that he agreed to do. The Vermont senator, after being hailed for his "modesty" by his costars and producers, was back in New Hampshire by 3 a.m., traveling via his charter plane, though until a month ago he was more accustomed to middle seats on cheap commercial flights.

It had been a nerve-racking day rehearsing a show with Secret Service agents on hand and even more celebrities and moving parts than usual, the *SNL* creator and executive producer Lorne Michaels told me. Besides Sanders, Ben Stiller and Owen Wilson dropped by *Weekend Update* as Derek Zoolander and Hansel—it was Wilson's first frightening experience with live TV—to mock Donald Trump's "Blue Steel" poses: "Orange Mocha Crappaccino," "Hot Mess" and "Second Place."

Just as in 2008, when Michaels woke up one day and was told by everyone—including his doorman—that John McCain's surprise vice-presidential pick was a dead ringer for one of the brightest graduates of *SNL*, this winter, he again woke up one day and realized that the cranky senator giving Hillary a Larry-David-and-Goliath fight in the Democratic primary was a dead ringer for the cranky comedian who had started his career, haltingly and briefly, at *SNL* in 1984 under a different producer, Dick Ebersol.

"My phone rang, and it was Ari and he said, 'Larry David would like to play Bernie Sanders,'" Michaels recalled, referring to David's swashbuckling agent, Ari Emanuel. "The audience cast him. It was the same with Tina. So I said to Larry, 'Can you be here Thursday?' And he said, 'Yes.'" Karmic revenge for '84, when David's sketches failed to get on air.

The 2016 presidential election has been so surreal that it sometimes seems beyond parody, but *SNL* is up for the challenge.

Donald Trump hosted in November, to "yuge" ratings. Hillary Clinton did a zesty turn as a bartender named Val in a scene with Kate McKinnon playing the beleaguered candidate. And Saturday, Sanders and David did their abrasively and bracingly honest twin act, including a hilarious merger of life and art called "Bern Your Enthusiasm."

"Bernie was here because of Larry," Michaels said. "And he embraced Larry's impression from the very beginning." (McKinnon likes Bernie, too, but she already has her Hillary "horse in the race.")

David said he enjoyed working with Sanders, and he praised his long record of authenticity as a politician. But he had some doubts about what a President Sanders defense policy would look like.

"Like Bernie, I'm from Brooklyn, and unlike Israeli Jews, we do not care for fighting," he told me dryly. "We run for the hills. On the other hand, if I had some football players backing me up or in this case, the US military, I probably would have instigated fights!" Asked if he's surprised that Bernie has turned out to be such a chick magnet, David replied, grinning: "Women like old Jewish men."

After the show, I sat down with Michaels at a back table at Dos Caminos, where he nursed a cranberry and vodka. At one point, the chairman of NBC Entertainment, Ted Harbert, rushed over from another table, waving a list of 55 presidential candidates running in New Hampshire who could complain to the FCC about equal time. His favorite was Vermin Supreme, a perennial candidate promoting zombie-apocalypse awareness, a zombie-based energy plan and time-travel research. As though that weren't enough, he's also promising a free pony for every American and pledging to pass a law requiring people to brush their teeth.

I talked to Michaels about whether reality in politics is now too much like satire to satirize, and whether, with Palin back in a transcendently nutty mix, 2016 is on track to Trump the mind-boggling *SNL* run in 2008.

MD:    How do you compare the 2008 election with 2016?

LM:    You have a lot of hot personalities this year. Obama was the essence of cool and minimalist, and you have people now who tend to spill over, and that is much easier because they're just bigger.

MD:    Then Sarah Palin suddenly pops back up in this flamboyant way. Did you have to talk Tina into doing it again?

LM:    No, Tina knew. She was happy. When you saw the tape of Sarah Palin, I think the hardest part of that was the jacket. We had to make it.

MD:    You once told me that you thought Will Ferrell's "backhand-edly affectionate" portrayal of W. helped sway the 2000 election, even though that didn't jibe with Ferrell's politics. Are you worried that you are making Sanders even more hip and popular with young people and that that will hurt Hillary?

LM:    You were at the Trump show, and the criticism there was that we were giving him a platform. I don't go along with the idea that the American people can't make up their own minds and that if you expose them to these things, they will just be swept along. I mean, we have another year of this. Sunlight is the best disinfectant.

I don't think anyone makes up their mind to vote for Bernie Sanders because he was on the show tonight. But his performance tonight, the fact that he was as good with Larry as he was, or the fact that Hillary was as good with Kate as she was—you can sort of tell that they have a sense of humor about themselves. My grandmother used to say that what's in you comes out. Their portraits reveal themselves as the months go on. It won't resonate unless there's some truth to it.

MD:    Bill Carter wrote in *The Hollywood Reporter* that when you saw a rehearsal in 2012 of the Romney-Obama debate sketch, you almost scrapped it. Was that year less scintillating?

**LM:** I think it's like the World Series. I don't mean to trivialize it. There are years you care about and years you don't. There are certain times when everybody is watching, and that's sort of where we are now. It's less about parties and doctrine and more about the personalities involved. It just transcends politics and becomes about who we are as a country.

**MD:** You've known Donald Trump for a long time. Were you surprised that he got in and has done so well?

**LM:** Whenever anybody is that quickly dismissed, you know the critics probably aren't right. I remember in '79, '80, Democrats said, "You know, Reagan's an actor." Like voters don't know that. There's a smugness to that attitude that causes the voting public to go, "We're smarter than that." Donald's giving voice to what polite society has sort of sat on for a while, things that are felt but that no one is articulating. There is something happening there, or it wouldn't be resonating.

**MD:** Do you think that Trump can go further?

**LM:** No idea. He could end up being the moderate. People are always looking for us to be on the side of Clinton, and that's not what we do. If Trump is ascendant, then we will be discussing that.

**MD:** Sometimes the visiting politicians want to play face-to-face with their doppelgängers, as with Trump and Darrell Hammond. Larry David said he didn't want to do his Bernie next to Bernie's Bernie. And Tina told me she thought it would be "sweaty" to do her impression with Palin on stage with her.

**LM:** No question. I think she thought that anything she did that was proximate would look like an endorsement, and I wanted to say that I think that was possibly overthinking it. Possibly.

**MD:** You handled the Larry-Bernie dueling impressions more obliquely, rather than using what the writer Jim Downey calls a "classic sneaker-upper."

LM:   It's like Dana Carvey's George Bush Sr. When you'd see the real president, it didn't sound like Bush, because Dana was such a definitive take. You never wanted to see them together, because Carvey was the real Bush. Larry's the real Bernie.

MD:   Are some pols harder to mimic?

LM:   There are some politicians you can't lay a glove on. It was really hard to get a funny take on Reagan. It helps when the audience thinks there's a hidden side of a politician.

MD:   So what have you learned from being the daddy of comedy all these years, working with so many generations of comics?

LM:   I think what you realize when you do my job is that you can pretty much tell how everyone was treated by their father. Sometimes you get stuck in your period of peak rebellion. If they were a girl and they were adored by their father, they just assumed that posture. They were very easy to be around. If they were a guy whose father was way too critical, whatever you said was a problem. Then you realize it has so little to do with you, it's just the role.

MD:   Are you actually as serene as you seem, or do you have to do that to calm other people?

LM:   Probably early on, I acted serene to calm others. But now, as I say every week, we are ready to go on because it's 11:30.

## Kate McKinnon

*I went to Boston in the summer of 2015 to the set of the* Ghostbusters *movie to interview SNL's Kate McKinnon about her star-making turn as Hillary. In addition to her roles as Angela Merkel and Justin Bieber, she plays a character called the Crazy Cat Lady. McKinnon does love cats and she has a feline manner. But she's much sexier and shyer than the cat lady.*

**MD:** Your colleagues at *SNL* say you wanted the Hillary impression to be funny but also vulnerable, not a mean-spirited takedown. How do you find the line between sharp and mean?

**KM:** That's the hardest thing. I truly would be so horrified if someone was upset at something that I did about them. I would have to retire at that point. It would really kill me. So I try, but you have to point something out about them. So that's something I just obsess about, and it causes me great heartache all the time, just wondering, "Is this too much?" "What would they think of this?"

**MD:** You're an outspoken Hillary Clinton supporter, but your impression sort of dovetails with the haters' assessment of Hillary: that she is pathologically ambitious and insincere. Do you fret about that?

**KM:** Um, yes. But it's my job to make comedy out of current events. I'm sorry I talk so slow.

**MD:** It's okay. People won't hear that in print.

**KM:** A good impression is sort of a juxtaposition of two disparate elements, which is surprising in some way. For instance, Angela Merkel, to me, is a very emotional German; she may not be in real life, but that's how the writers and I conceived of the character. With Hillary, it's that she's a staunch, passionate lady, and in our culture, unfortunately, there's something funny about that. There shouldn't be anything funny about that, but that tickles us for some reason. So that's what I've been working with, and her zeal is what I find delightful about her.

**MD:** You said you would be nervous to meet Hillary Clinton because you find her "resplendent." Why resplendent?

KM: Well, she's a bastion, a brilliant intellectual, a crusader for things I care deeply about. She's just ten million times smarter than me and has seen things and done things that I could never even comprehend. I just wouldn't know what to say. She's too smart.

MD: Well, you better get ready. I'm sure she'll be coming on the show.

KM: Maybe I'll find out what TV show she likes and I'll try to talk to her about that.

MD: In order to nail an impression, do you have to share some of that person's DNA? What part of Hillary Clinton is part of you?

KM: I think that what I connect to about her is the degree to which she wants to help the common man. Yeah, what I find so lovable about her is her staunch passion and her conviction. And I feel like I have that. I could never be a politician, but I just love how badly she wants to fix stuff. I would like to do that. I'm just not smart enough.

MD: That feral side of her that you portray, where she wants to get to the Oval Office so badly, is also probably a reflection of the fact, as she's said, that she's not as good as Bill Clinton at retail politics. That's not what she enjoys. She wants to leap up over that part.

KM: I guess I understand that as well. I'm an introvert and I have trouble schmoozing, and so I guess I relate to her on that level as well. That she just wants to get down to business. I'm very much like that as well.

MD: Do you have a server in your bathroom?

KM: No.

MD: You've been working on getting Hillary's laugh down. How are you doing?

KM: That's the thing that I latched onto first, was how hardy her laugh is.

MD:    Some guys I know love that laugh.

KM:    And how funny it is coming from a short woman. And I can say that because I am also a short woman.

MD:    I thought of your "Summertime" skit, because Hillary had to leave her vacation in Martha's Vineyard to go campaign in the Midwest because of Donald Trump and all the email stuff.

KM:    I just want her to sleep, to be able to sleep.

MD:    Would a male politician be similarly mocked for his ambition?

KM:    No, I don't think so at all. I think that what makes it surprising and ticklish is that she's a woman. If you had a man saying the same things, that would not qualify as a comedic character, and I think that's deeply problematic and speaks more about our culture than it does about her.

MD:    Tina Fey felt that "mean" was a word that tended to be thrown at women who do satirical humor more than guys. She said that nobody ever said that Dan Aykroyd was mean to Richard Nixon or Will Ferrell was mean to W., but she got hit with being "mean" to Sarah Palin.

KM:    That impression was not an exaggeration. It was just frighteningly accurate.

MD:    When Fey did Sarah Palin, she worried about having an effect on the election, pro or con, and she wanted to make sure she felt "clean" and had "fair hits." What do you worry about when you do Hillary?

KM:    I unequivocally want her to win, and I don't really think I have the power to sway anything.

MD:    Lorne Michaels thinks that Will Ferrell's good ol' boy impression of W. helped him win the 2000 election. Does that idea excite you or scare you?

KM:    That's the worst thing I could ever imagine. I don't want that on my shoulders. I'm just trying to make a lovable character out of her. What I'm doing, I don't think, bears much resemblance to the actual person. I just wanted to have a good time playing with what I find to be a good time about her.

MD: Do you ever use Hillary's voice in any other situation—a romantic situation or ordering food?

KM: No. That's what I found hardest about it. She doesn't have a silly voice at all. It's a pretty normal voice.

MD: Fey didn't want to do the impression at the same time as Palin. She felt it would feel "sweaty." If the real Hillary is on *SNL* this season, would you want to do it at the same time?

KM: I'm nervous. I don't feel like I have the right to be in the same room as her, frankly. I don't know what it would be like. We will see.

MD: Do you study a lot of videos?

KM: Yes, I don't know how people did a sketch show without You-Tube. I just look at YouTube clips all day. (*Her blouse slips a bit.*) God, my boobs are out.

MD: Do you go back to the '90s, Hillary as first lady, or do you stay with the post–Monica Hillary?

KM: I have watched mostly recent clips.

MD: When you see Hillary's poll numbers, do you start getting your Elizabeth Warren ready? Or would you do Bernie Sanders?

KM: I think she'll be fine.

MD: If you were Hillary's strategist, what advice would you give her?

KM: I would never be a strategist. I hate strategy. It should just be correct. The correct thing to happen should just happen without having to grab at it so hard.

MD: Should she just try not to act too cool?

KM: I don't know. I don't like to worry about presentation in my own life, and I hate to think of anyone having to worry about it in theirs. Yet it's a lot of what people care about.

MD: In one of your skits, your Hillary says, "Aren't we such a fun, approachable dynasty." What do you think of the idea of our dynasties?

KM: I think about what they do at night and what TV they watch and if they're okay and what they think about and what it must be like with that relentless schedule. I try to imagine their inner lives. I love playing any politician because all you have to do is give them any sort of human quality, allude to their inner life in any way, and that's funny because you don't think about that.

MD: Would you like to play Donald Trump?

KM: I would have a hard time.

MD: You've called your approach to impressions "empathetic mockery," and the *SNL* writers say the heart of your talent is that you bring an extra level of pathos to every scene.

KM: I came in not really knowing how to approach any of this and I still don't. I try to distill it down to some sort of science, but it keeps changing and I don't know what the (expletive) I'm doing. I do find it hard to do an impression of someone who I don't like or can't connect to. So I don't. So everyone that I've had the pleasure of doing, there's always something about them that I love and do feel is part of myself as well. You know with Lorne, there's a lot of pathos. He insists on it in everything that he's produced. And I've come to espouse that because I believe it's the correct approach. He's big on likability. And I didn't understand why until I got there and saw that it's just more fun to watch if you also like the person. You can be mocking them but there has to be a celebration of what's good about them as well or else you don't really want to go back and watch it again. I didn't see it at first but now it's the cornerstone of how I approach everything.

MD:   You are the first openly lesbian member of the *SNL* cast in its 40-year history. Does that bring with it any special obligation? Colleagues said that you were sensitive about using the word "dyke" in "Dyke and Fats," the '70s Chicago cops skit you do with Aidy Bryant, where you play Les Dykawitz and Aidy plays Chubbina Fatzarelli. Or does it feel good to be at a time in our history where it's not a big deal?

KM:   I hope that. I'm very happy to be living in a time where it has been mostly ancillary, and I credit the women before me for making that possible and I'm entirely indebted to them.

MD:   As your movie career takes flight, are you at all worried about the old biases that make gay actors stay in the closet because there's a fear that it would be less convincing if they played straight characters?

KM:   That's just one of the eight million concerns that I have.

MD:   In the Dan Aykroyd–Bill Murray days, *SNL* was known as a macho preserve, and there's still an overwhelming majority of men applying to be writers on the show. How are women doing in achieving parity?

KM:   Well, the arc of history is long but it bends towards justice. It's not appropriate to use that quote about something as trivial as comedy. But I find it to be generally true. It's slow, though. What a long arc.

MD:   I hear you honed your mimicry skills getting on the loudspeaker at North Shore High School in Glen Head, New York, and imitating your art history teacher, Anita Rabin-Havt, in eleventh grade. What were some other early impressions?

KM:    Where in the (expletive) did you find this shit? Oh, my God. You've gone deep. She's an incredible woman. She was so hilarious and very smart. And every time she spotted an injustice, she'd say, "That's going in my book, you'll read it in my book." I loved Cheri Oteri's Barbara Walters so much because it was so accurate and a caricature at the same time. That was the first impression I did. It was just a copy of hers. I just loved different accents and what they seemed to suggest about a person's character and internal desires, so I always just did as many accents as I could.

# 5

# Meanwhile on Planet Vulcan...

# Bring On the Puppy
# and the Rookie

I walked over to the White House Tuesday night and leaned against the fence. How can such a lovely house make so many of its inhabitants nuts?

There was no U-Haul in the driveway. I don't know if W. was inside talking to the portraits on the wall. Or if the portraits can vanish from their frames, as at Hogwarts School, if W. is pestering them about his legacy.

The Obama girls, with their oodles of charm, will soon be moving in with their goldendoodle or some other fetching puppy, and they seem like the kind of kids who could have fun there, prowling around with their history-loving father.

I was not surprised during the campaign by the covert racism about Barack Obama or by Hillary Clinton's subtext when she insisted to superdelegates: "He can't win."

But I was astonished by the overt willingness of some people who didn't mind being quoted by name in *The New York Times* saying vile stuff, that a President Obama would turn the Rose Garden into a watermelon patch, that he'd have barbecues on the front lawn, that he'd make the White House the Black House.

Actually, the elegant and disciplined Obama, who is not descended from the central African American experience but who has nonetheless embraced it and been embraced by it, has the chance to make the White House pristine again.

I grew up in Washington, and I love all the monuments filled with the capital's ghosts. I hate the thought that terrorists might target them again.

But the monuments have lost their luminescence in recent years.

How could the White House be classy when the Clintons were turning it into Motel 1600 for fund-raising, when Bill Clinton was using it for trysts with an intern, and when he plunked a seven-seat hot tub with two Moto-Massager jets on the lawn?

How could the White House be inspiring when W. and Cheney were inside making torture and domestic spying legal, fooling Americans by cooking up warped evidence for war and scheming how to further enrich their buddies in the oil and gas industry?

How could the Lincoln Memorial—"With malice toward none; with charity for all"—be as moving if the black neighborhoods of a charming American city were left to drown while the president mountain biked?

How can the National Archives, home of the Constitution, be as momentous if the president and vice president spend their days redacting the Constitution?

How can the black marble V of the Vietnam Memorial have power when those in power repeat the mistake of Vietnam?

How can the Capitol, where my dad proudly worked for so many years, hold its allure when the occupants have spent their days—and years—bickering and scoring petty political points instead of stopping White House chicanery and taking on risky big issues?

How can the FDR Memorial along the Tidal Basin be an uplifting trip to the past when the bronze statue of five stooped men in a bread line and the words of FDR's second inaugural—"I see one-third of a nation ill-housed, ill-clad, ill-nourished"—evoke the depressing present?

Obama may be in over his head. Or he may be heading for his own monument one day.

His somber speech in the dark Chicago night was stark and simple and showed that he sees what he's up against. There was a heaviness in his demeanor, as if he already had taken on the isolation and "splendid misery," as Jefferson called it, of the office he'd won only moments before. Americans all over the place were jumping for joy, including the block I had been on in front of the White House, where they were singing: "Na, na, na, na. Hey, hey, hey. Goodbye."

In the midst of such a phenomenal, fizzy victory overcoming so many doubts and crazy attacks and even his own middle name, Obama stood alone.

He rejected the Democratic kumbaya moment of having your broad coalition on stage with you, as he talked about how everyone would have to pull together and "resist the temptation to fall back on the same partisanship and pettiness and immaturity that has poisoned our politics for so long."

He professed "humility," but we'd heard that before from W., and look what happened there.

Promising to also be president for those who opposed him, Obama quoted Lincoln, his political idol and the man who ended slavery: "We are not enemies, but friends—though passion may have strained it must not break our bonds of affection."

There have been many awful mistakes made in this country. But now we have another chance.

As we start fresh with a constitutional law professor and senator from the Land of Lincoln, the Lincoln Memorial might be getting its gleam back.

I may have to celebrate by going over there and climbing up into Abe's lap.

It's a $50 fine. But it'd be worth it.

# Exit the Boy King

It was the Instant the Earth Stood Still.

Not since Klaatu the robot landed in a flying saucer on the Ellipse in the classic sci-fi film *The Day the Earth Stood Still* has Washington been so mesmerized by an object whirring through the sky.

But this one was departing, not arriving.

As W. ceased to be president, he flew off over the Capitol and across the Mall en route to Andrews Air Force Base, and then back to Texas.

I've seen many presidents come and go, but I've never watched a tableau like the one Tuesday, when four million eyes turned heavenward, following the helicopter's path out of town. Everyone, it seemed, was waving goodbye, with one or two hands, a wave that moved westward down the Mall toward the Lincoln Memorial, and keeping their eyes fixed unwaveringly on that green bird.

They wanted to make absolutely, positively certain that W. was gone. It was like a physical burden being lifted, like a sigh went up of "Thank God. Has Cheney's wheelchair left the building, too?"

The crowd was exuberant that George Bush was now an ex-president, and 43 himself was jovial "the way he always is," according to his last press secretary, Dana Perino.

It was like a catharsis in Greek drama, with the antagonist plucked out of the scene into the sky, and the protagonist dropping into the scene to magically fix all the problems. Except Barack Obama's somber mien and restrained oratory conveyed that he's no divinity and there will be no easy resolution to this plot.

It was a morning of such enormous emotion and portent—jaw-dropping, Dow-dropping and barrier-dropping—that even the cool new president had to feel daunted to see his blocks-long motorcade and two million hope-besotted faces beaming up at him, dreaming that he can save their shirts.

The optimism was tempered by pessimism, a vibe of "Maybe this once-in-a-lifetime guy can do it, but boy, there are a lot of never-in-our-lifetime problems here."

Unlike W., Obama is a realist. He knows there is the potential of letting all these blissed-out people down.

The day had its jittery moments: including Teddy Kennedy collapsing at the inaugural luncheon. There was also that match of the titan smarty-pants—the new Democratic president face to face with the conservative chief justice he voted against.

First John Roberts had to say "Easy, cowboy" after Mr. Obama jumped the gun on "I" at the start of the oath of office. Then the president, who had obviously been looking over his lines, graciously offered the chief justice a chance to correct his negligent syntax, when he put the "faithfully" and other words out of place.

Under the platform, near where I sat, Denzel Washington, Beyoncé, Jay-Z and P. Diddy looked on proudly as the new commander in chief showed he was in command of the script and the country.

After thanking President Bush "for his service to our nation," Mr. Obama executed a high-level version of Stephen Colbert's share-the-stage smackdown of W. at the White House Correspondents' Dinner in 2006.

With W. looking on, and probably gradually realizing with irritation, as he did with Colbert, who Mr. Obama's target was—(Is he talking about me? Is 44 saying I messed everything up?)—the newly minted president let him have it:

"As for our common defense, we reject as false the choice between our safety and our ideals," he said to wild applause, adding: "Those ideals still light the world, and we will not give them up for expedience's sake." He said America is choosing hope over fear, unity over discord, setting aside "false promises" and "childish things."

Letting a little air out of the highest hopes about what one man, even "The One," can do, he emphasized the word "our." He stressed that rebuilding after the wreckage of W. and Cheney will be a shared burden and that "giving our all to a difficult task" isn't as bad as it sounds.

I grew up here, and it was the first time I've ever seen the city wholly, happily integrated. The Obamas have made an unprecedented pledge to get involved in the real city that lies beyond the political Oz, and have already started doing so in many ways, including starting the night out at the DC Neighborhood Inaugural Ball.

Downtown was a euphoric pedestrian mall of commerce and communal kindness. The patience that America is extending to Mr. Obama, according to a *Times* poll, was reflected across the capital, as the cram of people sparked warmth rather than antsiness.

Strollers laughed as a peddler in a Rasta hat hawked his "Barack Obama incense." And revelers stepped up to a spot where you could pick out a colored magic marker and complete posters that began, "Mr. President, I hope for..."

Entries ranged from "burning less oil" to "health care for all" to "a cure for cancer" to this lofty and entirely understandable sentiment: "a sick inauguration party."

# No Bully in the Pulpit

The graying man flashing fury in the Rose Garden on behalf of the Newtown families, the grieving man wiping away tears after speaking at the Boston memorial service is not the same man who glided into office four years ago.

President Obama has watched the blood-dimmed tide drowning the ceremony of innocence, as Yeats wrote, and he has learned how to emotionally connect with Americans in searing moments, as he did from the White House late Friday night after the second bombing suspect was apprehended in Boston.

Unfortunately, he still has not learned how to govern.

How is it that the president won the argument on gun safety with the public and lost the vote in the Senate? It's because he doesn't know how to work the system. And it's clear now that he doesn't want to learn, or to even hire some clever people who can tell him how to do it or do it for him.

It's unbelievable that with 90 percent of Americans on his side, he could get only 54 votes in the Senate. It was a glaring example of his weakness in using leverage to get what he wants. No one on Capitol Hill is scared of him.

Even House Republicans who had no intention of voting for the gun bill marveled privately that the president could not muster 60 votes in a Senate that his party controls.

President Obama thinks he can use emotion to bring pressure on Congress. But that's not how adults with power respond to things. He chooses not to get down in the weeds and pretend he values the stroking and other little things that matter to lawmakers.

After the Newtown massacre, he and his aides hashed it out and decided he would look cold and unsympathetic if he didn't push for some new regulations. To thunderous applause at the State of the Union, the president said, "The families of Newtown deserve a vote." Then, as usual, he took his foot off the gas, lost momentum and confided his pessimism to journalists.

The White House had a defeatist mantra: This is tough. We need to do it. But we're probably going to lose.

When you go into a fight saying you're probably going to lose, you're probably going to lose.

The president once more delegated to the vice president. Couldn't he have come to the Hill himself to lobby with the families and Joe Biden?

The White House should have created a war room full of charts with the names of pols they had to capture, like they had in the *American President*. Soaring speeches have their place, but this was about blocking and tackling.

Instead of the pit-bull legislative aides in Aaron Sorkin's movie, Obama has Miguel Rodriguez, an arm-twister so genteel that the *Washington Post*'s Philip Rucker wrote recently that no one in Congress even knows who he is.

The president was oblivious to red-state Democrats facing tough elections. Bring the Alaskan Democrat Mark Begich to the White House residence, hand him a drink and say, "How can we make this a bill you can vote for and defend?"

Sometimes you must leave the high road and fetch your brass knuckles. Obama should have called Senator Heidi Heitkamp of North Dakota over to the Oval Office and put on the squeeze: "Heidi, you're brand-new and you're going to have a long career. You work with us, we'll work with you. Public opinion is moving fast on this issue. The reason you get a six-year term is so you can have the guts to make tough votes. This is a totally defensible bill back home. It's about background checks, nothing to do with access to guns. Heidi, you're a mother. Think of those little kids dying in schoolrooms."

Obama had to persuade some Republican senators in states that he won in 2012. He should have gone out to Ohio, New Hampshire and Nevada and had big rallies to get the public riled up to put pressure on Rob Portman, Kelly Ayotte and Dean Heller, giving notice that they would pay a price if they spurned him on this.

Tom Coburn, the Republican senator from Oklahoma, is one of the few people on the Hill that the president actually considers a friend. Obama wrote a paean to Coburn in the new *Time 100* issue, which came out just as Coburn sabotaged the bill.

Obama should have pressed his buddy: "Hey, Tom, just this once, why don't you do more than just talk about making an agreement with the Democrats? You're not running again. Do something big."

Couldn't the president have given his Rose Garden speech about the "shameful" actions in Washington before the vote rather than after?

There were ways to get to 60 votes. The White House just had to scratch it out with a real strategy and a never-let-go attitude.

Obama hates selling. He thinks people should just accept the right thing to do. But as Joe Manchin, the West Virginia Democrat, noted, senators have their own tough selling job to do back home. "In the end you can really believe in something," he told the *Times*'s Jennifer Steinhauer, "but you have to go sell it."

The president said the Newtown families deserved a vote. But he was setting his sights too low. They deserved a law.

# Lost Art of Loyalty

There is a futuristic cop show starting soon on Fox called *Almost Human,* produced by J. J. Abrams.

It's set in the year 2048, and it features an attractive black robot who is highly evolved, logic-based and designed to be as human as possible, partnering with an attractive white guy, who is all too human, prone to saying the wrong things and getting into scrapes.

Fox is billing the show as the first Robromance.

But, of course, it's not the first. We have one in the West Wing.

When Barack Obama partnered with Joe Biden, Biden felt it was his mission to inject humanity—or "intensity," as Hillary Clinton called it—into Obama's android air. The ebullient political veteran was eager to help interpret the erudite Obama to Joe Sixpack.

In a capital known for hogging credit and stealing turf, Joe Biden has provided his boss with a rare loyalty over the last five years. Even behind closed doors, the vice president tries to elevate the president. His friends stress that Biden is not a golden retriever but a sled dog, pulling his weight, chipping in, doing whatever he can.

And the two men, buffeted by problems, have grown closer after a rough start when Obama was dismissive or eye-rolling to his vice president often enough for it to merit a satirical takeoff on *Saturday Night Live.*

As Mark Halperin and John Heilemann write in *Double Down*, Biden worried that he would be cast as the buffoon, calling it the "Uncle Joe Syndrome," and he confronted the president about it at a weekly lunch.

It's fair to say that Joe Biden has not been given the respect he deserves in the White House. It's the story of the ultimate team player who has not been treated that way himself.

The West Wing young bucks never fully appreciated the fact that if you have a president who turns up his nose at working with Congress, it's nice to have a vice president who enjoys being a pol, who can pick up the phone and persuade Arlen Specter, at the cost of his political career, to help pass Obama's stimulus.

Biden has bent over backward to put the president in a good light, even as the president and Obamaworld have bent over backward to treat Hillary like the rightful successor to Obama.

They say loyalty is its own reward, and, in the case of Biden, it will have to be.

On the *CBS Morning Show* last week, Bill Daley, Obama's former chief of staff who is now a CBS News contributor, acknowledged the story in *Double Down* that he had pushed to poll to see if Biden should be dumped from the 2012 ticket and replaced with Hillary, something he never told Biden; this, even though the vice president was the best friend and one of the few defenders the unpopular chief of staff had in the White House. Daley had been Biden's national political director in his '88 presidential bid.

"The chief of staff and the vice president were a pair of plump green peas in a pod: both Irish Catholic sexagenarians with old-school tastes, old-school tendencies, and old-school values," write the *Double Down* authors. In the hypermodern Obama White House, they write, Biden and Daley "were like the gray-haired hecklers in the balcony on *The Muppet Show*, the Statler and Waldorf of the White House."

Except in this version, Waldorf considers pushing Statler off the balcony.

Daley defended himself to the *Times*'s Jonathan Martin this way: "You have to remember, at that point the president was in awful shape, so we were like, 'Holy Christ, what do we do?' "

You scapegoat Uncle Joe, of course, even though he had nothing to do with the president's low standing.

When Biden blurted out his support for gay marriage, after the poll-driven Obama had dithered about revealing his position in favor of it for eight years, controlling Obama staffers punished the vice president with friendly fire, anonymously trashing him. *Double Down* reports other slights to Biden: Obama, fearing leaks, cuts the size of his reelection strategy meetings, excluding Biden, even though, as a 40-year veteran of politics, he would have had plenty of insights. And David Plouffe dresses down Biden, who was going on a 2012 campaign fund-raising swing in California, for wanting to meet with Hollywood and Silicon Valley big shots who could help if he ran in 2016. "We can't have side deals," Plouffe tells him.

That's rich, given the fact that Obama let Hillary move her team of image buffers and political aides into the State Department. She was allowed to do side deals, like the time she had a political aide at State send invitations to prominent Irish Democrats who had raised millions for her past campaigns to accompany her on a diplomatic trip to Dublin and Belfast.

Biden loyalists believe Daley added insult to injury by dishing to the *Double Down* authors.

Noting with dark humor that in the *Boardwalk Empire* days, such disloyalty in the Irish tribe would have been met with a knee-capping in a dark alley, one asked: "How does Bill Daley get out of bed every morning?"

# Is Barry Whiffing?

Stop whining, Mr. President.

And stop whiffing.

Don't whinge off the record with columnists and definitely don't do it at a press conference with another world leader. It is disorienting to everybody, here at home and around the world.

I empathize with you about being thin-skinned. When you hate being criticized, it's hard to take a giant steaming plate of "you stink" every day, coming from all sides. But you convey the sense that any difference on substance is lèse-majesté.

You simply proclaim what you believe as though you know it to be absolutely true, hoping we recognize the truth of it and, if we don't, then we've disappointed you again.

Even some of the chatterers who used to be in your corner now make derogatory remarks about your manhood. And that, I know, really gets under your skin because you think they just don't get your style of coolly keeping your cards to yourself while you play the long game. Besides, how short memories are. You were the Ice Man who ordered up the operation that killed Osama bin Laden.

I also appreciate the fact that it's harder for you than it was for

JFK, W. and all those other pols who had their rich daddies and their rich daddies' rich friends to buy anything they needed and connect them up and smooth the way for them. That gives them a certain nonchalance in the face of opprobrium and difficulty, a luxury that those who propel themselves to the top on their own don't have.

We understand that it's frustrating. You're dealing with some really evil guys and some really nutty pols, and the problems roiling the world now are brutally hard. As the Republican strategist Mike Murphy says, it's not like the campaign because you have "bigger problems than a will.i.am song can fix."

But that being said, you are the American president. And the American president should not perpetually use the word "eventually." And he should not set a tone of resignation with references to this being a relay race and say he's willing to take "a quarter of a loaf or half a loaf," and muse that things may not come "to full fruition on your timetable."

An American president should never say, as you did to *The New Yorker* editor, David Remnick, about presidents through history: "We're part of a long-running story. We just try to get our paragraph right."

Mr. President, I am just trying to get my paragraph right. You need to think bigger.

An American president should never say, as you did Monday in Manila when you got frustrated in a press conference with the Philippine president: "You hit singles; you hit doubles. Every once in a while, we may be able to hit a home run."

Especially now that we have this scary World War III vibe with the Russians, we expect the president, especially one who ran as Babe Ruth, to hit home runs.

In the immortal words of Earl Weaver, the Hall of Famer who managed the Baltimore Orioles: "The key to winning baseball games is pitching, fundamentals, and three-run homers." A singles hitter doesn't scare anybody.

It doesn't feel like leadership. It doesn't feel like you're in command of your world.

How can we accept these reduced expectations and truculent passivity from the man who offered himself up as the moral beacon of the world, even before he was elected?

As Leon Wieseltier wrote in the latest *New Republic*, oppressed and threatened swaths of the world are jittery and despairing "because the United States seems no longer reliable in emergencies, which it prefers to meet with meals ready to eat."

The *Times*'s Mark Landler, who traveled with the president on his Asia trip, reported that Obama will try to regain the offensive, including a graduation address at West Point putting his foreign policy in context.

Mr. President, don't you know that we're speeched out? It's not what we need right now.

You should take a lesson from Adam Silver, a nerdy technocrat who, in his first big encounter with a crazed tyrant, managed to make the job of NBA commissioner seem much more powerful than that of president of the United States.

Silver took the gutsy move of banning cretinous Los Angeles Clippers owner Donald Sterling for life, after many people speculated that there was little the NBA chief could do except cave. But Silver realized that even if Sterling tries to fight him in court (and wins) he will look good because he stood up for what was right.

Once you liked to have the stage to yourself, Mr. President, to have the aura of the lone man in the arena, not sharing the spotlight with others.

But now when captured alone in a picture, you seem disconnected and adrift.

What happened to crushing it and swinging for the fences? Where have you gone, Babe Ruth?

# Where's the Oval Avatar?

The White House likes to use a phrase of tingling adventure to describe the president's recent penchant for wandering the country talking to people: "The bear is loose."

There are three problems with this unbearable metaphor: Barack Obama is not in captivity, he's not a bear and he's not loose. As Voltaire said of the Holy Roman Empire, it was "neither Holy, nor Roman, nor an empire."

When our whippetlike president travels on Air Force One from staged photo-op to staged photo-op and then to coinciding fund-raiser to coinciding fund-raiser, encased by the White House travel behemoth and press centipede, that's kind of the opposite of breaking loose.

Somehow, I thought that the tech revolution in campaigns would usher in fresh ways for presidents to communicate. In the age of Snapchat, I didn't think presidents would still be crisscrossing the country to do hokey snaps of chats.

As David Plouffe wrote in the *Wall Street Journal* last week, "With advancements in artificial intelligence, you could soon have holograms of presidential candidates at your door, interacting with you and asking and answering questions." He noted that Narendra

Modi used holograms to extend his reach during his successful campaign to become the Indian prime minister.

So where's the Oval Office holodeck?

Besides the fact that the posed pictures end up on Twitter as well as in the paper, prescreened and sanitized political tableaus seem stuck in the 20th century. 44 does rallies and roundtables and has Kabuki sit-downs with people in coffee joints just the same way 41 did.

In the sixth year of his presidency, the White House is still trying to cast Barack Obama as a regular guy, playing pool and drinking beer (even though he only took a few sips) in Denver with Governor John Hickenlooper of Colorado. This, when the one thing we know, and that Obama wants us to know, is that he's no regular guy.

As Julie Hirschfeld Davis wrote in the *Times* on Tuesday, the president has been seeking out the intellectual, artistic and tech elite at private dinners around the globe.

"Sometimes stretching into the small hours of the morning, the dinners reflect a restless president weary of the obligations of the White House and less concerned about the appearance of partying with the rich and celebrated," Davis wrote.

In Dallas last week, Obama did a short roundtable with Governor Rick Perry of Texas on the border imbroglio followed by a barbecue DCCC fund-raiser with five round tables of fat cats. Explaining why he was staying away from the heart-wrenching scene on the border, the president said, "This isn't theater. This is a problem," adding, "I'm not interested in photo ops. I'm interested in solving a problem."

Yet, even as the world is roiling, the president's desk is clean. As he flees gridlock and a Boehner lawsuit in Washington over executive power, the best news for Democrats is that Republicans are talking impeachment. The Democrats can actually make money on that. Obama seems fixated on both the photo ops he's doing and the ones he's not doing.

He didn't go to the LBJ play on Broadway and meet its

Tony-winning star, Bryan Cranston, after Cranston suggested that if he went, he might learn some methods for getting his way with Congress. And the president doesn't want to be pictured on the border in shots that look as if he's welcoming children, many fleeing violence in Central America, who are illegally entering the country, even though Pope Francis has advised that "the humanitarian emergency requires, as a first urgent measure, these children be welcomed and protected."

By now, Americans are so habituated to stagy things, it's hard to imagine that many people don't see the president's roving photo ops as posed and theatrical.

But Plouffe, who helped devise Obama's technologically groundbreaking campaign, contends that such events are more important than ever because for younger people, if you don't have the visual with the words, it's almost as though it doesn't exist.

"People like to see their president or their governor or their mayor out mixing it up in the community and not behind the ivory gates," he told me, adding that he could see a day when a campaign could have a candidate's hologram materialize in the kitchen of a swing voter in Lorain, Ohio, to talk education.

"It's not going to be a 2016 thing," he said. "But it could be a 2020 or a 2024 thing."

(Microsoft's Jaron Lanier waggishly suggests that political avatars be saved for fund-raising, where their algorithms could be fine-tuned to deliver individual, if hypocritical, pitches that would get the maximum donations.)

"My suspicion," Plouffe said, "is that unless the Republicans shed some of their intolerance, Hillary Clinton will get all the great tech talent."

The president's odysseys are meant to illustrate that he's still relevant. But do they actually underscore irrelevance by conveying his view that if Republicans in Congress are going to keep blocking him, he may as well go fishin'?

August 19, 2014

# Alone Again, Naturally

Affectations can be dangerous, as Gertrude Stein said.

When Barack Obama first ran for president, he theatrically cast himself as the man alone on the stage. From his address in Berlin to his acceptance speech in Chicago, he eschewed ornaments and other politicians, conveying the sense that he was above the grubby political scene, unearthly and apart.

He began *Dreams from My Father* with a description of his time living on the Upper East Side while he was a student at Columbia, savoring his lone-wolf existence. He was, he wrote, "prone to see other people as unnecessary distractions." When neighbors began to "cross the border into familiarity, I would soon find reason to excuse myself. I had grown too comfortable in my solitude, the safest place I knew."

His only "kindred spirit" was a silent old man who lived alone in the apartment next door. Obama carried groceries for him but never asked his name. When the old man died, Obama briefly regretted not knowing his name, then swiftly regretted his regret.

But what started as an affectation has turned into an affliction.

A front-page article in the *Times* by Carl Hulse, Jeremy Peters and Michael Shear chronicled how the president's disdain for politics has alienated many of his most stalwart Democratic supporters on Capitol Hill.

His bored-bird-in-a-gilded-cage attitude, the article said, "has left him with few loyalists to effectively manage the issues erupting abroad and at home and could imperil his efforts to leave a legacy in his final stretch in office."

Senator Claire McCaskill of Missouri, an early Obama backer, noted that "for him, eating his spinach is schmoozing with elected officials."

First the president couldn't work with Republicans because they were too obdurate. Then he tried to chase down reporters with subpoenas. Now he finds members of his own party an unnecessary distraction.

His circle keeps getting more inner. He golfs with aides and jocks, and he spent his one evening back in Washington from Martha's Vineyard at a nearly five-hour dinner at the home of a nutritional adviser and former White House assistant chef, Sam Kass.

The president who was elected because he was a hot commodity is now a wet blanket.

The extraordinary candidate turns out to be the most ordinary of men, frittering away precious time on the links. Unlike LBJ, who devoured problems as though he were being chased by demons, Obama's main galvanizing impulse was to get himself elected.

Almost everything else—from an all-out push on gun control after the Newtown massacre to going to see firsthand the Hispanic children thronging at the border to using his special status to defuse racial tensions in Ferguson—just seems like too much trouble.

The 2004 speech that vaulted Obama into the White House soon after he breezed into town turned out to be wrong. He misdescribed the country he wanted to lead. There is a liberal America and a conservative America. And the red-blue divide has only gotten worse in the last six years.

The man whose singular qualification was as a uniter turns out to be singularly unequipped to operate in a polarized environment.

His boosters argue that we spurned his gift of healing, so healing is the one thing that must not be expected of him. We ingrates won't let him be the redeemer he could have been.

As Ezra Klein wrote in Vox: "If Obama's speeches aren't as dramatic as they used to be, this is why: the White House believes a presidential speech on a politically charged topic is as likely to make things worse as to make things better."

He concluded: "There probably won't be another Race Speech because the White House doesn't believe there can be another Race Speech. For Obama, the cost of becoming president was sacrificing the unique gift that made him president."

So The One who got elected as the most exciting politician in American history is The One from whom we must never again expect excitement?

Do White House officials fear that Fox News could somehow get worse to them?

Sure, the president has enemies. Sure, there are racists out there. Sure, he's going to get criticized for politicizing something. But as FDR said of his moneyed foes, "I welcome their hatred."

Why should the president neutralize himself? Why doesn't he do something bold and thrilling? Get his hands dirty? Stop going to Beverly Hills to raise money and go to St. Louis to raise consciousness? Talk to someone besides Valerie Jarrett?

The Constitution was premised on a system full of factions and polarization. If you're a fastidious pol who deigns to heal and deal only in a holistic, romantic, unified utopia, the Oval Office is the wrong job for you. The sad part is that this is an ugly, confusing and frightening time at home and abroad, and the country needs its president to illuminate and lead, not sink into some petulant expression of his aloofness, where he regards himself as a party of his own and a victim of petty, needy, bickering egomaniacs.

Once Obama thought his isolation was splendid. But it turned out to be unsplendid.

*August 23, 2014*

# The Golf Address, Channeling President Obama

Fore! Score? And seven trillion rounds ago, our forecaddies brought forth on this continent a new playground, conceived by Robert Trent Jones, and dedicated to the proposition that all men are created equal when it comes to spending as much time on the links as possible—even when it seems totally inappropriate, like moments after making a solemn statement condemning the grisly murder of a 40-year-old American journalist beheaded by ISIL.

I know reporters didn't get a chance to ask questions, but I had to bounce. I had a 1 p.m. tee time at Vineyard Golf Club with Alonzo Mourning and a part-owner of the Boston Celtics. Hillary and I agreed when we partied with Vernon Jordan up here, hanging out with celebrities and rich folks is fun.

Now we are engaged in a great civil divide in Ferguson, which does not even have a golf course, and that's why I had a "logistical" issue with going there. We are testing whether that community, or any community so conceived and so dedicated, can long endure when the nation's leader wants nothing more than to sink a birdie putt.

We are met on a great field of that battle, not Augusta, not Pebble Beach, not Bethpage Black, not Burning Tree, but Farm Neck Golf Club in Martha's Vineyard, which we can't get enough of—me, Alonzo, Ray Allen and Marvin Nicholson, my trip director and favorite golfing partner who has played 134 rounds and counting with me.

We have to dedicate a portion of that field as a final resting place for my presidency, if I keep swinging from behind.

Yet it is altogether fitting and proper that I should get to play as much golf as I want, despite all the lame jokes about how golf is turning into "a real handicap" for my presidency and how I have to "stay the course" with ISIL. I've heard all the carping that I should be in the Situation Room droning and plinking the bad folks. I know some people think I should go to Ferguson. Don't they understand that I've delegated the Martin Luther King Jr. thing to Eric Holder? Plus, Valerie Jarrett and Al Sharpton have it under control.

I know it doesn't look good to have pictures of me grinning in a golf cart juxtaposed with ones of James Foley's parents crying, and a distraught David Cameron rushing back from his vacation after only one day and the Pentagon news conference with Chuck Hagel and General Dempsey on the failed mission to rescue the hostages in Syria.

We're stuck in the rough, going to war all over again in Iraq and maybe striking Syria, too. Every time Chuck says ISIL is "beyond anything we've ever seen," I sprout seven more gray hairs. But my cool golf caps cover them. If only I could just play through the rest of my presidency.

ISIL brutally killing hostages because we won't pay ransoms, rumbles of coups with our puppets in Iraq and Afghanistan, the racial cauldron in Ferguson, the Ebola outbreak, the Putin freakout—there's enough awful stuff going on to give anyone the yips.

So how can you blame me for wanting to unwind on the course

or for five hours at dinner with my former assistant chef? He's a great organic cook, and he's got a gluten-free backyard putting green.

But, in a larger sense, we can dedicate, we can consecrate, we can hallow this ground where I can get away from my wife, my mother-in-law, Uncle Joe Biden, Congress and all the other hazards in my life.

The brave foursomes, living and dead, who struggled here in the sand, in the trees, in the water, have consecrated it, far above our poor power to add or subtract a few strokes to improve our score. Bill Clinton was Mr. Mulligan, and he is twice as popular as I am.

The world will little note, nor long remember, what we shot here, or why I haven't invited a bunch of tiresome congressmen to tee it up. I'm trying to relax, guys. So I'd much rather stay in the bunker with my usual bros.

Why don't you play 18 with Mitch McConnell? And John Boehner is a lot better than me, so I don't want to play with him.

It is for us, the duffers, rather, to be dedicated here to the unfinished work which they who played here have thus far so nobly advanced to get young folks to stop spurning a game they find slow and boring.

It is rather for us to be here dedicated to the great task remaining before us of getting rid of our slice on the public's dime—that from this honored green we take increased devotion to that cause for which Bobby Jones, Jack Nicklaus, Tiger Woods and Rory McIlroy gave their last full measure of devotion—and divots.

We here highly resolve that these golfing greats shall not have competed in vain, especially poor Tiger, and that this nation, under par, shall have a new birth of freedom to play the game that I have become unnaturally obsessed with, and that golf of the people, by the people, for the people shall not perish from the earth.

So help me Golf.

# He Has a Dream

As he has grown weary of Washington, Barack Obama has shed parts of his presidency, like drying petals falling off a rose.

He left the explaining and selling of his signature health-care legislation to Bill Clinton. He outsourced Congress to Rahm Emanuel in the first term, and now doesn't bother to source it at all. He left schmoozing, as well as a spiraling Iraq, to Joe Biden. Ben Rhodes, a deputy national security adviser, comes across as more than a message-meister. As the president floats in the empyrean, Rhodes seems to make foreign policy even as he's spinning it.

But the one thing it was impossible to imagine, back in the giddy days of the 2009 inauguration, as Americans basked in their open-mindedness and pluralism, was that the first African American president would outsource race.

He saved his candidacy in 2008 after the "pastor disaster" with Jeremiah Wright by giving a daring speech asserting that racial reconciliation could never be achieved until racial anger, on both sides, was acknowledged. Half black, half white, a son of Kansas and Africa, he searchingly and sensitively explored America's ebony-ivory divide.

He dealt boldly and candidly with race in his memoirs, *Dreams from My Father*. "In many parts of the South," he wrote, "my father could have been strung up from a tree for merely looking at my mother the wrong way; in the most sophisticated of Northern cities, the hostile stares, the whispers, might have driven a woman in my mother's predicament into a back-alley abortion—or at the very least to a distant convent that could arrange for adoption. Their very image together would have been considered lurid and perverse."

Now the professor in the Oval Office has spurned a crucial teachable moment.

He dispatched Eric Holder to Ferguson and deputized Al Sharpton, detaching himself at the very moment when he could have helped move the country forward on an issue close to his heart. It's another perverse reflection of his ambivalent relationship to power.

He was willing to lasso the moon when his candidacy was on the line, so why not do the same at a pivotal moment for his presidency and race relations? Instead, he anoints a self-promoting TV pundit with an incendiary record as "the White House's civil rights leader of choice," as the *Times* put it, vaulting Sharpton into "the country's most prominent voice on race relations." It seems oddly retrogressive to make Sharpton the official go-between with Ferguson's black community, given that his history has been one of fomenting racial divides, while Obama's has been one of soothing them.

The MSNBC host has gone from *The Bonfire of the Vanities* to White House Super Bowl parties. As a White House official told *Politico*'s Glenn Thrush, who wrote on the 59-year-old provocateur's consultation with Valerie Jarrett on Ferguson: "There's a trust factor with The Rev from the Oval Office on down. He *gets it*, and he's got credibility in the community that nobody else has got."

Sharpton has also been such a force with New York's mayor, Bill de Blasio, in the furor over the chokehold death of a black Staten Island man that the *New York Post* declared The Rev the de facto police commissioner. The White House and City Hall do not seem concerned about his $4.7 million in outstanding debt and liens in federal and state tax records, reported by the *Post*. Once civil rights leaders drew their power from their unimpeachable moral authority. Now, being a civil rights leader can be just another career move, a good brand.

Thrush noted that Sharpton—"once such a pariah that Clinton administration officials rushed through their ribbon-cuttings in Harlem for fear he'd show up and force them to, gasp, shake his hand"—has evolved from agitator to insider since his demagoguing days when he falsely accused a white New York prosecutor and others of gang-raping a black teenager, Tawana Brawley, and sponsored protests against a clothing store owned by a white man in Harlem, after a black subtenant who sold records was threatened with eviction. A deranged gunman burned down the store, leaving eight people dead.

Sharpton also whipped up anti-Semitic feelings during the Crown Heights riots in 1991, denouncing Jewish "diamond dealers" importing gems from South Africa after a Hasidic Jew ran a red light and killed a seven-year-old black child. Amid rioting, with some young black men shouting "Heil Hitler," a 29-year-old Hasidic Jew from Australia was stabbed to death by a black teenager.

Now Sharpton tells Thrush: "I've grown to appreciate different roles and different people, and I weigh words a little more now. I've learned how to measure what I say."

Obama has muzzled himself on race and made Sharpton his chosen instrument—two men joined in pragmatism at a moment when idealism is needed.

We can't expect the president to do everything. But we can expect him to do something.

# From Pen and Phone to Bombs and Drones

The president was at the United Nations on Wednesday urging young people across the Muslim world to reject benighted values, even as America clambers into bed with a bunch of Middle East potentates who espouse benighted values.

President Obama has been working hard to get a coalition that includes Saudi Arabia, Qatar, Bahrain, Jordan and the United Arab Emirates because they provide cover in the fight against the brutal, metastasizing threat of the Islamic State, a "network of death" known as ISIS, that our blunders—both of action and inaction—helped create.

He and Secretary of State John Kerry have cajoled this motley crew for the coalition—American warplanes are doing most of the airstrikes in Syria—even though in countries like Saudi Arabia and Qatar, powerful elements are financing some of the same terrorists that their governments have been enlisted to fight.

At the UN on Tuesday, in a scene in a fancy old New York hotel that evoked Marlon Brando making the peace with the heads of the five families in *The Godfather*, President Obama offered a tableau of respect to the leaders of Saudi Arabia, Bahrain, Jordan, Qatar and the United Arab Emirates.

"This represents partners and friends in which we have worked for very many years to make sure that security and prosperity exists in the region," he said.

When American presidents rain down bombs on Muslim countries, they use the awful treatment of women in the Middle East as one of their justifications.

In his speech at the United Nations, President Obama said he wanted "to speak directly to young people across the Muslim world" and urged them to create "genuine" civil societies.

"Where women are full participants in a country's politics or economy, societies are more likely to succeed," he said. "And that's why we support the participation of women in parliaments and peace processes, schools and the economy."

Yet, because we need the regressive rulers in the Persian Gulf to sell us oil and buy our fighter jets and house our fleets and drones and give us cover in our war coalitions, we don't really speak out about their human rights violations and degradation of women as much as we should. The Obama administration was sparked to action by the videos of ISIS beheading two American journalists. Yet Saudi Arabia—wooed to be in the coalition by Kerry with a personal visit this month—has been chopping off heads regularly, sometimes for nonlethal crimes such as drugs or sorcery.

The president should just drop the flowery talk and cut to the chase. Americans get it. Let's not pretend we're fighting for any democratic principles here.

America failed spectacularly in creating its democratic model kitchen with Iraq. So now we have to go back periodically and cut the grass, as they say in Israel, to keep our virulent foes in check.

It is preemption. But the difference with President Obama's preemption is that there is an actual threat to the globe from a vicious, maniacal army. President Bush, Dick Cheney, Donald Rumsfeld, Paul Wolfowitz and Condoleezza Rice made up a threat to America from a contained and diminished Saddam Hussein to justify pre-emption and serve their more subterranean purposes.

Eight months ago, the president was reduced to threatening to act without Congress, warning: "I've got a pen, and I've got a phone."

Now he's brandishing bombs and drones on a scale he's never done before. The ex-community activist elected on a peace platform has grown accustomed to coldly ordering the killing of bad guys.

"It's hard to imagine that in his wildest dreams—or nightmares—he ever foresaw the in-box he has," said Richard Haass, the president of the Council on Foreign Relations.

But, as Harold Macmillan, the former British prime minister, said once, when asked what disrupted his best-laid plans: "Events, dear boy, events."

As the US woos the Arab coalition, Arab leaders are not speaking out against the atrocities of ISIS against women.

"It is the obligation and duty of Arab countries, where men always feel so possessive about their mother, their wife, their daughter, to condemn ISIS's violence against women," said Haleh Esfandiari, the director of the Middle East Program at the Wilson Center. "Why don't they say a word?

"I've been working with women in the Middle East for forty years, and I've never seen such brutality, such barbarism as that which ISIS is committing against women. It is unbelievable."

We are so far from where the dunderheads of the Bush administration were in 2003, with George W. Bush bragging about his cakewalk of weakening dictators, forging democracies and recognizing the rights of women. As it has rampaged like a flesh-eating virus through the region, ISIS has been targeting professional women. An Iraqi lawyer who worked to promote women's rights was grabbed from her home last week after she posted complaints on her Facebook page about ISIS's "barbaric" destruction of mosques and shrines in Mosul. Sameera Salih Ali al-Nuaimy was tortured for days; then a masked firing squad executed her on Monday and then told her family she could not have a funeral.

In a *Wall Street Journal* piece headlined "ISIS's Cruelty Toward Women Gets Scant Attention," Esfandiari toted up a litany of horrors, including the tragic story of a woman who was tied to a tree, naked, and repeatedly raped by ISIS fighters, who are "rewarded" with droit du seigneur as they assault and pillage their way toward an Islamic caliphate.

She noted that even though ISIS propaganda emphasizes protecting the morality of women, it has taken little girls playing with dolls and married them off to fighters three times older, set up "marriage bureaus" in captured Syrian towns to recruit virgins and widows to marry fighters, and tied together women with a rope as though "they were being led to a makeshift slave market."

She told me that "it's a strategy to shame women and undermine their families. In our part of the world, a woman who has been raped, whether once or fifty times, feels ashamed, her family feels ashamed. Some commit suicide. Others become pregnant and are ostracized by their family and community, with no fault at all of their own."

Haass noted that one of the lessons we should have learned in fighting halfway around the world, from Vietnam to Iraq, is "the power of local realities."

"One of the things we've learned is that we can't deliver fundamental social and cultural transformation in this part of the world," he said. "Our ability to influence the position or status of women in the Arab or Muslim world is limited."

He said the Arab coalition is necessary because "our priority has got to be to push back and weaken ISIS.

"Even if we're not in a position to give women the better life they deserve," he concluded, "we are in a position to save many of them from what ISIS would do to them. And that's significant."

# Running for Daylight
# (Obama, Not Brady)

The talk up in Boston is all about deflation while the talk down here in Washington is all about inflation.

Our sleek, techie president, whose battery dies faster than an iPhone's, was fully charged Tuesday night for the State of the Union.

He was so puffed up, with such a bristling sense of self, that it was hard to believe this was the same guy who spent the last year clenched like a fist, beset by ISIS, beheadings and Ebola, shunned by his own party and slammed by the other party in the fall election.

The murmur went up from grateful Democrats gathered at the Capitol: "Wow, he's got a pulse."

Proving once again that he is a different kind of cat, Barack Obama is oddly pumped by his party's defeat. Even in the House chamber, surrounded by hundreds of people and watched by millions, he seemed to delight in his detachment as he laid down his own markers to drive up his own numbers.

He doesn't mind splendid isolation. He really thinks it's splendid. He's free to revert to being the consummate outsider who doesn't see himself in the context of a system.

He likes the game better when he's up against an opposing team. To him, Harry Reid was as big a problem as Mitch McConnell.

Now it's easier for him to see who he is and where he stands vis-à-vis the Republicans because he doesn't have to make intellectual compromises or negotiate the jagged shoals of the old-school Democratic Party. Now he can define himself against modern conservatives such as Rand Paul and Scott Walker.

President Obama feels he will be able to finally float above it all, more singular and more interesting and more separate, debating enlightened progressive topics like criminal justice reform and child care infrastructure while those off-kilter conservatives fight it out for 2016.

Unlike FDR, Obama was not determined to give Americans heart and courage at times of crisis. Instead, his White House tended to take on the coloration of his funks and the clouds spread worldwide.

He only began to really brag on the economy Tuesday night, when he felt certain of the numbers, rather than before the midterms, when it might have helped his party. He could have done a better job all along explaining where we stood and where we were hopefully headed. As one top White House official says about the Obama inner circle, "They'd rather be right than win."

He's alone on the stage—always his preferred setting. As an isolato, he can say what he thinks and define himself on his own terms. He can ascend to the mountaintop and ignore us when we pester him to come down.

He doesn't have to negotiate with Republicans anymore. He doesn't have to stroke Democrats anymore. He doesn't have to hawk himself to voters anymore. He isn't concerned about Hillary, as he yanks the party to the left. He has forged no lasting links to foreign leaders. And he can have the "vacation from the press" that he told NBC News's Chuck Todd he yearns for.

"Barry got his groove back," as Larry Wilmore, the droll host of Comedy Central's *The Nightly Show*, put it.

We got the guy we've been yearning for only when he was able to blow us all off. He can finally do and say whatever he wants.

One Democrat who saw Obama in the White House said the president was so buoyant he had an air of "senioritis."

It seemed a shame, the Democrat said, that Obama couldn't have a third term, now that he was, at long last, fired up and ready to go. Of course, if there was a third term, he would be waiting another four years to show the mojo.

Thrilled to sidestep the press, he felt liberated enough, even as Yemen spiraled, to go on YouTube and make his case to the appealing GloZell Green, a YouTube star wearing glowing green lipstick who got famous eating cereal out of a bathtub.

Remarkably, The One has ended up in the same place the unpopular W. found himself at the end of his two terms: casting his lot with history.

Now that it's all about him, he doesn't get languid and reflective. He rolls up his sleeves and crisscrosses the country.

Anyone expecting Clintonesque triangulation or even a conciliatory nod to the winning team Tuesday night was disappointed. Instead, they got the State of the Veto Threat Address.

The president goaded Republicans, who chortled when he reminded them he was done running for office. He shot back with his favorite snarky rejoinder to Republicans: I won.

Obama won the presidency by creating a magnetic narrative. But then, oddly, he lost the thread of his story and began drifting. He didn't get to the point Bill Clinton did, where he had to insist he was relevant, though last summer, some of his frustrated hopey-changey acolytes talked about having an intervention with the rudderless president. But others argued against it, pointing out that, while

Obama might not have the presidency that was giddily anticipated, during the 2008 enphoria, he was doing what he wanted.

He wanted to do what he saw as right and have the public and the pols come along simply because he said it was right.

But when the Potomac didn't part when he was elected, he got grumpy and decided not to play the game.

As David Axelrod said, and as Obama concurred, the president was resistant to the symbolism and theatrical aspect of his office. He never got it that the emotional component of the presidency is real, whether it's wooing lawmakers or comforting the nation.

When the public was jittery about ISIS, Ebola and Ferguson, Obama responded like a law professor. He made a stunning speech on race to save his 2008 campaign, but he has stayed largely detached from the roiling race drama that stretched from St. Louis to New York.

In Year 7, when everyone else has started focusing on 2016, he suddenly popped up with a full-throated narrative and rationale for his presidency: It is time for the middle class to share the wealth and the Republicans are still protecting the rich.

The State of the Union was not so much too little, too late as too much, too late.

Republicans said Obama was in "Fantasyland." While free community college educations, money for child care, new roads, new taxes on the rich, initiatives on climate change and partying in Cuba are all feel-good ideas for Democrats, a lot of that isn't going to happen and he knows it.

Though President Obama's numbers are up, the results are likely to be pretty meager. When he trolled Republicans in his speech, it felt good to him, and Democrats jumped for joy. But Republicans will have their revenge—and not just Netanyahu's visit.

In the end, the speech told us less about the state of the union than the state of Obama. The state of Obama is strong, if solitary.

# Obama's Flickering Greatness

On Saturday mornings, I love to watch reruns of the TV Western *The Rifleman*. Each show is a little moral fable, with Chuck Connors's widowed rancher and crack shot, Lucas McCain, teaching his son, Mark, about actions and consequences.

*If you neglect to do this now, you will pay a penalty later. If a corner is cut here, you will regret it there.*

The president might want to catch some shows, as the lame duck's chickens come home to roost.

At this pivotal moment for his legacy at home and abroad, his future reputation is mortgaged to past neglect.

Like Prufrock, Obama must wonder if the moment of his greatness is flickering.

The president descended from the mountain for half an hour on Thursday evening, materializing at Nationals Park to schmooze with Democrats and Republicans at the annual congressional baseball game.

It was the first time he had deigned to drop by, and the murmur went up, "Jeez. Now? Really?"

Obama has always resented the idea that it mattered for him to charm and knead and whip and hug and horse-trade his way to leg-islative victories, to lubricate the levers of government with personal loyalty. But, once more, he learned the hard way, it matters.

His last-minute lobbying trips to the ballpark for his trade package—with a cooler of home-brewed beer from the White House—and to Capitol Hill Friday morning to lecture Democrats about values reaped a raspberry from House Democrats.

The Democrats—even most of the Congressional Black Caucus, which Obama courted aggressively and which has been protective of him—showed their allegiance to themselves, their principles and their labor allies, and not to their aloof president.

A flustered Nancy Pelosi abruptly and stunningly deserted Obama in a floor speech, saying, "We want a better deal for America's workers." She has been loyal to the president. It was her high-heeled toe on the scale that helped a first-term senator scoot past the heavy-weight Hillary Clinton in 2008.

But you could almost see the thought bubble above her head as she spoke on Friday: "I've done a lot of heavy lifting for this guy and I'm not going to do this. He's on his way out. I may be on my way out, too, but I want to keep my friends."

The White House may yet find a way around this with another vote or a maneuver in the Senate. But this was a striking personal rejection, with the House Democrats—many still smarting more than 20 years after Clinton successfully allied with Republicans to push through NAFTA—proving their relevance at the president's expense.

The Obama White House has managed Congress poorly, with arrogance—or worse, neglect.

Pelosi had to bail out Obama on health care after the Democrats lost Teddy Kennedy's seat to Scott Brown, with the White House once more being caught by surprise when it wasn't a surprise.

The president also showed his ineptness at vote counting, working the system and leveraging when he got only 54 votes in the Senate for gun curbs that 90 percent of Americans wanted.

Obama casts himself as the man alone in the arena, refusing to let Democrats stand on stage with him at key moments or even give them a lift in his limo.

House Democrats resented the way Obama pushed so hard on trade when he hadn't pushed for their priorities, like the highway bill, and when he cut a big deal with the Republicans who have done everything in their power to undermine him.

Some were angry, as Representative Peter DeFazio told *Politico*, that Obama had "tried to guilt people and impugn their integrity."

The attitude of many was "OK, go have fun with your Republican friends."

As he was stymied from pivoting to Asia on trade, he was stymied from fleeing the Middle East to focus on China.

Because he was elected partly on his promise to pull American troops from Iraq, he had a distaste for unraveling the Gordian knot tied by W., Dick Cheney and Donald Rumsfeld (despite Rummy's attempts last week to weasel out of it).

So Obama failed to keep his foot on the throat of our Shiite puppets, who balked at leaving an American troop presence there, with immunity, and who treated the Sunnis badly to punish them for the decades when Saddam treated the Shiites badly.

Many Sunnis, including Saddam's former fighters put out of work by the American viceroy Paul Bremer, felt exposed and unprotected and joined up with Al Qaeda and ISIS.

As the French ambassador to the United States, Gérard Araud, put it to me recently: "Why would a Sunni soldier want to die fighting Sunnis to defend a Shiite government?"

President Obama has vowed to degrade, destroy and defeat ISIS, but it seems more like delay, so it won't look as though he lost Iraq on his watch. He's putting a bandage on the virulent gash, sending

American advisers to work with Iraqi troops and tribesmen in "lily pad" bases near the front lines.

It appears to be a sad, symbolic move by a country and president fed up with endless war and at wit's end about how to combat the most murderous terrorists on the face of the earth. If we drowned in quicksand going full-bore for a dozen years beside Iraqi soldiers who did not want to fight, what good will 450 more American trainers do?

A lame duck sending sitting ducks to lily pads is not a pretty sight.

# What Would Beau Do?

A pattern of cutting corners, a patina of entitlement and inevitability, has led to this.

Destroying digital messages and thwarting official investigations while acting all innocent about wiping out sensitive material.

Avoiding reporters after giving disingenuous explanations at uncomfortable news conferences. Claiming egregious transgressions are a private matter and faux controversy while sending out high-power lawyers and spin doctors to deflect and minimize.

Two controlling superstars with mutable hair and militant fans, married to two magnetic superstars who can make a gazillion an hour for flashing their faces and who have been known to stir up trouble.

A pair of team captains craving a championship doing something surreptitious that they never needed to do to win.

It turns out Tom Brady and Hillary Clinton have more in common than you would think.

Brady had his assistant terminate his Samsung phone the day before he talked to an investigator about Deflategate. Hillary set up a home-brew private server, overruling the concerns of her husband's aides, and erased 30,000 emails before the government had a chance to review them to see if any were classified.

Brady and Hillary, wanting to win at all costs and believing the rules don't apply to them, are willing to take the hit of people not believing them, calculating that there is no absolute proof.

They both have a history of subterfuge—Brady and the Patriots with Spygate, Hillary with all her disappearing and appearing records.

Robert Kraft, the owner of the Patriots, is out there rabidly defending Brady. The crafty Hillary has her own rabid defender in David Brock. Kraft and Brock both have a financial interest, of course, in bleaching the images of their quarterbacks. Hillary and Brady have billion-dollar operations, and their sketchy value systems force people around them into seamy Faustian bargains.

These may be mere speed bumps for these top players. But in the case of Hillary, problems of style and substance are starting to scuff her sheen of inevitability.

There are tensions in her campaign that echo the failed 2008 campaign. Her rare interviews have seemed robotic and infused with the queenly attitude that put off people last time, before she melted in New Hampshire and decided, as in *Frozen*, to Let it go.

Once more, she has figuratively and literally roped off the press, sloughing off her promise at a journalistic dinner four months ago for a fresh start.

Her strategists worry about surveys showing that voters do not trust her. But her private server is a metaphor for her own lack of trust and a guarded, suspicious mind-set that lands her in needless messes.

*The Wall Street Journal* on Thursday offered yet another unsavory saga of what appears to be Clinton back-scratching. After Hillary, as secretary of state, intervened to help make a deal where UBS had to turn over only a small fraction of the account information sought by the IRS, UBS amped up its donations to the Clinton Foundation and paid Bill Clinton $1.5 million to do some Q and A's for the company.

Hillary is lucky that she faces a crowded, absurdist Republican field cowering in the shadow of the megalomaniacal showman Donald Trump.

But two recent Quinnipiac University polls show her unfavorability rising in swing states. She now trails Jeb Bush by one point, after leading him by 10 in May, and Joe Biden leads Jeb by one point.

Many Democrats fret that she seems more impatient than hungry, more cautious than charismatic. They are increasingly concerned that, aside from the very liberal Bernie Sanders, who could be approaching his ceiling in the early states, there is no backup if something blows up—no Jimmy Garoppolo to step in while Brady is suspended for four games.

Potent friends of America's lord of latte, Howard Schultz, have been pressing him to join the Democratic primary, thinking the time is right for someone who's not a political lifer. For the passionate 62-year-old—watching the circus from Seattle—it may be a tempting proposition.

After coming up from the housing projects in Brooklyn, Schultz reimagined Starbucks and then revived it. He has strong opinions, and even position papers, about what he calls the fraying American dream. While he was promoting his book on veterans last year, he honed a message about making government work again and finding "authentic, truthful leadership."

Joe Biden is also talking to friends, family and donors about jumping in. The 72-year-old vice president has been having meetings at his Washington residence to explore the idea of taking on Hillary in Iowa and New Hampshire.

He gets along with Hillary and has always been respectful of the Democratic Party's desire to make more history by putting the first woman in the Oval Office.

But going through the crucible of the loss of his oldest son, Beau, to brain cancer made the vice president consider the quest again.

As a little boy, Beau helped get his father through the tragedy of losing his beautiful first wife and 13-month-old daughter in the car crash that injured Beau and his brother, Hunter.

When Beau realized he was not going to make it, he asked his father if he had a minute to sit down and talk.

"Of course, honey," the vice president replied.

At the table, Beau told his dad he was worried about him.

*My kid's dying,* an anguished Joe Biden thought to himself, *and he's making sure I'm OK.*

"Dad, I know you don't give a damn about money," Beau told him, dismissing the idea that his father would take some sort of cushy job after the vice presidency to cash in.

Beau was losing his nouns and the right side of his face was partially paralyzed. But he had a mission: He tried to make his father promise to run, arguing that the White House should not revert to the Clintons and that the country would be better off with Biden values.

Hunter also pushed his father, telling him, "Dad, it's who you are."

It could be awkward for President Obama, who detoured from the usual route—supporting your vice president—and basically passed the torch to Hillary. Some in Obama's circle do not understand why he laid out the red carpet for his former rivals. "He has no idea how much the Clintons dislike him," said one former top White House official.

But the president has been so tender and supportive to his vice president ever since learning that Beau was sick, it's hard to say how he will react. Since the funeral, Obama has often kept a hand on Biden's back, as if to give him strength.

When Beau was dying, the family got rubber bracelets in blue—his favorite color—that said "WWBD," What Would Beau Do, honoring the fact that Beau was a stickler for doing the right thing.

Joe Biden knows what Beau wants. Now he just has to decide if it's who he is.

# Obama's Last Tango

Barack Obama is tangoing into history, and there's something perfect about that.

The tango has been described as vertical solitude. And this president is all about vertical solitude.

Republicans are frothing and comics are tweaking about the baseball diplomacy in Cuba and the tango diplomacy in Argentina, juxtaposed with the terrorist attack and manhunt in Brussels.

Comedy Central's Larry Wilmore mocked Obama's "spring break world tour." He chided the president for doing the wave with Raúl Castro and remarked on Obama's sinuous, take-charge tango partner. "OK, Republicans, now he's leading from behind," Wilmore said. Rush Limbaugh accused the president of flamenco dancing and "doing the tango with women not even his wife."

Yes, that outrageous sin of being polite to your foreign hosts at a state dinner.

Barack Obama started off as a man self-consciously alone on stage and that's how he is exiting. He is, for better and worse, too cool for school. His identity is defined by his desire to rise above the fray. Unfortunately, he is in politics, which is the fray.

Obama shot to prominence at the 2004 Democratic National Convention with a rousing speech about boldly moving past our barriers—red and blue, black and white. But those divisions are more pronounced than ever. So now he brings people together and gets things done when he can, like importing modernity to Cuba and inveigling China on climate change.

The president has a bristling resistance to what he sees as cheap emotion. (See: flag pin, 2008.) That has led him, time after time, to respond belatedly or bloodlessly in moments when Americans are alarmed, wanting solace and solutions.

The Christmas bomber; the BP oil spill; James Foley beheaded by ISIS, the Paris attacks, the San Bernardino attacks and now Brussels, which he discussed rationally and briefly with ESPN at the baseball game, wearing cool $485 Oliver Peoples sunglasses beside a cool Derek Jeter.

He feels that fanatics who are not an existential threat to us want to disrupt our lives and we should not let them; that more people die slipping in their bathtubs than in terrorist attacks.

That anthropological detachment—the failure to viscerally connect and vigorously persuade, the lip-curling at needy lawmakers, jittery Americans or anyone else who does not see things as he does—may keep him from being a Mount Rushmore president.

Obama went to a baseball game with Raúl Castro just 15 months into their working relationship. It took him six years, with his trade bill—one of his top foreign policy initiatives—on the line, to go to the congressional baseball game, toting some White House home brew.

If he were up for reelection, the president probably would have forced himself to appear more emotionally responsive to the terrorist attacks, urged on by his staff.

But he clearly feels liberated in the homestretch, relishing what he can do alone, venting privately about world leaders, lawmakers and pundits who have not risen to his lofty standards. Once he read about FDR's legislative prowess. Lately, he has been buffing up on Teddy Roosevelt blowing a raspberry at Congress and expanding executive power.

I traveled with the president to Havana to watch as he did the logical thing, bypassing the inane and antiquated congressional embargo to help move Cuba past its sepia arrested development.

There was a muted excitement in repressed Havana around the low-risk trip, a precursor to opening the Cuba wing in the Obama presidential library.

Obama, with his elegant family along, deftly maneuvered in the chaos of communism, charming the 84-year-old Raúl Castro even though the White House did not know which bits of historic pageantry the Cuban would play along with.

After months of intense negotiations, the dictator told the president at the last minute that he would do a news conference—the first anyone could remember in Cuba. But clearly Castro had not been briefed that the two American journalists' multipart questions would include tart ones for him. Standing at a lectern flanked by plush burgundy drapes with "RP" embossed in gold on them in the Revolutionary Palace—which sounds like an oxymoron—Castro bridled when Andrea Mitchell asked him about human rights. Afterward, Latin correspondents noted that if Mitchell were not American, she would be spending the afternoon in jail.

When the Cubans bobbled a photo op at the José Martí memorial in Revolutionary Square, President Obama took over and directed the group to its picture in front of a Che Guevara mural.

He was a long way from 2008, when a Fox TV channel in Houston blew up a story about an Obama volunteer who had the unpatriotic temerity to have a Cuban flag with a picture of Che at her desk.

Conservatives then were trying to smear Obama as a socialist. Now many Democratic voters, especially young ones, are disappointed that

Obama wasn't liberal enough and are gravitating toward a real socialist rather than the president's preferred successor.

Obama is trying to untangle the Gordian knots in a Middle East shattered by his predecessor; it was W.'s unwarranted invasion of Iraq that unwittingly created ISIS, as the veteran war correspondent Michael Ware points out in his new movie, *Only the Dead*.

While Republicans who would succeed Obama talked loco last week—Ted Cruz vowed to carpet-bomb ISIS and Donald Trump refused to rule out nuclear strikes—Obama's military leaders announced that they had killed two top ISIS leaders.

The president can go to a ballgame and still keep his eye on the ball.

# Interlude

## *Is Trump the Hero or the Enema?*
## by Kevin Dowd

*My conservative brother, Kevin, explains why he plans to vote for Trump.*

It is a tale of wickedness, madness and dynastic twists better suited to *King Lear* or *Hamlet*. The election for president of the United States in 2016 will be contested between businessman and showman Donald Trump and the Queen Cersei of the Democratic party, Hillary Rodham Clinton.

The current startling state of both political parties reflects, in many ways, where our culture has gone over the past 10 years. If you don't believe me, turn on your television and see what passes for a sitcom these days, which are all sexual double entendres and no intelligent writing. We now live in a world of tweets and texts that supply all the misinformation you need in a phone that appears to be permanently attached to your hand.

The mission was clear from the beginning for every Republican voter: Nominate the most electable candidate to beat Hillary Clinton. My personal choices were Marco Rubio and John Kasich. These two men were experienced, likable and electable. Rubio would help with the party's Hispanic gap and appeal to younger voters. Kasich wrote the budget for Ronald Reagan and was the popular governor of Ohio, a state the Republicans have always needed to win the presidency.

The year began with media outlets reporting that the Republican Party was splintering into uncontrollable factions that could not be governed, that it would be destroyed in the upcoming elections and might cease to be a major party. The narrative went that the GOP was self-destructing with its colliding conservative and libertarian wings, driving the Speaker of the House into early retirement, unable to agree on budgets and tilting at windmills with calls to shut down the government.

Republicans were portrayed as consistently overmatched against a president who either out-bluffed them or went around them with his egregious use of executive orders. The entire Congress had sunk to an approval rating in the teens.

The debates began and Trump swept aside the other nine people on the main stage with a combination of rudeness and incivility never seen in debate history. Ted Cruz temporarily restored order with a narrow victory in Iowa, but Trump swamped the field in New Hampshire. It was a shock to me but not as great as the one that awaited me when I had my usual Friday happy hour at the bar at the Knights of Columbus hall, where an overwhelming majority of the room was solidly for Trump.

Back in 2012, my Maryland golf club held a mock election and Mitt Romney won with 78 percent of the vote. As Trump began to have upset wins in primaries, I took an informal survey of the members and found a strong Trump presence, even among the women.

Sixteen men and one woman entered the race to become the party's nominee. All appeared battle tested and competent, but the one that emerged was a man whose unconventional style and untethered rhetoric shattered all previous rules of decorum. Donald Trump gave voice to a new silent majority, crushed financially by the last seven years of Democratic rule and fed up with political gridlock and myriad mindless social regulations shoved down their throat. These Americans had a yearning captured in the 1984 Bonnie Tyler song: "I'm holding out for a hero 'til the end of the night…And he's gotta be larger than life." Trump was their man.

The Republican primary voters have delivered the message the media and talking heads all missed. The country is fed up with the status quo and wants big changes. They see in Trump a man who says what is on his mind, boldly walking through the minefield of political correctness carefully cultivated over the past seven years by the president and his Democratic allies. America is more than ready for some red meat after being force-fed Barack Obama's tofu. This all came into clear focus when Trump voiced his unconditional support for the police and veterans while President Obama was being sued by 11 states for trying to do away with the sanctity of the bathroom.

Full disclosure: I have been a Republican since I began my professional career and discovered that my twin reimbursements—net and gross pay—did not resemble each other. I was skeptical of Trump at the beginning of the process but was happy he was included because his presence guaranteed giant ratings, which would benefit the other candidates. Every single media outlet, print and electronic, said Donald Trump was an illusion and would be a forgotten footnote to history in short order. They claimed that he did not command the facts and would be chewed up by policy wonks like John Kasich and Jeb Bush, humiliated by seasoned debaters like Ted Cruz and Rand Paul and outcharmed by the more likable Mike Huckabee and Marco Rubio.

Whoops.

Trump dispatched the other 16 candidates in short order, cresting the 1,237 delegate benchmark before Memorial Day. His message echoed Jack Nicholson's great Joker line in the original Batman movie: "This town needs an enema." He won 36 states in the primaries and totaled more votes than any Republican in primary history. His main appeal was his outlaw approach. The liberal media gasped at his remarks about Megyn Kelly, John McCain and debate opponents and predicted his immediate demise, but he only grew stronger. His one-line slogan, "Make America Great Again," reverberates in places the Republicans have not been competitive in decades. He gives the GOP a chance to widen its narrow electoral-college path to the presidency, a Valhalla his vanquished opponents could only dream about.

Trump easily held his own on the debate stage, consistently frustrating his opponents to the point of madness. His ability to immediately tweet his nine million followers distilled everything into 140 characters. Make no mistake: This election will not be fought under the Marquess of Queensberry rules. It will be more like a WWE steel-cage match.

Trump wants the doyenne of the Democratic Party to be a piñata at his Cinco de Mayo party, complete with taco bowls as appetizers. She is a weak campaigner with a documented history of unsavory dealings. She is declared unlikable by 55 percent of the electorate and untrustworthy by 67 percent. And she was investigated by the Obama Administration and the FBI for arrogantly setting up her own email system while Secretary of State. When the director of the FBI laid bare her gross negligence for arrogantly setting up her own email system while secretary of state and announced there would be no prosecution, you could hear the heavens thunder for justice. Not since O.J. Simpson had someone so obviously guilty by the facts, walked away. A separate investigation tying Clinton Foundation contributions to speeches made by Bill adds to the pungent aroma of shiftiness and entitlement that routinely hovers above them. Bill only added to it with his surprise thirty-minute visit to the attorney general on the tarmac at the Phoenix airport, a stunt even a first-year law student knows is verboten. The DNC thought it was lining her up with a weak sparring partner she could destroy, marching into Philadelphia with momentum and money for the general campaign.

Whoops.

Bernie Sanders, the 74-year-old socialist senator from Vermont, won 22 states and exposed Clinton's weakness among young women and men. He routinely railed against Hillary's cozy connections with Wall Street and obscene speaking fees. He claimed the system was rigged with superdelegates already in the bag for Clinton. He blamed the acerbic head of the DNC, Debbie Wasserman Schultz, for orchestrating the whole thing and suggested she be ousted. (His best idea, by far.) As an announced Democratic socialist, he should be the logical candidate to take over eight years of socialist rule as Hillary limps out of the arena like a gored bull.

Anyone placing a bet in Las Vegas could have gotten long odds on Trump winning the Republican nomination. But his winning it over 16 seasoned politicians should give a clear message that the voting public is fed up with political insiders. Bad news for Cersei, the ultimate insider who is running solely on the fact she is the ultimate insider. She has been in the public eye for 25 years. The voters' perceptions of her are cast in concrete.

My wife, Ellen, a registered Democrat, told me that her friends were offended by Trump but more offended that Hillary Clinton might become the president of the United States. At first, I was waiting for common sense to take control and for people to realize that Trump is not a politician. It turns out that is one of his greatest strengths. I did not fully appreciate the anger simmering barely beneath the surface. Trump has tapped a supersensitive nerve that exploded like an oil well. Many people are willing to overlook his rudeness, his childish outbursts, his petty feuds and his bad manners because they see what has been missing for seven years: a leader who is not worried about being liked, someone who would stand up to our enemies and who has actually created real jobs.

Trump is a force of nature blasting through uncharted waters with total confidence. He sees a severely diminished America—weaker, less respected and burdened by endless government regulation. He sees Europe collapsing under the weight of the Middle East refugee crisis and an illegal immigration crisis threatening to sink our own economy. He sees $19 trillion dollars of debt and a Democratic Party pandering to every liberal whim.

Trump is a conundrum more complex than a Rubik's Cube. He is not the traditional or ideal candidate. His incivility and bombast would have eliminated him from a spelling bee, never mind the presidency. His overreaction to imagined slights is absurd and his insults are too cruel and personal. And most alarmingly, he too often flirts with race-baiting, as he did with the unnecessary and offensive comments about the judge in the Trump University trial.

He thinks he can win without the help of the party, a fatal mistake. My decision to support Trump is not an easy one and not made because I blindly vote Republican in every election. It is because I believe Hillary Clinton does not have the moral authority to be president. The Supreme Court is a vitally important issue this year because the new president could change the balance to 7–2 in his or her first term. This could affect an entire generation.

I believe the race is competitive, even though Trump has made several maddening missteps that have caused some Republicans to rethink their endorsements. He has made unity way more difficult than it should be and wasted the 50 days since he clinched the nomination. He must stop the unnecessary insults to his own party members for previous slights, real or imagined. He could have made a compelling case for Trump University on the merits. Instead, he reduced it to needless insults of Judge Curiel's ethnicity. And above all, he cannot turn Hillary Clinton into a victim, a role that launched her political career.

Trump's best bet now is that his opponent is asking voters for four more years of misery, served up by someone they don't like or trust. Trump's lightning-quick responses regarding Bill Clinton have neutralized Hillary's best weapon. Some of Trump's instincts are brilliant. When President Obama said our allies were rattled, Trump said that was a good thing. He correctly predicted the Brexit result and predicted it was a preview of the US election. He flirted with having a debate with Sanders, further diminishing Hillary, and published his own list of his Supreme Court nominees. No one knows what his ideology really is, so he has great latitude in changing voters' opinion about him. He has already defied traditional expectations but he must stop wasting time. He has just been given another golden opportunity with the FBI excoriation of Clinton. Trump's charge of a "rigged system" for the Clintons was verified by the Wikileaks revelation that the DNC did indeed try to hinder Sanders, a threat to Democratic unity that resulted in the quick departure of Wasserman-Schultz. His speech at the convention was thorough and disciplined. It perfectly outlined the dangers the country faces if it continues the Obama vision. He would also be wise to have the voters imagine a Clinton presidency with Hillary in charge of the FBI.

Reagan once remarked that one of the most important aspects of the presidency was its symbolic power. The people want a president they can be proud of on the world stage. The nuts and bolts were left to the thousands of people around him. Trump has created a huge and complex company that employs thousands of people. He is a very smart man. I do not think the job is too big for him. We are finishing eight years with a man who literally had barely any job experience outside politics when he won the White House. I am hoping Trump will clean up and tone down his act because it would be a shame to lose an election to such an uninspiring and unworthy candidate. I hope to vote for Donald Trump not just as a civic duty but to save our country for my grandchildren.

The Republicans need a hero. The question is: Is it Trump?

# 6

# Gasping Old Party

# Romney Is President

It makes sense that Mitt Romney and his advisers are still gob smacked by the fact that they're not commandeering the West Wing.

(Though, as the *Daily Show* correspondent John Oliver jested, the White House might have been one of the smaller houses Romney ever lived in.)

Team Romney has every reason to be shell-shocked. Its candidate, after all, resoundingly won the election of the country he was wooing.

Mitt Romney is the president of white male America.

Maybe the group can retreat to a man cave in a Whiter House, with mahogany paneling, brown leather Chesterfields, a moose head over the fireplace, an elevator for the presidential limo and one of those men's club signs on the phone that reads: "Telephone Tips: 'Just Left,' 25 cents; 'On His Way,' 50 cents; 'Not Here,' $1; 'Who?' $5."

In its delusional death spiral, the white male patriarchy was so hard-core, so redolent of country clubs and Cadillacs, it made little effort not to alienate women. The election had the largest gender gap in the history of the Gallup poll, with Obama winning the vote of single women by 36 percentage points.

As W.'s former aide Karen Hughes put it in *Politico* on Friday, "If another Republican man says anything about rape other than it is a horrific, violent crime, I want to personally cut out his tongue."

Some Republicans conceded they were a *Mad Men* party in a *Modern Family* world (although *Mad Men* seems too louche for a candidate who doesn't drink or smoke and who apparently dated only one woman). They also acknowledged that Romney's strategists ran a 20th-century campaign against David Plouffe's 21st-century one.

But the truth is, Romney was an unpalatable candidate. And shocking as it may seem, his strategists weren't blowing smoke when they said they were going to win; they were just clueless.

Until now, Republicans and Fox News have excelled at conjuring alternate realities. But this time, they made the mistake of believing their fake world actually existed. As Fox's Megyn Kelly said to Karl Rove on election night, when he argued against calling Ohio for Obama: "Is this just math that you do as a Republican to make yourself feel better?"

Romney and Tea Party loonies dismissed half the country as chattel and moochers who did not belong in their "traditional" America. But the more they insulted the president with birther cracks, the more they tried to force chastity belts on women and the more they made Hispanics, blacks and gays feel like the help, the more these groups burned to prove that, knitted together, they could give the dead-enders of white male domination the boot.

The election about the economy also sounded the death knell for the Republican culture wars.

Romney was still running in an illusory country where husbands told wives how to vote, and the wives who worked had better get home in time to cook dinner. But in the real country, many wives were urging husbands not to vote for a Brylcreemed boss out of a '50s boardroom whose party was helping to revive a 50-year-old debate over contraception.

Just like the Bushes before him, Romney tried to portray himself as more American than his Democratic opponent. But America's gallimaufry wasn't knuckling under to the gentry this time.

If 2008 was about exalting The One, 2012 was about the disenchanted Democratic base deciding "We are the Ones we've been waiting for."

Last time, Obama lifted up the base with his message of hope and change; this time the base lifted up Obama, with the hope he will change. He has not led the Obama army to leverage power, so now the army is leading Obama.

When the first African American president was elected, his supporters expected dramatic changes. But Obama feared that he was such a huge change for the country to digest, it was better if other things remained status quo. Michelle played Laura Petrie, and the president was dawdling on promises. Having Joe Biden blurt out his support for gay marriage forced Obama's hand.

The president's record-high rate of deporting illegal immigrants infuriated Latinos. Now, on issues from loosening immigration laws to taxing the rich to gay rights to climate change to legalizing pot, the country has leapt ahead, pulling the sometimes listless and ruminating president by the hand, urging him to hurry up.

More women voted than men. Five women were newly elected to the Senate, and the number of women in the House will increase by at least three. New Hampshire will be the first state to send an all-female delegation to Congress. Live Pink or Dye.

Meanwhile, as Bill Maher said, "all the Republican men who talked about lady parts during the campaign, they all lost."

The voters anointed a lesbian senator, and three new gay congressmen will make a total of five in January. Plus, three states voted to legalize same-sex marriage. Chad Griffin, the president of the Human Rights Campaign, told the *Washington Post*'s Ned Martel that gays, whose donations helped offset the Republican super PACs, wanted to see an openly gay cabinet secretary and an openly gay ambassador to a G-20 nation.

Bill O'Reilly said Obama's voters wanted "stuff." He was right. They want Barry to stop bogarting the change.

# That's Not Amore
## (*A Satire*)

John Boehner wakes up in his English basement apartment on Capitol Hill, his head still in a merlot fog.

It's a glorious autumn morning, but Boehner doesn't want to open his baby blues. He lies there, in his "Man of the House" T-shirt and Augusta National gym shorts.

He wishes he didn't have to go to work. He reaches for his Camel Ultra Lights in his supposedly smoke-free apartment.

"Oh, Lord," he growls. "How did I become that idiot Newt?"

He takes a deep drag as he drags himself out of bed. "My whole career was about not becoming Newt," he mutters. "You'd think our getting bounced from the leadership in '98, in the backlash after the last shutdown, and then the Clinton impeachment, would have taught me something."

He dresses with his usual care. He's not going to let the press pests, with their cheap haircuts and bad ties, see that he's down.

"People call me the Dean Martin of DC, and I'm certainly getting roasted," he tells his image in the mirror, perfectly knotting his sea-green tie on a crisply ironed shirt. "Old Dino was from Ohio, too."

The security detail picks up Boehner in an SUV, and, as usual, he heads to Pete's Diner for breakfast.

The congressman who grew up in the Rust Belt with 11 siblings, mopping up his dad's bar, likes his perks and loves being the Speaker. But as he picks at his sausage, eggs and rye toast, his head aches.

"Boy, I really gotta start wondering if it's worth it," he muses. "I'm being led around by the nose by goofballs like Michele Bachmann, Ted Cruz and Louie Gohmert when all I wanna do is wield my really big gavel—right on the heads of a couple of these dingdongs. I enjoyed it a heckuva lot more when the Big Ted in the Senate was Kennedy. Me and Teddy, doing No Child Left Behind with No Wine Left Behind. Ha! That Washington has been snuffed out."

He gulps his coffee. "I'm so tired of Obama," he keens to himself. "The president says he wishes he had Kevin Spacey to deal with. Well, so do I. I've been here for twenty-two years and that cat acts like I don't know what I'm doing. He wafted through Congress like a cool breeze, while I spent years sweating out big deals with Democrats. The only thing that guy gets right is shellacking me in the Rose Garden. At least I showed him up at golf.

"Hey, I could go down to Hains Point for eighteen holes. I need to relax, get some rays. Aw, never mind. I closed it as part of the government shutdown."

He scans *Politico*. "As if things weren't bad enough, Harry Reid's office leaked these emails to show what a hypocrite I was for raising hell about Congress's special subsidy for health insurance this week after he and I had wheeled and dealed to keep the darn thing," he rumbles. "I can't stand Harry, but you gotta admire his methods. That's how they do it in Vegas, baby. While I was hoping Democrats would slip on a banana peel, Harry labeled us banana Republicans."

The phone rings. It's Eric Cantor, in his oleaginous Richmond drawl, assuring Boehner that if the Speaker wants to defy the Tea Party and make a deal with the Democrats, Cantor will be behind him all the way.

Ending the call as he leaves the diner, Boehner cracks to a member of his security detail, "Hey, pal, pull the knife out of my back."

He calls an aide to ting-a-ling-a-ling his rat pack, Senators Saxby Chambliss and Richard Burr and Congressman Tom Latham, and maybe a lobbyist or three, for an early dinner at Trattoria Alberto on Barracks Row. The government is closed, after all.

"I'm just a business guy," he thinks, staring out the tinted window of the SUV, barely noticing government workers streaming out of their agencies to go home. "I came to look out for business, not to shut down the zoo's Panda Cam. These Tea Party wacko birds are in la-la land.

"Washington used to be an adult place where you could slug it out during the day and have a few slugs at night, making deals in rooms that I personally filled with smoke. Now Congress is a crap sandwich. We used to pretend to hate each other. Now we really do.

"Paul Ryan sure has headed for the hills. Isn't he the big budget genius? In 2011, I kept these loony tunes at bay. But maybe I don't have any more tricks up my sleeve. Now the kooks have overpowered me, made me look like one of the weakest speakers ever. Not exactly the legacy I was shooting for.

"I knew this shutdown was trouble. I've gotta decide if this job is even worth it if I have to be Cruz's sock puppet."

As the speaker arrives at the Capitol, he reaches for his hankie. "It's enough," he blubbers, "to make a grown man cry."

# Welcome to Ted Cruz's Thunderdome, The Detritus of the Government Shutdown

## A Place Once Called Washington

An ape sits where Abe sat.

The year is 2084, in the capital of the land formerly called North America.

The peeling columns of the Lincoln Memorial and Abe's majestic head, elegant hands and big feet are partially submerged in sludge. Animals that escaped from the National Zoo after zookeepers were furloughed seven decades ago migrated to the memorials, hunting for food left by tourists.

The white marble monuments are now covered in ash, Greek tragedy ruins overrun with weeds. Tea Party zombies, thrilled with the dark destruction they have wreaked on the planet, continue to maraud around the Hill, eager to chomp on humanity some more.

Dead cherry blossom trees litter the bleak landscape. Trash blows through L'Enfant's once beautiful boulevards, now strewn with the detritus of democracy, scraps of the original Constitution, corroded White House ID cards, stacks of worthless bills tumbling out of the Treasury Department.

The BlackBerrys that were pried from the hands of White House employees in 2013 are now piled up on the Potomac as a flood barrier against the ever-rising tide from melting ice caps. Their owners, unable to check their messages, went insane long ago.

Because there was no endgame, the capital's hunger games ended in a gray void. Because there was no clean bill, now there is only a filthy stench. Because there was no wisdom, now there is only rot. The instigators, it turned out, didn't even know what they were arguing for. Macho thrusts and feints, competing to win while the country lost.

Thomas Jefferson's utopia devolved into Ted Cruz's dystopia.

Law and order broke down as police, who were not getting paid, eventually decided to stay home. The fanatics barricaded in the Capitol dug in, determined to tear down what their idols, the founding fathers, had built. Darkness soon devoured the rest of the country.

Unlike Suzanne Collins's *The Hunger Games*, where the capital thrived as the nation withered, here, the capital withered first, as the federal city shriveled without federal funds. But, in other ways, it mirrors the fantasy dystopias depicted by Hollywood and Cormac McCarthy in his novel *The Road*, "bloodcults" consuming one another in "an ashen scabland," a "cold illucid world."

In 2084, there's little sign of life in the godless and barren lost world. The insurance exchanges are open and the kinks are almost ironed out. But there is no one to sign up. Koch brother drones patrol the skies. A Mad Max motorcycle gang wielding hacksaws roars through the CIA, now a field of dead cornstalks, and the fetid hole that was once Michelle Obama's organic vegetable garden. Will Smith and Brad Pitt are here, hunting aliens and monsters.

The Navy–Air Force game goes on, somehow, and there are

annual CrossFit games on the Mall, led by flesh-eating Dark Seeker Paul Ryan, now 114 years old. CrossFit is still fighting the Department of Agriculture's food pyramid, even though there's no Department of Agriculture and no food.

A gaunt man and sickly boy, wrapped in blue tarps, trudge toward the blighted spot that was once the World War II monument, scene of the first shutdown skirmishes. They know they may not survive the winter.

"How did this happen, Papa?" the boy asks.

"Americans had been filled with existential dread since the 9/11 attacks, but they didn't realize the real danger was coming from inside the government," the man says. "It started very small with a petty fight over a six-week spending bill but quickly mushroomed out of control."

"Whose fault was it, Papa?" the boy presses.

The man tries to explain: "The Grand Old Party, the proud haven of patriots who believed in a strong national security and fiscal responsibility, was infected with a mutant form of ideology. It was named the Sarahcuda Strain after the earliest carrier. Remember when you saw that old science fiction movie, *I Am Legend*? A scientist described the virus that burned through civilization as being like 'a very fast car driven by a very bad man.' That's what happened: In the infected Tea Party politicians, brain function decreased and social de-evolution occurred. They began ignoring their basic survival instincts.

"It's hard to believe now, but they were fixated on stopping an effort to get health care to those who couldn't afford it. It eventually led them to destroy all the things they said they held most dear."

The boy is confused. "They killed America because they didn't care about keeping Americans alive?" he asks.

The man sits down. His voice grows faint. "Well, they didn't seem to understand themselves or what they were doing," he continues. "In the face of overwhelming evidence to the contrary, many of the feverish pols believed they were waging the right and moral fight even as GOP party elders like Jeb Bush, John McCain, Karl Rove and James Baker warned them that they were dragging the country toward catastrophe. The Tea Party leaders liked to refer to themselves as the Children of Reagan. But as Baker told Peggy Noonan, Reagan always said, 'I'd rather get eighty percent of what I want than go over the cliff with my flag flying.' "

The boy frowns. "But Papa, didn't the healthy Republicans realize the infected ones had lower brain functions?"

"Well, son, they knew there was something creepy about the ringleader, Ted Cruz," the man replies. "His face looked pinched, like a puzzle that had not been put together quite right. He was always launching into orations with a weird cadence and self-consciously throwing folksy phrases into his speeches, like 'Let me tell ya,' to make himself seem Texan, when he was really a Canadian."

The boy looks alarmed. "A Canadian destroyed the world, Papa?"

"Once the government shut down, a plague came, because they had closed the Centers for Disease Control," the man says. "Storms, floods and wildfires raged after FEMA was closed down, and the National Guard got decimated.

"Once we went into default, the globe got sucked into the economic vortex. With a lot of the Defense Department, FBI and intelligence community on forced leave, the country became vulnerable to terrorist attacks. Without the CIA to train the moderate Syrian rebels, Syria fell to Al Qaeda.

"After the final American president, Barack Obama, canceled his trip to Asia, that part of the world decided we were weak. China moved quickly to fill the vacuum. Obama grew so disgusted, he spent his final years in office isolated in the White House residence. When he stopped returning the calls of Hassan Rouhani and Bibi

Netanyahu, it was only a matter of time before the Middle East went up in flames.

"What is left of the world is being run by Julian Assange from what is left of the Ecuadorean Embassy in London and by some right-wing nut in a cabin in Idaho."

The boy begins to cry. "Papa, stop. You're making me sad. Are all the good guys gone?"

Looking through the gray skies toward the ashen Lincoln Memorial, where an ape sits in Abe's chair, the man replies sadly, "Yes, son."

# Mitt's White Horse Pulls Up Lame

When the Mitt Romney documentary premiered here at the Sundance Film Festival last year, one member of the audience was especially charmed by the candidate up on the screen.

That guy is great, Mitt Romney thought to himself. That guy should be running for president.

It was an "aha" moment that came to him belatedly at age 66, after two failed presidential runs that cost more than $1 billion.

Mitt had a revelation that he should have run his races as Mitt—with all the goofiness, Mormonism, self-doubt and self-mockery thrown into the crazy salad.

Some of his strategists had argued against the movie. But wasn't it endearing, when the tuxedo-clad Romney ironed his own French cuffs while they were on his wrists? When he listened to *This American Life* on NPR with his family? When he wryly called himself a "flippin' Mormon"? When he and Ann prayed on their knees just before the New Hampshire primary? When he went sledding with his grandkids?

He was himself as a moderate Massachusetts governor. But

when he ran for president in 2008, he was "severely conservative," as he would later awkwardly brag, and that wasn't him.

In 2012, he was closer but still not truly himself, putting his faith and centrist record off to the side. He had surrounded himself with Stuart Stevens and other advisers who did not have faith that the unplugged Mitt could win, and the candidate did not have enough faith in himself to push back against them.

"It's a sad story of discovery," said a Republican who is friends with him. "He kept going through campaigns and evolving closer to himself. Then he saw the documentary and it was liberating, showing 100 percent of himself instead of 80. But it was too late. You don't really get three shots."

Romney got bollixed up by dueling fears that the unkind arena would rage at him if he put up his guard and rage at him if he dropped it. He was haunted by the collapse of his father's 1968 campaign for president after his father dropped his guard, telling a Detroit TV broadcaster that he thought he had been brainwashed into supporting the Vietnam War by American commanders and diplomats there.

But after Romney saw the documentary *Mitt*—by Mormon filmmaker Greg Whiteley—and felt that he could be Mitt "all the way," as one friend put it, he was ready to run "a hell of a race."

Mormons learn firsthand that rejection—as the young Mitt learned in Paris on his mission when he got fewer than 20 converts in two and a half years—doesn't mean you should stop trying.

Recent polls had Romney ahead of Jeb Bush and other Republican contenders. He was more in demand on the trail than President Obama during the 2014 campaign. He had shied away in 2012 from explaining the role of faith in his life, worried that Mormonism might still sound strange to voters if he had to explain lore like the white horse prophecy, that a Mormon white knight would ride in to save the US as the Constitution was hanging by a thread.

But, in the last few weeks, Romney had seemed eager to take

a Mormon mulligan. Less sensitive about his great-grandparents fleeing to Mexico to preserve their right to polygamy, Romney began joking to audiences that when he learned about the church at Brigham Young University, "Emma was Joseph Smith's only wife."

It was foolish to ever think he could take his religion—which is baked into every part of his life—and cordon it off.

In Park City Wednesday, I talked to Jon Krakauer, the author of *Under the Banner of Heaven*, a history of Mormonism, and executive producer of *Prophet's Prey*, a Showtime documentary, which was premiering at Sundance, about the most infamous Mormon polygamous cult.

"I don't think he has a choice," Krakauer said. "I don't know how people will react, but he has nothing to be ashamed with, with his faith. And by not talking about it, it looks like he does."

It was the same mistake Al Gore made in 2000 when he listened to advisers who told him he would seem too tree-huggy if he talked about the environment. When that was off-limits, Gore lost the issue he was least likely to be wooden on; it was the one topic that made him passionate—not to mention prescient.

If Mitt was 100 percent himself, he began to think this time, he could move past the debacles of his 47 percent comment caught on tape and his cringe-worthy 13 percent tax rate—both of which had made him seem like the pitiless plutocrat conjured by Democrats.

Two weeks ago, at a Republican meeting in San Diego, Romney talked about his decade as a Mormon bishop and stake president, working "with people who are very poor to get them help and subsistence," finding them jobs and tending to the sick and elderly.

He changed his residency to Utah and started building a house in a wealthy suburb of Salt Lake City. He got a broker for the luxe La Jolla oceanfront home with the four-car elevator.

It was reported that a 2016 Romney campaign could be based here. Romney had been burning up the phone lines with donors and past operatives and was reassembling his old campaign team. But Jeb Bush popped Mitt's trial balloon by peeling off the money and the talent.

"He thought there was more interest than there was," one strategist close to Romney said. "There wasn't a big groundswell. The donor-activist-warlord bubble had moved on. It's a tough world. Mitt didn't want to claw and slug."

Or as his 2008 presidential campaign adviser Alex Castellanos put it, "Mitt Romney found he had walked out on stage without his pants."

At an appearance Wednesday in Mississippi, where he seemed to be honing talking points and attack lines for a possible run, he said Hillary Clinton had "cluelessly" pushed the reset button with Russia.

He blamed the news media and voters for concentrating on the wrong things. "It would be nice if people who run for office, that their leadership experience, what they've accomplished in life, would be a bigger part of what people are focused on, but it's not," he said. "Mostly it's what you say—and what you do is a lot more important than just what you say."

But both in what he said and did, Romney came across as clueless in 2012. He was hawking himself as a great manager, but he couldn't even manage his campaign. His own advisers did not trust him to be himself. They did not adapt what the Obama team had taught everyone in 2008 about technologically revolutionizing campaigns. His own campaign was in need of a Bain-style turnaround and he was oblivious.

The reel Mitt could have told the real Mitt, as Romney said in the documentary, that the nominee who loses the general election is "a loser for life."

He seemed shocked, the night of the election, to learn that his White Horse was lame. But how could he have won? The wrong Mitt was running.

*October 3, 2015*

# The Speaker, the Pope and the Exorcism (A Satire)

John Boehner stands smiling in front of the mirror in the bathroom of his English basement apartment on G Street on Capitol Hill. He breaks into song as he fastidiously ties the four-in-hand knot in his bright green tie to get the perfect dimple.

"Zip-a-Dee-Doo-Dah, Zip-a-Dee-A, My, oh my, it's almost my last day," he belts. "Plenty of golf and sunshine heading my way."

The Speaker speaks: "I'm almost free of these knuckleheads. That visit by Pope Francis was a blessed exorcism. I'm casting out the demons. Begone, Ted Cruz, you jackass! Away, Louie Gohmert! In the name of the Father, the Son and the Holy Spirit, out you unclean devil, Mark Meadows. You wanted to get rid of me and I'm soon going to be rid of you."

Boehner chuckles as he heads out to meet his security detail and the black SUVs that won't be at his disposal after October 30. "You're the only part of the job I'm going to miss," he tells the Capitol police officer at the wheel. "There's just nothing like being driven right up to my private smoking room at Trattoria Alberto."

His BlackBerry ring-a-ding-dings. He rolls his blue eyes. It's another panicked call from Kevin McCarthy. Boehner is beginning to wonder if the kid just doesn't have it, if he's bombsville. McCarthy styled himself as one of the "young guns," along with Eric Cantor, who misfired, and Paul Ryan, who can't pull the trigger. Now Boehner's worried that McCarthy might be a pop gun.

"Kevin, did you make another mess I gotta clean up?" the Speaker growls. "Stop blubbering. That's my department. Obviously, you really stepped in it with that Benghazi crack on *Hannity*. You told Sean that I get a B-minus as Speaker? I give you a D for Dumbo.

"We've spent sixteen months and a lot of taxpayer dough persuading people that the Benghazi committee is a legitimate attempt to get to the bottom of what happened, not a way to drag down Hillary so whichever lamebrain we nominate has a chance against her. As I like to say, always do the right things for the right reasons, unless you need to do the sneaky things for the wrong reasons.

"You can't just go blurt out the truth—even on Fox. It still gets around to regular people. You managed to give Hillary the first break she's had in months. I may have to email her my congratulations. But that's classified.

"Stop hyperventilating, man. Haven't those mixed martial arts you practice manned you up? As your Mr. Miyagi, here's my advice: Try yoga. It's done wonders for unclenching me. And the sphinx pose has fixed my backswing. In fact, you should start acting like a sphinx and shut your big trap. Your colleagues and my soon-to-be-ex-colleagues are ripped about you undermining their Benghazi scam.

"You ran around and recruited all these Tea Party crazies so we could win the majority and now you're going to have to live with this pack of rats. You better watch how far you go trying to show you're one of them, like you did on *Hannity*, because you're really not and all it's going to do is get you in trouble.

"Now some of those bozos think you're 'untrustable,' to use one of your mangled words. Jason Chaffetz may not have made the cut to get into the Secret Service but he could be a headache for you. Not like Daniel Webster. The actual dead Daniel Webster could get more votes than that guy."

The SUV pulls up on the Capitol plaza and Boehner hops out, still trying to soothe the distraught McCarthy.

"Consider yourself lucky that the Draco Malfoy look-alike, Trey Gowdy, didn't run. He could totally beat you and he would have reason to, since you made him look like a chump as the head of the House Select Committee to Drive Down Hillary's Poll Numbers. You should be thankful Draco didn't hit you with the Cruciatus Curse.

"And Kevin, you might want to freshen up your wardrobe, get rid of that Bakersfield chic and hit Joseph A. Bank. And quit sleeping in your office. What did you do with that lottery money you won? Use your raise as Speaker to pop for an apartment. Even a gym rat shouldn't use the House gym as his actual house. No rent is low rent.

"I gotta go. Remember: A leader who doesn't have anybody following him is just a guy taking a walk."

Boehner hangs up and tears up as he walks alone through Statuary Hall, recalling how he tenderly accompanied Pope Francis there only a week ago, after the pontiff blessed the Speaker's first grandson.

"It was a miracle," he thinks to himself. "It suddenly hit me that I didn't have to tough it out with these losers anymore. I've told reporters that garbagemen get used to the smell of bad garbage. But twenty-five years in, this place stinks to high heaven. The institution is filled with people who should be in an institution.

"Back in the day, me and heavyweights like Ted Kennedy and Ted Stevens actually got together on big bills, hashing out policy issues. Now the famous Ted in the Senate is Cruz. Guys like him don't give a whit about policy. Neither does McCarthy for that matter. I'm not sure Kevin has even passed a bill naming a post office.

"The pope made me see the light. I can go down to my condo on Marco Island, eat oranges and get as orange as Trump's hair. I can get some board seats. If I can't tee up bills, I can tee up at Augusta.

"Geez. People think I'm gonna become a lobbyist. How wigged out is that? I didn't like hanging with most members of the House when I could tell 'em what to do. You think I'm going to come up here and beg those goofballs for stuff?"

Boehner fires up a Camel Ultra Light as he enters his office and heads out to the balcony to stand in the Shoes of the Fisherman.

"I have four weeks to clean out the barn," he muses. "I guess it's up to me to save the Republic because absolutely nothing is gonna happen once I'm gone. The false prophets going for profits at Heritage and other non-think tanks, the guys egging on my right-wing members to spread chaos, are going to make sure of that. I need to try one last time to strike some kind of bargain with Obama before I leave and he becomes an even lamer duck. We've at least got to increase the federal debt limit to keep these clowns from tanking the economy. After all, I'm gonna need some income, too."

The Dean Martin of DC begins crooning the Disney lyric again. "Mister bluebird on my shoulder—oh wait, I don't want some bird pooping on my Brooks Brothers suit and that's the truth. But everything else, as the song says, is satisfactual."

# Interlude

## *The Loathsome Trump*
## by Rita Beamish

*Donald Trump stirred up such strong feelings that some of my friends could not even bear to read my interviews with him. One girlfriend suggested I call my book* Revulsion. *Another, Rita Beamish, sent me passionate emails about why Trump was such a corrosive force in politics. I asked Rita, who covered the Bush I White House with me for the Associated Press and who is now a freelance writer based in California, to hit me with her best rant against the man she calls "the vulgarian shape-shifter." Here it is.*

It isn't as if I set the bar for politicians so high.

I covered politics as an AP reporter, not a pundit. My job was not to hold pols to lofty standards but to report on their records, words and actions—how they measured up to expectations that they planted in the minds of the electorate. Most all of them tend to disappoint at some level—caving in, weaseling out, covering up or pussyfooting around with questionable personal or professional dalliances—all part of a week's news.

But I realized I did have a certain bar, after all, when Donald Trump, the vulgarian shape-shifter, set his sights on the White House and in the process shredded not just political conventions but also a generic, nonpartisan, American value set that I thought was embedded in the national psyche, at least as aspiration.

I guess my assumptions were naïve. The more Trump got away with what would have sunk other presidential candidates, the more I was struck that the Trump army, inflamed by his venom, or maybe just sucked in by his strutting, reality-TV bombast, was willing in their disgust with Washington to cast aside requirements for basic values and decency, things that now apparently were the province of the hated establishment.

Things like: Racism and religious intolerance are horrific. And so is mocking the disabled.

So, for instance, a leader doesn't publicly malign an entire ethnic or religious group or bellow out like some proud plantation owner, "Look at my African American over here"—as Trump did in Redding, California—or insist beyond all rationality that an American-born judge's heritage negates his ability to be fair. Nor does a would-be president stand on a stage and mimic the physical disability of a reporter he doesn't like, as Trump also did, or refer to women as dogs, fat pigs or slobs, rating their looks on a scale of 1 to 10. Or possess such blind, overt narcissism that he turns a stunning national tragedy—the mass murder of 49 people in Florida—into a platform to crow about himself, in lieu of a leaderly message of sympathy and healing.

Call me crazy, but I thought a serious twenty-first-century presidential aspirant should have more than a schoolboy's understanding of geopolitical complexity and the domestic policy realm. Rudimentary knowledge, at least.

And just on a basic TMI level, if ever I had imagined such a bizarre grotesquerie, I'd have thought a small veneer of decorum would preclude a major candidate from yammering on in defense of his anatomical manliness, disrespecting voters who are concerned about issues like jobs, security and education.

That Trump upended all of this, blatantly and unashamedly, purposely offending in every direction in a craven appeal to fear and divisiveness, provides a sobering view into the Trumpian Great America. It's a vision without the ideals of tolerance, compassion or policy nuance that we generally expect presidential candidates to have in their repertoires by the time they assume their party's mantles. Even Presidents Bush, father and son, who both ended up going to war, at least gave a nod to the value of a "kinder, gentler" America and "compassionate conservatism." But kindness and thoughtfulness apparently are for wimps in the waterboarding, wall-building, judge-bashing, nuke-spreading world of Trump.

Trump has been the horror movie that keeps getting scarier. His bottomless spew of vitriol, designed, successfully, to rouse his crowds, is complemented by knee-jerk pronouncements that other candidates wouldn't attempt—like threats to First Amendment free press protections and notions of turning back the clock on decades of nuclear nonproliferation.

Inevitably, we look to our political leaders as examples. If all politicians have their foibles, even reprehensible moments, Trump, who rose on a uniquely Teflon arc, takes it to a new level. It's hard to imagine Jeb Bush, derided for several news cycles for using the term "anchor babies," getting away with sneering Trumplike and routinely mocking the appearance of people he didn't like. Or President Obama insulting reporters and calling them names rather than answering their questions.

It was big news when candidate George W. Bush, thinking he was off mic, told his running mate, Dick Cheney, that a veteran *New York Times* reporter was a "major-league asshole." But Trump brings the incivility front and center, making his relationship with journalists—seen by other politicians as an annoying but accepted part of the political process—intensely personal, like everything else. To Trump, reporters are just another useful foil—"the most dishonest people I've ever met," derided as sleazes, incompetent, third-rate, no-talent dopes whose news organizations deserve public belittling.

His tone demeans the presidential campaign as it calls up dark impulses in a divided nation. "Get 'em the hell out," he growls from the stage as hecklers are ejected. Lurching from one toxic topic to the next—let's ban all Muslims from crossing our borders; arm Japan, Saudi Arabia and South Korea with their own nukes; punch out people we don't like; torture foes beyond waterboarding—he pushes the buttons that validate hate. With sledgehammer slyness, he injects insinuation into minds, suggesting that Obama somehow has "something going on" when it comes to being tough on terror.

What message do his words send to children? Where are the aspirations for unity, healing and working together for solutions to the nation's problems? Trump's hard vision is anathema to what many of us try to instill in our kids—thoughtfulness, understanding, the merits of doing good for others.

The Trump model also puts "me" first, alarmingly skewing his worldview so that every relationship is seen through a lens of self-adulation. He can't utter a bad word about global pariah Vladimir Putin because Putin "called me a genius," for instance.

In kicking aside the long-taught idea that our immigrant culture enriches us, Trump even has me wondering if one day his penchant for indicting entire ethnic groups might target my adopted daughter as less than American, simply because she spent the first seven months of her life in China.

As his sneering, bullying style emboldens violence and vulgarity at home—some Trumpsters sport T-shirts labeling Hillary Clinton a bitch—I even found people in the streets of Tanzania, during a trip the June before the election, alarmed about how a Trump presidency might affect their continent. One story, apparently made up on the Internet, had him opining that Africa should be recolonized—ludicrous except that we've come to expect just about anything from Trump's mouth.

Who else could skate to a major political party nomination on the back of this brutish behavior and easily disprovable wedge-issue lies—like that he witnessed thousands of Muslims celebrating in New Jersey on 9/11, and that illegal immigration is responsible in some disproportionate way for crime?

The carnival barker keeps reeling people in, partly for the unmatched spectacle of it but also because he blasts the status quo and makes up platitudes that people want to believe. Americans do feel angry, let down by Washington, and the system does need a lot of fixing. But Trump, indefensible and dangerous, does not meet the bar for a national leader.

Hardly.

# 7

# Escape from Bushworld

# "Cancel My Subscription."

*Tom Friedman and I in our days as Bush White House reporters, interviewing the president as* Times *photographer Paul Hosefros captures the moment.*

We were both disappointed at first.

When our career arcs intersected at the White House, we each wanted something different.

I yearned for a more Shakespearean leader to cover, someone deeper, darker and more complicated, a Johnson or a Nixon. Not an airy Wasp propelled to the top by the old boys' network, a preppy in the mold of Bertie Wooster whose biggest news story during his first few months in office was that he showered with his dog, Millie.

He was expecting an old-school *New York Times* White House correspondent, someone with a byline like Franklin Farnsworth III, the sort of chap with whom he could chummily sit on Air Force One, sipping a vodka martini and palavering off-the-record about the North Atlantic Alliance.

Improbably, though, somewhere along the way, George Herbert Walker Bush and I grew to appreciate each other. Over the decades, our relationship came to resemble a '30s screwball comedy, where a jaded working-class newspaper gal (Jean Arthur) and a buoyant Ivy League big shot (Jimmy Stewart) reach across class and cultural chasms, past spirited disagreements, to discover real affection.

"We have a love-hate relationship," he told me when I saw him in 2001 at a party at the Georgetown home of his former White House counsel, Boyden Gray. "I talk to my shrink about it," he joked, knowing that I was well aware of his allergy to introspection.

In postpresidential notes, a cache which I chose to keep private while his sons were still running for office, he kept it up as a theme. He let me know where I was ranking that week on the anger Richter scale and pleading "Dr. Freud, Dr. Jung, Dr. Phil—Help. Help me please.... Signed, 'a troubled-mixed-up-100% correct—80 year old – GB.'"

In one note, he said, "I like you. Please don't tell anyone." He began another "Darn you Maureen Dowd." Sometimes he signed off, "con afecto, GB," or depending what I was writing about his sons, "Con Afecto, still, just barely though! gb." Or "Love" crossed out and replaced with the handwritten admonition, "not quite there yet."

At the start, the mismatch grated.

"We just don't see you as the *New York Times* White House reporter," President Bush's usually genteel pollster, Robert Teeter, told me one night over dinner at a Washington restaurant, as he

JANUARY 3, 2002

Dear Maureen,
Thanks for the great book. I'll be nice if you'll be nice.

I did this all by
Myself- the fancy
Art work, but I cannot
Get this message down below
the "be nice". I am calling Bill
Gates.
    In 2002 please be kinder and gentler to
the Bush family. There is much room for
Improvement, says this very objective
Father of "43" and father of Governor Jeb.

sipped his second martini. "We see you more at a newspaper like the *New York Daily News* or the *Chicago Tribune*."

Astonished, I asked: "You mean because I'm a woman with an ethnic, working-class background?"

Teeter nodded.

Didn't they see enough rich white men in their cloistered White House fraternity, I wondered to myself. The president, after all, belonged to four all-male clubs and one all-male golf club, Burning Tree.

Brent Scowcroft, the slender, serious National Security Adviser, and Marlin Fitzwater, the portly, witty White House spokesman, invited me out to dinner one New Year's Eve in Houston, where President Bush was spending the holidays.

"We have a request," Scowcroft announced in his soft voice. "Can you please stop calling the president 'goofy'?"

H.W. did enjoy acting goofy, though, recalling Tom Hanks playing a boy exuberantly bursting out of the body of an adult in *Big*.

What other CIA director signed notes "Head Spook"?

What other commander in chief wore a bunny tie on Easter and a pumpkin tie on Halloween?

What other president would have taken Hosni Mubarak to his first baseball game in Baltimore? (The crowd cheered when spectator Ted Williams was introduced and reacted in confused silence when the announcer boomed "the President of Egypt—Mubarak.")

Who else would sit in the White House reading women's magazines with his wife and then look up to ask, "Bar, what's a bikini wax?"

Who else would be game enough to do his birthday parachute jump at 90, years after he was confined to a wheelchair with a form of Parkinson's disease? (Standing on the landing pad on the lawn of their church in Kennebunkport, Barbara mordantly noted that if something went wrong, at least they wouldn't have far to go for the funeral.)

H.W. had a metabolism so fast that when he was the UN ambassador in the '70s, the Chinese press compared his frenetic debating style to "ants on a hot pan."

When the first President Bush went to Maine, he was manic. One Sunday, he explained that he was wearing white socks to church so he could save time afterward getting to his tennis game. He drove his cigarette boat, *Fidelity*, so demonically, yelling, "Those bluefish are dead meat!" that he threw out an NBC reporter's back. François Mitterrand refused to get on the boat with him, predicting mal de mer. I sensed a little disappointment on the president's part when I came back from our *Fidelity* outing in one piece.

H.W.'s golf was so galloping, it was dubbed "golf polo" or "aerobic golf." (Scores were tallied by strokes and time.) Even when it was pounding rain and the Secret Service was insisting he go inside, he would race around and play sand traps as water hazards. His nom du golf was Mr. Smooth.

He personally delivered some cease-and-desist requests to me.

When I asked him which movies and TV shows he liked, he accused me of trying to psychoanalyze him and said he didn't want to be put "on the couch." He finally confessed that, as a teenage navy pilot in World War II, he had a sneaker for Doris Day, though he was quick to add that four of his planes were named *Barbara*. He also admitted that he once fell asleep in the middle of the Ronald Reagan movie *Santa Fe Trail*.

President Bush did not like it when I silently watched him during impromptu press conferences on Air Force One. He abruptly stopped one gaggle to testily ask why I was staring at him. Finally, he realized I was too nervous to ask him a question in public, so he threatened to ask me one during a national press conference.

I was so tired at 7 a.m. one morning in Kennebunkport that I plopped down on the grass to watch him tee off at the Cape Arundel Golf Course. He thought I was trying to figure him out and that gave him the yips.

On one of his "blue notes" from the Oval dated 7-27-90, he wrote to Fitzwater complaining that I was sitting in a "hinayanistic" Buddha pose on the first tee—"off meditating in Sri Lanka"— staring at him as he tried to hit a straight drive.

"I'd tee it up and as I got ready to swing, I saw her giving me the 'Gail Sheehey' treatment," he said. "She sat cross legged, inscrutable, slightly severe but not menacing. Indeed she was trying to figure out what makes this crazy guy tick." (Any slight misspellings in his notes are included.)

He mused whimsically, "Will Maine air save Maureen? Can Scowcroft help out by an in-depth seminar on Europe at Mabel's." That was the president's favorite lobster joint.

He put great faith in his rank. He loved wearing navy windbreakers with his name and title. On his final parachute jump, he wore a patch on his flight suit that read 41@90. Sometimes he ended arguments with advisers by saying, "If you're so damned smart, why are you doing what you're doing and I'm president of the United States?"

Yet he was modest for a politician, so thoughtful as a child that he was nicknamed "Have Half" because he always offered his older brother, Prescott, half of his snacks.

His eager, loyal air caused some to treat him like a dupe. Nixon and Henry Kissinger secretly schemed to open up China while an oblivious H.W., the UN ambassador, was fighting for Taiwan. As head of the Republican National Committee, Bush was one of Nixon's last defenders. (Nixon dismissed him as a "worrywart.") But when Bush discovered the extent of the cover-up, he privately sent Nixon a letter urging him to resign for the good of the country.

Karl Rove, who began his career at 22 as a special assistant to H.W. when he was running the RNC, said Watergate was "agony" for Bush. "He was one of the most extraordinarily moral and good people I've ever met," Rove told me.

In 1974, as Watergate peaked, Poppy wrote his sons a long letter about the scandal's lessons. "Don't confuse being 'soft' with seeing the other guy's point of view," he advised. (W. said he tried to live by that standard, but if he had, his presidency would have been much different. He might have realized that, in a tough Middle East neighborhood, Saddam needed to pretend he still had WMDs to keep Iran at bay.)

When H.W. was Ronald Reagan's vice president, he actually managed to make himself look shorter, even though he was an inch taller, in a self-effacing maneuver his speechwriter Christopher Buckley called the "deferential Episcopal tilt."

In 1985, when Fitzwater came aboard as Vice President Bush's press aide, he told Bush he needed to work on his photo ops with dignitaries, so that he smiled for the cameras for a moment before turning his attention to the VIP.

At his next photo op, with King Hussein of Jordan, Bush made a point of turning his back to the cameras and taking the king to look out the window at some trees.

"He did the whole damn thing to defy me and let me know he wasn't a piece of meat to be pushed around," Fitzwater said, laughing. "He didn't like anything that looked phony or was phony."

As president, 41 refused to be handled like a Macy's Day balloon, as Reagan had been. He wouldn't walk down the most photogenic White House hallway, with windows to give depth—a site picked out by Reagan media wizard Mike Deaver—for press conferences. He stood in front of a blank wall instead.

Poppy was so imprinted with his mother's admonition not to brag and bask in "the big I" that he often sliced personal pronouns off the front of his sentences, shunning the subject and sometimes the verb.

"Can't act," he told me once on his boat. "Just have to be me." Asked what his summit meeting with Mikhail Gorbachev in Malta would mean for the world, he replied: "Grandkids. All of that. Very important." In his 1990 State of the Union message, he summed up what he called "the vision thing" this way: "Ambitious aims? Of course. Easy to do? Far from it."

Always his mother's son, he rejected aides' pleas to do a Reaganesque speech in the ruins of the Berlin Wall, fearing that any grandstanding would cause problems for Gorbachev with the hardliners. But when critics used the word "tepid" to refer to his muted but effective management of the sweep of democracy in Eastern Europe, he was hurt.

Before an interview with the *Times*'s redoubtable political writer Johnny Apple, President Bush gratefully accepted a list of less pejorative synonyms from his suave Las Vegas image meister, Sig Rogich.

H.W. told Apple he was being "prudent," "cautious," and "diplomatic." Those words ended up shaping Dana Carvey's "Wouldn't be prudent...nah-gah-da-it" impression on *Saturday Night Live*—a video Bush later delightedly installed in his presidential library in College Station.

He declined to go to the New York ticker-tape parade after the Gulf War, telling Colin Powell, "This parade is for the troops."

"He always heard his mother saying 'George, now don't you gloat,'" Powell told me.

Hilariously, one of the few things H.W. ever bragged about was when he began claiming, after he got out of office, that he had coined the phrase "You da man" in the '60s. "He maintains he was inspired to shout it to the Houston Astros' Rusty Staub as he rounded third base following a home run, and it slowly caught on from there," his daughter Doro wrote in her book on her dad.

Although the president loved the idea of his political dynasty, from Prescott to himself to George W. and Jeb to George P., he was sensitive to any talk of elitism or entitlement. He would wrinkle his nose and instruct me not to use "the d word."

As much as he denied dynastic dreams, 41 wrote a long letter to *Time*'s Hugh Sidey after 43 became president, comparing himself to John Adams, the only other president whose son, John Quincy, attained the Oval Office.

"A prolific reader, he loved the classics, prided himself on his ability to speak Latin, and had a library of extraordinary proportions," H.W. wrote of Adams, adding: "I couldn't wait to stop studying Latin. Big difference there between me and John."

He said he appreciated the fact that Thomas Jefferson and John Adams overcame their differences at the end of their lives and became friends again. "Should I make up with Ross Perot?" he wrote about the kooky Texas billionaire, the spoiler in the 1992 race against Bill Clinton. "The answer is no. Perot is no Jefferson, and I am not trying to say that I am a John Adams."

My brothers Michael and Martin were Senate pages in the late 40s and 50s, working with a group that included JFK, Nixon and Prescott Bush, the six-foot-four craggy senator from Connecticut. Michael often talked about how the Bush patriarch "was straight out of central casting," and Martin said Senator Bush's pin-striped suits were so impressive that "every day he looked like he was about to go to a wedding."

Senator Bush would sometimes snitch one of the Hershey's chocolate almond bars that Senator John Williams of Delaware kept in his desk for the pages and then grin with an upper lip stained with chocolate as Williams made a show of "catching" him.

One day Michael was with another boy in the mail room. Holding up a letter addressed to Prescott Bush, the other kid wryly observed, "You just know a guy with a name like Prescott Bush is not driving a bus."

In a 2000 letter to my brother Martin, who had sent 41 a T-shirt with a caricature of 43 as a cowboy shooting me as a cobra (W.'s nickname for me), H.W. said, "I hate the word 'legacy' as applied to my family." And in another note to me he accused me of "legacying" him and fretted about whether the "legacy crud" could hurt Jeb.

In January of 2002, he wrote me to "please be kinder and gentler to the Bush family" and lay off "the Gatsby stuff."

"There is much room for Improvement, says this very objective Father of '43' and father of Governor Jeb," he said. "We are not in quest of 'legacy'—just trying to 'hep out from time to time in the affairs of our nation, in the affairs of Florida, too. Please discuss this with your sensible sister if she is still on our side."

It annoyed him to be labeled a patrician, even though it fit him to a T. He could shed his preppy striped watchband, but not his stripes. Out of office, he tweaked me about the characterization, writing that he was going to climb into his "elitist boat, out of touch up there in swanky Kennebunkport, and escape."

Although Fitzwater told me once that the tension between the Greenwich side and the Texas side may have hurt Mr. Bush, the ex-president insisted that his Lone Star coloration was real. Even though I knew he liked popcorn better than pork rinds and martinis better than beer, he rejected my view that all the talk about pork rinds and country music was a blatant attempt by his bad-boy strategist, Lee Atwater, to play down the effete Eastern side and play up the mesquite Western side.

"Can I name drop right here?" H.W. wrote in one note, dropping country singer Reba McEntire's name as a reference. "I am mad about Reba and she likes me, too—so there!"

In another blast from Houston retirement, he offered: "As you know we Ivy League preppies were taught to reply to letters— 'Always be nice, George.' 'Do not be mean, George.' But then there is the other side of me. The West Texas oilfield side that the damn *New York Times* and those all-important weekly magazines never understood or wanted to understand. 'How could this Brooks Brothers Ivy Leaguer possibly like BBQ, Mexican food, or, God Forbid, country music?' It is all a fraudulent hoax—just to get votes.

"But that 'other side' is in control now. It really is, but it is not a bad side, honest. It is a side free from the political correctness you must live with every day up there."

He did put Tabasco sauce on his tuna fish sandwiches and wear cowboy boots emblazoned with "GB" and go quail hunting at his rich friend's spread in Beeville, Texas.

But he also asked for "a splash" more coffee at a New Hampshire truck stop and wore white socks and off-white leather shoes with a gray suit to church in Kennebunkport (and in a weird touch that was neither Western nor Eastern, he sometimes sprinkled Butterfingers on his oat bran).

Poppy—"I've gotten used to you having resurrected my nickname that I dumped way back in the 50s," he wrote me—often golfed with a family foursome chock-a-block with Roman numerals and names like Hap and Bucky, and his curses on the course were "Golly!" "Darn!" and "Oh, shoot!"

Like President Obama, he loved going off with the boys on the links. Goaded by reporters into playing with Barbara one day, he muttered to us afterward: "She stank."

The entitlement was bred in the bone. The president's brother, Jonathan, a friendly man who had played a hayseed in *Oklahoma* off-Broadway, tried and failed to revive minstrel shows off-Broadway in the '60s.

Ralph Lifshitz made a fortune by changing his name to Ralph Lauren and peddling Wasp tableaus and pseudo-English gentility. H.W.'s '88 campaign ad shot in part by Roger Ailes in Kennebunkport with the Bush family evoked that aesthetic so strongly that Alessandra Stanley did a *New Republic* cover story called "Presidency by Ralph Lauren."

The president was so fond of his youthful odyssey with Barbara to infuse some red blood into his blue blood, his adventure almost making a killing as a Midland oilman (albeit funded with help from his father's wealthy Wall Street friends), that he winced when I noted that he had taken a limousine to kindergarten in Greenwich. He preferred his saga of roughing it with Barbara and young W., sharing a duplex in Odessa with a mother-daughter prostitute team.

He bonded with Rogich, James Baker and the other men in his White House by trading dirty jokes. Once, showing a group of male guests around the White House residence, President Bush pointed to a portrait of Dolly Madison in the Queen's bedroom and awkwardly remarked: "How do you like the rack on that woman?"

He exhibited a wacky sense of humor with women, too. The renowned broccoli hater sent me a Polaroid of himself wearing a T-shirt that read "Broccoli Lover." Another time, he sent me a photo of himself, wearing coral slacks and engaging in a mock-passionate clench with the Silver Fox, as he called his wife, squeezing her derrière. It was a priceless send-up of the superawkward, superattenuated smooch that Al Gore gave Tipper at his convention in 2000.

When he was 79, in July of 2003, he sent a Polaroid of himself standing in front of a sign that read "I DON'T BELIEVE The New York Times." On Walker's Point stationery, with a drawing of his sprawling, gray-shingled house, he wrote that he was "risking" two things:

"One, in sending you this letter on this stationery I may be reinforcing the Times long held view that I am an out of touch elitist. But on this score I do not care any more.

"Two, I am risking being known as a whiner by those on the top floor of the NYT building. I read the NYT every day. It is a truly great paper, but let's face it, it is a paper with a point of view. They don't trust or like conservatives, say nothing of Ivy Leaguers who do not embrace the politically correct social values that the NYT espouse."

I was still writing searing columns about the "mendacity" and "dissembling" of W.'s White House on getting us into the Iraq war when Saddam had nothing to do with 9/11 or Osama, and when he wasn't threatening our national security, as W. claimed.

And H.W. was still conflicted. "Why do I continue to read you, to like you?" he wrote, signing off. "Help me Lord!"

My own conservative siblings agreed with him. My sister, who volunteered for W.'s first convention and carried a sign reading "W Stands for Women," canceled her *Times* subscription and put the guest room where I was staying under construction. My brothers relentlessly mocked me. One Christmas, my oldest brother, Michael, sneered, "If there was a hurricane, you'd blame it on W." And then Katrina hit, and I did.

H.W. loved tricks and pranks. He replaced a friend's martini onion with a rubber one, and once switched out Scowcroft's golf ball for a chalk one.

Poppy was a loyal customer of the magic store near the White House. He went himself as vice president and sent someone over for coin tricks and props when he was president. He was known for one trick he used at fancy dinner parties, where he'd put a dollar attached to string on the floor and then, when someone would reach down to pick it up, he'd yank it away.

Just before his inauguration, he relaxed by showing off tricks in his West Wing office: a red rope that turned white, a calculator that squirted water, a crystal ball with a disembodied voice that gave Delphic answers to questions about tax increases: "The images are cloudy. Have someone else ask."

Once, in Kennebunkport in the summer of '89, I decided to play a prank on the president. I donned my blue Dole for President '88 T-shirt and a white Jesse Jackson for President '88 cap.

Unfortunately, 41, zooming around the bend in his golf cart at the ninth hole, did not look my way. But Junior, as the future President Bush was known back then, was riding shotgun, and he gave me a squinty blue glare. I would have been alarmed had I not been absolutely certain that the Roman candle and black sheep of the Bush brood would never rise to a position where he could wreak revenge on me. Jeb, after all, was the comer in those days.

When W. announced for president in 1999, I was invited to a family gathering by the gleaming ocean in Kennebunkport. The candidate recalled that day at the golf course and charmingly asked, "Are you still holding that against me?"

Some of my H.W. stories were positive; some were not. During his campaign, I wrote about his expedient dash to the right—including the race-baiting Willie Horton business, which was prefigured by his opposition to the 1964 Civil Rights Act when he unsuccessfully ran for the Senate in Texas. I also wrote about his dubious choice of the overcaffeinated and underqualified Dan Quayle, and chronicled one of his first trips as vice president, where he kept leaders around the world waiting on tarmacs and in offices while he went diving and played golf. Even Nixon sent him word afterward to leave the clubs home next time.

In 1991, I covered the even more objectionable choice of Clarence Thomas and the mind-boggling Anita Hill hearings. I also wrote about how H.W. had claimed a moral imperative in attacking Saddam and then deserted the Shiites and Kurds he had encouraged to rise up after the Persian Gulf War, letting Saddam mow them down. And of course, there was Scowcroft's unsavory midnight champagne toast on his secret trip to Beijing, kowtowing to the perpetrators of the Tiananmen Square massacre.

H.W.'s governing mantra was a lofty "Trust us, we know best," and in the '92 reelection campaign he had a bumper sticker that said "Annoy the Media: Reelect Bush." But he liked the press far more than his three successors or Dick Cheney, who wanted to do away with checks and balances altogether. He was a news junkie. He read every story and column about his White House, and watched TV news shows, complaining to Fitzwater about a word here or a sentence there, even in otherwise positive pieces.

His son was the opposite, ignoring what was written about him, mostly watching sports on TV and sometimes eschewing newspapers. W. did care what was written about his parents, though, and in 1994 he told me I had impressed him with my review of his mother's memoir.

If W. acted like the bristly First Rebel, H.W. was the Last Gentleman, as his biographer Jon Meacham called him.

"He honestly and without irony believed in duty, honor and country," Meacham told me. "He represented a tradition of politics and public service that was not perfect but was about governing over perpetually campaigning." The anarchic trend among Republicans, from Newt Gingrich to Ted Cruz and the Tea Party crowd, to burn down the Capitol and tear down the president, "was beyond his imaginative capacity to understand," Meacham said.

"He just enjoyed governing," Marlin Fitzwater agreed. "He didn't hook politics onto everything he did like other presidents."

While 43 had to insist that he was "the Decider," 41's many high-level jobs gave him the experience to move quickly on things.

"He was very decisive in an odd kind of way," Powell told me. H.W. would listen to everyone sitting on the Oval Office couches and chairs talk while he said nothing. Then afterward he would either decide to do it or not do it.

W., on the other hand, would act more on his gut, without gathering as much information or encouraging full-throated debates. No one can tell you when he decided to go to war in Iraq; he personally came to the conclusion and people found out at different times. He told Bob Woodward that they went to war on body language.

H.W. never wrote a memoir but he kept up a stream of consciousness correspondence with all kinds of people, including his erstwhile sparring partner, the one he claimed to have "kicked a little ass" with in their debate, Geraldine Ferraro.

He would send me emails, typed letters on "my little IBM", as he called it, and handwritten notes from steamy Houston and "sparkling" Maine, referring to himself as the "Dana Carvey-talk-alike," "the ex-Potus" and "George HW Bush (41), formerly just plain George Bush" and "GB 41, obh, old but happy."

He regularly complained that while the *Times*—the favorite newspaper of his father—was "still the best paper in the land," it had gone too far "LEFT" and was letting opinion bleed into news stories.

"Piling on gets a 10-yard penalty," he chided. And in another note, "Booh!, editorial page."

Another time, in a letter with a wacky font at the top that said "me again," he called the *Times* "a great newspaper particularly its coverage of foreign affairs."

When I asked the ex-president if he would like to meet with our editorial board, he replied "Only after 3 root canal jobs. Thanks anyway."

Recalling the days when the Taylor family owned the *Boston Globe*, he observed that he was not as irate a press basher as his younger sister, Nancy Ellis, who lives in Boston.

*Dear Maureen,*                                                    *January 6th*

*our 57th wedding anniversary, thus my*          *conciliatory tone!*

"I am not like my beloved sister who has re-cancelled her Boston Globe subscription four different times," he said, "and who once took on one of the sacred Taylor family in a letter-to the ed as a 'Droopy Drawers.'"

He would wonder why my Reagan-and-Bush-loving mother had not baked "better conservative views" into me and offered to write her if it would help.

"Resign from the Times!" he demanded in December 2004. "Turn red (as in red state)! Trade jobs with Bill Kristol!" [the editor of the conservative *Weekly Standard*]

Referring to my brother, he continued: "Make Kevin happy— your Mom, too. Befriend Karl Rove. Turn your back on the liberal elite! Go hear James Dobson tell it! Do all this so our relationship, yours and mine, can come out of the closet." He signed off "Sincerely, My Excellency, GHWB, Eastern Elitist."

He would make tart observations about those on his hit list— George Will, Dan Rather, Michael Moore, Paul Krugman, Frank Rich, Andy Rosenthal and Molly Ivins ("Throw up!") He complained about liberals who had criticized W. and Jeb, and any "he/she who refuses to wear the big 'L' but is one. Moderate is their preferred word while we are right wing nut cases."

He joked that he had a voodoo doll "that already looks like a porcupine" for *Times* publisher Arthur Sulzberger Jr. But then, in a 2002 letter, which began with big wavy font saying, "I'll be nice if you'll be nice," he went off on a tangent about how "Arthur is very nice."

"Did you know Arthur covered my campaign way back in 1980," he wrote. "We liked him, but then he got to be an editor then top gun—publisher. A lib, yes, but not a mean one."

He complained about Gerald Boyd, who covered his White House with me and went on to be managing editor before he died. Gerald, he said, had often written the phrase "dogged by Iran Contra" about him. Then Poppy melted, noting "but, darn it all, I like the guy."

In one 2004 note from Kennebunkport, he wrote: "Out on my boat I will hark back to that horrible Terry McCauliffe's attacks on our President and my second oldest son two years ago. I will be saying, 'I am a lucky Dad. And, Lord, thanks for giving me two boys who are willing to serve, with honor, in these tough, nasty, trying times.'"

In the same note, 41 returned to the love-hate theme: "You see, I like this exchange with you, but, as confessed before, I get angry with you."

Another time he joked, "Now I am off to the clinic to take a little Prozac, stretch out, and get some shrinkster to figure out this love/hate thing about you that plagues me." In a different note, he pleaded: "Do not prescribe shock therapy!"

But he reassured me once: "I am not a hate kind of guy," "there is not any hate—none, zero, zed, zilch!" and "I am not even the Angry American."

He wrote me many times how deeply it hurt him when his "boys," as he called them, using quote marks, were criticized about anything.

"I am trying to stay 'out of it,' on the sidelines, off the op-eds, off the talk shows, out of the news, out of the way," he wrote about 43 at one point. "I have strong views on what The President is doing. I strongly support him, of course; but if I see a need for fine tuning based on my own experience, I might tell him, but I won't go public.

I am even very careful around close friends having learned that the propensity to leak is stronger than the sex drive."

Even when "double dip angry," as he put it, he was upbeat. He said he felt "young at heart" and frisky as "a spring colt."

Once in a 2005 email, he teased: "If you promise to write only GOOD stuff about #43 I'll tell you what I know about Deep Throat. Meeting in those garages was fun. Once I saw both authors in the back seat of a stretch limo with a real bimbo. Haig was driving. Gergen – well I am afraid I can say no more, because he was on both sides of the limo…Enough!!" It was signed "Your sometimes admiring friend, your sometimes, make that 'often', at least recently, angry critic ghwb #41."

In a postscript, he used the epithet "ass," typed as "a—," adding that his indispensable chief of staff Jean Becker told him: "never use the 'a' word, use butt, rear, or heinie instead. g."

When I brought my mom, who was on crutches by then, to one of his White House Christmas parties, he leaned down and gave her a big kiss.

"I knew he had a cold," she said in the car on the way home, "but he was so handsome, I just went for it." Then she muttered ominously, "I don't want you to write anything mean about that man ever again."

When my mom died in 2005 at 97, he sent a moving email. "It hurts to lose a parent," he said, "It hurts an awful lot. When my own Mom died I went up to Greenwich to check on her. She was close to death and her breathing was so labored that I literally prayed to God, as I knelt right there by her bed, that she would go on to heaven. She was prepared to do just that.

"I hope your own Mom had a peaceful passing; and that she too felt joyous about going on to heaven. Heck with politics. Heck with the NYT and all my hang ups about" it.

The next year, he sent me a note saying he was giving up on *The*

*New York Times*—even though he didn't—and once more analyzing our relationship.

"Where do you and I stand," he mused. "It is not hate. [underlined] How can I feel a warm spot in my heart for someone who day in and day out brutalizes my son? I don't know but I do. End of Confession—Con Afecto, GB #41."

Jean Becker joked that the former president and I needed "couple counseling."

In 2011, after I sent him a note congratulating him on getting the Medal of Freedom, he wrote back that he was still "enjoying life a lot. My legs seem to have gone out from under me. It's called Parkinsonitis. Nothing hurts, though I did have to cancel my application for the Olympics. I had planned to enter the butt-kicking contest, but I have no balance."

Even irritated, he couldn't help his politesse. Once, when my assistant Ashley Parker (now a *Times* reporter) accidentally sent the former president her own drug-store hand warmers for Christmas 2008 instead of the lobster-embroidered glasses case I had intended, he wrote me a nice thank-you note for the cheap hand warmers.

"I shall use the handwarmers as Pres. Obama comes in and we Bushes leave town," he said.

When I wrote to apologize for the mix-up, he teased back, "Do you suppose some Jihadist slipped them into your care package for me?"

Another time, I had to snatch back an envelope with a pink-feathered headband for a friend's daughter who was named Poppy, when Ashley started to send it to Bush senior. But even if it had been sent, I have no doubt that Poppy Bush would have mailed back a courteous note and picture telling me how fetching he looked in pink maribou.

By the time the son rose, I was a columnist and my critiques intensified in keeping with the scale of W.'s transgressions. Given H.W.'s protectiveness toward his family, even I was surprised that we were able to stay on good terms throughout my run of tough takes on W. and the 2004 publication of *Bushworld*, in which I asked about the Iraq invasion: "Is this what happens when international strategy is reduced to a psychodrama of family competition?"

One of Bush père's associates asked me with amusement: "Wonder what 43 would say if he knew his dad was corresponding with you?"

Certainly, the impish 41 knew he was playing with fire, writing me: "Sometimes I found it better around my family to go 'Maureen who?'"

Shortly after W. became president—dragged over the Tallahassee finish line by Poppy's best friend, James Baker—41 invited me to be on a panel at a Leadership Forum at the Bush Library for Texas A&M students. He joked that he had to wait to invite me to Texas until Barbara, who kept close tabs on my critiques, was not around.

In return for making the trip to Aggieland, Bush gave me a maroon T-shirt from the conservative Texas school—"Use it for a nightie if it is not suitable for the New York Times newsroom," he joked about the memento—and a copy of *A World Transformed*, a policy book he wrote with Scowcroft—in lieu of a memoir—and recommended as "better than Sominex if you ever need a tranquilizer." He inscribed it: "Please write nice things about my boy, Quincy."

He also mock-apprehensively handed over a letter he had been debating sending me.

It was a hilarious, quirky, racy 11-page typed parody of my Bush parodies painting W. as a Boy Emperor in the clutches of his Machiavellian regents, Dick Cheney and Donald Rumsfeld.

H.W.'s satire was sprinkled with "forsooths," "lyres," "nobles and peasants," "courtiers," "verilys" and other Old English flourishes.

It brought alive a *Game of Thrones* Bushland with Poppy as "the old warrior king," or "HW, formerly King George," Barbara as the old "Queen Bar," and a blazing tapestry of other characters—King Prescott of Greenwich, "now in heaven;" Princess Doro; Earl Jeb of Tallahassee, Lady Dowd, "charming princess" of Op-ed land; Queen Hillary of Chappaqua and George of Crawford, "the new King" who took the throne thanks "to those foes who have just fought and lost the Battle of Chads in November."

The Old King deemed *The New York Times*, which supported "Sir Algore," vanquished, even though the paper refused to admit it, a denial that so irritated him that he foreswore his usual martini on the rocks and told a servant to bring one "on the stem."

Were liberal *Times* reporters angry, the Old King wondered, "that I, of their Eastern province background and past, now have progeny from the Great Western Plains willing to fight on? Why can't they say 'You won. We lost. We pledge you 2000 sheaves of grain and 100 barrels of Famous Grouse.'"

The send-up recalled "Maid Monica" frolicking with "King Bill" in the Oval Office, ushering in "a new permissiveness, a new standard that confuses the old man."

The Old King mused, "Hedonism must not be the standard of the day" and predicted that his oldest son would "restore honor to the Palace."

But, typically for a man who embraced former antagonists—except for the loathed Perot, whom he blamed for his losing a second term—H.W. softened when Bill Clinton came a wooing. Bubba, as Poppy called him, treated the older man like the father he never had as the two teamed up for philanthropic causes.

"Don't start with me," he would preemptively tell astonished former aides. "I like being with Bill Clinton."

The most cloak-and-dagger episode of our love-hate relationship came in 2006. I was covering a rare trip to Kennebunkport by W., who had largely avoided the Maine family compound but had come up one weekend for a wedding, a christening and a funeral.

I may have been persona non grata in W.'s White House, but I was not papa non grata.

In Maine, I was startled to get a message to call Karl Rove, W.'s political guru and White House adviser. Rove had mischief in his voice as he explained that he was playing a surreptitious go-between. He told me that, if it could be arranged so that W. would not get wind of it, Bush senior would like to meet me for a chat over the weekend.

I was eager to do it because it felt so preposterous, like two kids—one of them 82—sneaking around behind the back of a stern president.

But it's hard to have a secret assignation in a small town with an ex-president and his Secret Service detail without the other president and his Secret Service detail hearing about it—especially when they're staying in the same compound.

I thought the former "Head Spook" might still have a few clandestine tricks up his sleeve. Though we didn't pull it off in the end, I admired the sheer daring of the scheme, and the Skull and Bones skullduggery of it.

"I don't like it that you don't like my oldest son; but it's a bit of a stand off cuz he doesn't like you either," he wrote me once. "But then he doesn't know you as well as I do. Time may heal."

In one note H.W. wrote me after 9/11, when it turned out that 15 of the 19 hijackers were Saudis, he went off on a rant defending Saudi Arabia, inspired by a postcard with a camel that I had bought in the Kingdom and sent to him.

"That raises another bitch I have," he said. "Why does the New York Times want to make an enemy out of a friend, Saudi Arabia? How would you like it if the rest of the world judged the Catholic religion by the misdeeds of a handful of Catholic priests?

"How would we like it if those who kill in the name of Christ— the abortion clinic doctors' murderers, the Klan, you name it—were seen by others around the world as typical of Christianity itself? David Duke, the hater and anti-Semite. McVeigh who destroyed a building and killed many people—do you suppose our friends in the Gulf look at these folks and many more and conclude that the USA is evil. And when the murders are committed in the name of Christ or God do they knock Christianity like so many of the Eastern elite now knock Islam.

"The Saudi bashers better wake up or we might well find ourselves with more and more extremists in power, more Talibans, more wild Mullahs. I remember with shame how we treated the Shah of Iran and look what we got in his place!"

In 2011, I flew down to Houston and met up with my friend Rita Beamish, who covered 41's presidency for the AP—and who taught Bush the proper way to do sit-ups on one trip to Kennebunkport—so we could have lunch with the former president at his favorite pizza dive.

It made me sad to see the 87-year-old who had always bounded around like a yellow lab confined to a wheelchair. But he was still upbeat and even told some racy jokes. He spoke fondly of Bill Clinton, highly of President Obama and not so highly of Donald Trump. "He's an ass," H.W. said flatly, never dreaming that Trump would easily dispatch Jeb with withering insults in 2016 and attract more primary votes than any Republican candidate in history.

Smiling, he asked me: "Did you come because you think I'm going to die?"

"No," I replied. "I want to come on your ninetieth birthday parachute jump." Thank God he didn't take me; that windy landing, with his face sliding in the grass, looked terrifying.

When 41 was in the hospital in 2012, I sent him a gag gift, the classical music soundtrack selected by the author of *Fifty Shades of Grey*.

Barbara Bush, such a literary soul that she sometimes used a plastic book holder to read while she swam laps, wrote back that it had caused a lot of lively conversation.

"Did you by chance read those books?" she asked. "I did not, because I was told they were poorly written and pornographic."

\*    \*    \*

In the end, I got to cover a Shakespearean saga after all, an astonishing and parlous subordination of American history to particular psyches in one family. But it was sad to chronicle a burgeoning tragedy that cost so many lives, limbs and trillions, and that sucked America into such quicksand when we should have been quickening our pace against China.

The father-son drama that began in 1972, when a smashed W. smashed his car into a neighbor's garbage can at the family's Washington home and challenged his father "You want to go mano a mano right here?" climaxed when W. used his father as a reverse playbook to win the presidency and go to war.

"Never underestimate what you can learn from a failed presidency," W. told his Texas media strategist.

After many years of being "a juvenile delinquent, damn near," as James Baker jokingly put it to Meacham, the Prodigal Son finally got his act together and raced past the Good Son. Jeb was the careful, driven one whom their parents had anointed to be president someday.

W. not only stopped drinking, became a disciplined campaigner and poached the role reserved for Jeb in family lore, taking back what he felt was his birthright as eldest. He relied on his brother, then governor of Florida—though the two were not particularly close—to boost him to the Oval Office by reeling in the pivotal state during the protracted recount in 2000 in Tallahassee over hanging chads and butterfly ballots.

When W. superseded Jeb and became the comer, H.W. moved to

shore up the raffish son who had squandered so many years carousing. He swaddled W. with his friends, like Saudi Arabia's Prince Bandar, and his former advisers—Cheney, Colin Powell, Condi Rice—thinking they could add some gravitas and school W. in foreign policy.

But W. never wanted to be seen as the political heir of his father, who had alienated the ascendant conservatives. He had become born-again, inspired by the Reverend Billy Graham. Rove positioned W. in 2000 as the scion of Reagan, which must have smarted for his own dad. Poppy and Barbara, after all, had never been invited by Ron and Nancy to have dinner at the White House residence in the eight years he was vice president.

Poppy had written Jeb and W. in 1998: "At some point both of you may want to say 'Well, I don't agree with my Dad on that point' or 'Frankly I think Dad was wrong on that.' Do it. Chart your own course...so do not worry when the comparisons might be hurtful to your Dad for nothing can ever be written that will drive a wedge between us—nothing at all."

And 41's friends gave W. the benefit of the doubt. As one said, "He could not be seen as a clone of his father and expect to win."

But W.'s attempts to look flinty at the expense of his dad could sting.

The younger President Bush's White House Chief of Staff, Andy Card, even went so far as to suggest that W. was tougher than his courtly dad because he had been raised in Texas. "His training was dealing with problems on the streets of Laredo or Dallas or Houston or Midland or Austin," Card said. "This president came with a kind of street smarts and recognition of the importance of the resolve of America."

W.'s elaborate and absurd attempts to distance himself from his father so that he wouldn't seem like a juvenile posing in his dad's suit—H.W. had once caused a stir by referring to him as "this boy—this son of ours" in New Hampshire during the son's tight primary race against John McCain in 2000—spoke to his continuing insecurity and simmering frictions. W. didn't let his father, the last Republican President, speak at either of his conventions.

In the jittery time after 9/11, W. turned away from the sound advice his own father could have given, instead relying on the demented counsel of his dark father, Darth Cheney, as well as the wrongheaded advice of Donald Rumsfeld, who pushed to invade Iraq, where these were better targets than did the moonscape of Afghanistan.

I always thought it was strange for W., who had first come into his dad's '88 campaign as "a loyalty enforcer," to bring in Rumsfeld, who had maneuvered against 41 at every turn, mocking him as a lightweight. Bush felt that Rumsfeld pushed for him to get the top CIA job because it was, as the senior Bush put it in a letter to his siblings, "a graveyard for politics." Rummy also supported Dole against Poppy in the '88 Republican primary.

The Bushes had been traumatized by the 1987 *Newsweek* cover headlined "Fighting the Wimp Factor." H.W. met with Katharine Graham, the publisher of *Newsweek*, and cited the exact number of times the dreaded word had appeared in the article. W. cringed when his dad was labeled a "lapdog" or compared to a "jellyfish." He was so determined to be the antiwimp that he was susceptible when Cheney and Rumsfeld used that to manipulate him, telling him that he would seem weak if they didn't Shock-and-Awe Baghdad after 9/11, to make sure the Arabs never looked cross-eyed at America again.

W. had spent his life chafing against his dad's shadow. H.W. was captain of the soccer and baseball teams and on the editorial board of the school paper; W. was the head cheerleader and self-appointed stickball commissioner at Andover. H.W. was the Phi Beta Kappa baseball captain at Yale; W. received the gentleman C's at Yale.

(In a rich Oedipal moment, W. wrote in *41: A Portrait of My*

*Father* that his dad "didn't have a big enough bat to make the major leagues.")

H.W. was a navy pilot who got shot down in World War II heroically dropping bombs and was nearly captured by the Japanese; W. was a lackadaisical National Guard pilot in the Vietnam era. H.W.'s career as an oilman in Midland was middling; his son's even more so.

As one of W.'s Yale fraternity friends put it, "George grew up laboring in the shadow of his parents' disappointment in him."

Once, when the White House press corps for the first President Bush was in Kennebunkport, George and Barbara gave reporters a tour of their house. Two things surprised me. First, 41 had a framed *Doonesbury* cartoon, even though he resented Garry Trudeau for portraying him as putting his manhood in a blind trust. The second shock was when a reporter asked if the younger George Bush was going to run for Texas governor. Barbara barked a negative.

*The Bushes: Portrait of a Dynasty*, by Peter and Rochelle Schweizer, offered two illuminating moments:

When W. told his parents in 1993 that he was running for governor, his mother blurted out that he couldn't win.

After W. triumphed on the same night that Jeb lost the Florida governor's race, his father called his oldest son but sounded preoccupied with Jeb.

"The joy is in Texas," Poppy told reporters, "but our hearts are in Florida."

A wounded W. told his aunt Nancy, "It sounds like Dad's only heard that Jeb lost. Not that I've won."

Maybe fed up with or fearful of his parents' skepticism, W. was determined to run without his father's counsel. Although his father went on to help him raise money with his golden Rolodex, he once more had doubts about whether W. could win. Barbara later said that her first thought when her son announced his presidential ambitions was "He doesn't have a chance," former Bush senior aide Roman Popadiuk recounted in his book.

W. saw his presidency as an opportunity to finally outshine and impress his dad, getting the two terms H.W. was denied partly because the base turned on him after he broke his "Read my lips" pledge to never raise taxes.

Poppy also failed to fathom the threat of Bill Clinton, assuming that Americans would not elect a rogue, and he was not feeling well during his second run, possibly because the White House doctor was tinkering with 41's medicine for Graves disease.

The weekend after he lost, H.W. walked in the woods with Colin Powell in Camp David at twilight, their wives following a few steps behind, and admitted, "Colin, it hurts. It really hurts. I didn't think I'd lose."

W. wanted to snatch back the laurel his parents had awarded Jeb and his campaign was right out of the Joseph Campbell playbook. He ran as the son of Ronald Reagan, all but airbrushing his father from history, as if the presidential line of succession went straight from Reagan to Clinton.

For W., the Iraq invasion was an opportunity to not only avenge his father—Clinton had ordered missile strikes following intelligence that Saddam had plotted to assassinate H.W.—but to one-up the old man by taking out the villain his dad had left in place. W. would keep Saddam's 9-millimeter Glock 18C as a trophy in the Oval Office.

From the beginning, the Bush I crowd was alarmed at the belligerent, black-and-white, looking-for-boogeymen attitude of the Bush II administration.

Scowcroft talked with his protégé, Condi, and tried to talk sense to her. But Condi, taking her cue from the collapse of the Soviet empire, offered the Cheney-Rummy doctrine, saying that the US was the only superpower in the world and it could remake things in any way it wanted if it just pushed ahead.

Scowcroft urged her to think about coalitions and acting behind the scenes, but she was sprinting away from her multilateral mentors.

The always correct Bush père did not want to hover and be a helicopter parent. But as the war drums grew louder in 2002, he fretted to his sister, Nancy: "But do they have an exit strategy?"

He expressed his anguish to friends, fearing that his son had been captured by the neocons and did not fully understand the consequences of what he was doing. He worried that W. wasn't gathering enough information or taking the best advantage of all his advisers. Poppy stewed about Cheney, Rummy, Scooter Libby and Paul Wolfowitz controlling the paper flow and stacking the deck to lead W. to calamitous decisions.

But W. told a group of conservative journalists that he admired the "brass balls" of Cheney and Rummy.

Bush senior was an establishment guy who listened to realpolitik pros like Baker and Scowcroft. They had decided an invasion of Baghdad in '91 would have created more instability.

Struggling to figure out why aides such as Libby and Wolfowitz had so much sway, Poppy interrogated and cross-examined old colleagues about the neocons and about whether his son fathomed their influence.

"The neocons have never found a war they didn't like," said one of the members of Poppy's inner circle. "We don't need to be sending young women and men to die needlessly."

Suffering heartburn and angst watching his son take so many hits, Poppy blamed Cheney and confided to friends that he did not understand what had happened to his former defense secretary. Cheney seemed to have turned from "a delight" in his administration, as one H.W. friend put it, to a Dr. No seeking global domination in his son's administration. Some in the father's circle speculated that Cheney had had, as one Bush I veteran put it, "one triple bypass operation too many."

In 1991, Cheney justified not going into Baghdad to try to eliminate Saddam, noting, "I think for us to set American military personnel involved in a civil was inside Iraq would literally be a guagmire." In 2003, he pushed W. to do the opposite.

Some who had worked with Cheney when he was 41's defense secretary during the first Gulf War did not think he had gone through any metamorphosis. He had dished up cockamamie hard-line, belligerent, world domination scenarios then, too. He hadn't wanted to go to the UN before the first Gulf War, either. But 41, Baker, Scowcroft and Powell all were of one realpolitik mind, so Cheney never won any arguments.

At times, 41 delicately offered his son advice. On 9/11, as Cheney was telling W. to keep flying around while the vice president stayed in the bunker playing president, 41 said he told 43 "the sooner he got back to Washington the better." Great advice that W. belatedly took.

Rove contended to me that "the son asked Bush 41 for more insight and counsel and wisdom than people give him credit for doing. But the father was reluctant to give it because he did not want to subvert the process within the cabinet and government.

"All this stuff about competition is baloney. They have as healthy a father and son relationship as you would hope to see in your life."

But most others in Bushworld saw a more complicated family portrait. Despite his Texas swagger, W. was insecure at times— reminiscent of the little boy playing a spangly cowboy in *Willy Wonka & the Chocolate Factory*. He went so overboard trying to show that he was not dependent on his father that, on the most critical issues, he lost the benefit of 41's unvarnished counsel. And Poppy Bush bent over backward not to encroach or overshadow, especially on Iraq, where their approaches differed.

"W. was afraid to talk to his dad and his dad was afraid to talk to W., frankly," said one friend of the family. "The big gorilla in the room was that W. did not want to get advice contrary to what he was doing."

H.W. was determined, as one friend put it, "not to put his finger in the pie, to let his son run his own shop." So 41 would be indirect, saying stuff to his son like, "I had a meeting with so-and-so and this is what he had to say" or "Did you read this?"

As one of H.W.'s intimates noted: "There was never any doubt in my mind of the love and affection between them. But you've got to ask yourself: Why didn't the son call and specifically ask the father about whether to go into Iraq?"

Another Bush I official observed that the twin impulses braided in Bushes were love and competition.

"One thing President Bush 41 had was enormous self-discipline," said the former official. "If he decided that the right way to do it was just to be a loving father and never raise the issue, he wouldn't. W. was motivated by a different issue. He wanted to prove himself. You put those two things together—and you throw in some insecurity on the part of W.—and you have these two immovable forces who, I believe, spent a lot of time together and never talked about policies for their own reasons."

Poppy used oblique methods. When W. told his dad that he wanted to run for Congress in Midland in 1977, Sr. asked Jr. to go talk to his friend, Allan Shivers, the influential Democrat and former Governor of Texas, to get his advice on the race. Shivers told W. straight up that he couldn't win.

W. ignored the warning, ran and lost.

Poppy may have employed a similar technique on Iraq to get 43 to reconsider a doomed path.

His pal Scowcroft wrote a *Wall Street Journal* op-ed piece headlined "Don't Attack Saddam."

"There is little evidence to indicate that the United States itself is an object of his aggression," Scowcroft wrote of Saddam, adding that he did not have much in common with "the terrorists who threaten us." Scowcroft accurately warned that it would not be "a cakewalk," as the neocons claimed, but an expensive and bloody exercise that could destabilize the region and hurt the US and global economies. He wisely suggested that we would be better off resolving the Israel-Palestine issue.

But W. got furious at this attempt to pry him from the hawks and neocons and bring him back to reality.

"Bush speaking through Scowcroft to his son turned loose a lot of unpleasantness," said one H.W. friend, adding that W. sent Condi Rice to upbraid her old mentor, Scowcroft. W. called his dad to complain, Meacham reported, and the elder Bush replied, "Brent's a good man. He's a friend—Brent's your friend."

Bob Gates recalled, "There was all this speculation that Brent did the op-ed as a cat's paw for 41. And that kind of thing made 43 and his people especially sensitive."

Another Bush I foreign policy official observed: "W. was a born-again who believed in missions and he knew absolutely nothing about the world. He was like a dog with a bone. He was going to prove daddy was wrong and he was right, even if he had to stuff a square peg into a round hole."

The day before Cheney gave a speech blowing off the UN and the notion of containment, Baker chimed in to urge caution in an op-ed piece in the *Times*: "Unless we do it the right way, there will be costs to other American foreign policy interests, including our relationships with practically all other Arab countries (and even many of our customary allies in Europe and elsewhere) and perhaps even to our top foreign policy priority, the war on terrorism . . . we should try our best not to have to go it alone, and the president should reject the advice of those who counsel doing so."

The Saudis also tried in vain to warn W. and prevent war. Prince Bandar and Prince Saud, the foreign minister, told the president that

Saddam would allow inspectors in, and explained that the Iraqi dictator was only blustering that he had weapons to deter Iran. They also told the White House that if it proceeded with an invasion, after three to six months America would be seen as an occupier. The Saudis, again vainly, advised the White House to leave the Iraqi institutions in place, replace the top layer of military generals and then hand everything over to the UN and international forces.

"Richard Perle and his buddies were salivating over pipelines and cell phones and the idea that the whole region would be transformed into a pro-American democracy," one top Saudi official told me a couple of years ago. "It was all wishful thinking by the neocons."

W.'s Middle East policy was a direct rebuke to his dad, a simplistic and naïve gambit designed to transplant democracy into the Middle East.

W. criticized previous administrations—including his dad's—for policies that indicated that "stability is more important than form of government."

The father dealt with the corrupt Saudi monarchy and Middle Eastern dictators while he was tough on Israel. So the son would try something else, getting rid of Saddam to establish a democracy and uncritically siding with Israel, a democracy.

In 2004, as the war in Iraq soured, W. told *The Washington Times* that America should not send mixed signals to the Iraqis or "cut and run early, like happened in, '91"—scapegoating his own father for showing weakness that encouraged the terrorists. He used his father's bête noire against him, suggesting that 41 had wimped out on Saddam.

On Don Imus's show during the 2004 Republican convention, the usually reticent Poppy admitted, "I didn't like that much ... Frantely, it hurt a little bit."

After dismissing "all this psychobabble stuff," the older Bush psychobabbled: "These damn issues now for me, they don't matter. What does matter to me, though, is if they have assigned things to him in some salon in the Upper East Side of New York that he is trying to get out from under some shadow to escape his father and to have his own legacy and not his dad. Maybe there were people around four years ago who felt that way." He added that he didn't want to sound like "the nutty father unleashed out there. We don't need that. I had my chance."

Or as one of his close friends said: "It wasn't the father's responsibility to rein in the son."

The way H.W.'s intimates saw it, Cheney called the shots and with Iraq, Cheney and Rumsfeld handed W. "a doo-doo ball," as one friend and adviser to Bush senior put it.

H.W. kept any difference of opinion with his son to himself, no matter how people tried to provoke him. Jeb also did not openly express any envy of W. for upending him in the family narrative.

In *41*, his "love letter" to his dad, W. tried to make H.W.'s war with Saddam and his own part of a logical continuum. But they were not. One war was about restoring the world order. The other was about imposing democracy.

The father attacked Saddam to establish the principle that one nation cannot unilaterally invade another. The son attacked Saddam to establish the principle that one nation can unilaterally invade another.

"I never asked Dad what I should do," W. wrote in *41*. "We both knew that this was a decision that only the President can make." Instead, he would "update" 41 on his decisions.

Even Fox News commentators were at a loss to understand how a Republican president could go to war against Saddam without hashing it out with the last Republican president who went to war against Saddam—especially if it was a beloved father. How could you not want to hear that unique perspective?

But W. told Brit Hume that he saw his dad more as a loving parent than an adviser, casting the knowledgeable ex-president in the role of blankie. He protested at another point that his father did not have the right security clearance to be briefed the way a sitting president would be—a risible excuse. Bush senior knew more about the region than most of those who might brief him.

W. told Bob Woodward that he preferred to consult "a higher father."

The Bush I crowd was dumbfounded when the Iraq viceroy, Paul Bremer, disbanded the Iraqi Army, laying the groundwork for all the Sunni insurgencies right up through ISIS, after W. had stated that the army would not be dissolved. Bremer told W. over videoconference that he was going to do it, but W. didn't object—seeming not to comprehend that he was abandoning his own strategy. Once more, the Old King and his courtiers fretted that W. was not in control.

Poppy and Barbara blamed the bad stuff on Cheney. "W. was dependent on him," said one family intimate. "So Cheney felt free to pursue his own policy prescriptions, which were neocon-ish and forceful. Don't forget Cheney had been a congressman from Wyoming and nobody is more conservative than a congressman from Wyoming."

As Iraq and Afghanistan cratered, W. too began to get angry at Cheney and Cheney's pal and mentor from back in the Gerald Ford days, Rumsfeld.

In the second term, at Laura's urging, W. fired Rumsfeld and replaced him with Bob Gates, H.W.'s CIA director and president of Texas A&M University.

W. also distanced himself from Vice, as he called him, infuriating Cheney by refusing to pardon Libby, the veep's chief of staff known as "Cheney's Cheney," who had been convicted of lying to the FBI and a grand jury in the Valerie Plame case. Bush commuted his two-and-a-half-year prison sentence.

"You are leaving a good man wounded on the field of battle," Cheney stormed at W.

One Bush family friend said that, at the beginning of W.'s second term, the president "began to ask himself, 'How did all this happen?'" That led to a more honest conversation between 41 and 43 about the deleterious effect of W.'s sulfurous advisers. One H.W. pal referred to this as "the reconciliation." Others agreed that once W. had gone through his own crucibles with Iraq and Katrina, he was mature enough to have a more mellow relationship with his father.

But the friction and competition between the two would never totally melt away, as illustrated by this stunning anecdote in *Duty*, Gates's memoir.

"The one somewhat touchy area between us—never openly discussed—was my close relationship to the president's father. When Bush 41 was in Washington in late January 2007 and wanted to come over to the Pentagon to see me and meet some of the military leaders, I got a call from Josh Bolten that Bush 43 thought such a visit might become a news story and he did not want that. Josh urged me to call off the visit. I said I would defer to 43's wishes. So 41 and I had breakfast the next day at the White House instead. A few weeks later I was returning from a meeting at the White House when my secretary called to tell me that 41 was on his way to the Pentagon. I barely arrived in time to welcome him, and he went around shaking hands and talking with the folks in my immediate office. He was there only about fifteen to twenty minutes, but I think he wanted to make a point about his own independence."

Laughing, Gates told me that he had to tell the driver to put on flashing red lights and sirens so he could get to the Pentagon in time to see 41.

I asked what on earth the 43 crowd was afraid of, as W.'s second term drew to a close. Wouldn't it have simply looked like 41 supporting 43's surge in Iraq, which started then?

"I suppose it was the continuing sensitivity that the father was somehow substantively engaged," Gates replied.

But most Americans would have liked 43 to get some guidance from his father, I suggested.

Gates said that, while there was "a deep underlying love" between the two men, they were very conscious of "the uniqueness of managing this relationship between two presidents in the era of social media. John Adams and John Quincy Adams were separated by a quarter of a century. The two Bushes were separated by only eight years."

He said that the father was extremely sensitive not to give the impression that he was a behind-the-scenes counselor, and the son was extremely sensitive not to be seen as a protégé.

"During that whole period I was the president of Texas A&M, and I was seeing 41 very frequently and he almost never talked about foreign policy," Gates said about the man who loved nothing better than dishing about foreign affairs. "He was very sensitive not to express his views on things, even to friends, for fear somehow it would get out, and that he might be seen as having a different view."

As an example of how bizarre and byzantine the father-son dynamic could get, Gates told me about the "triangular deception" that occurred when 43 summoned him to the Bush ranch for a secret meeting in 2006 to talk about the Pentagon job.

The only person Gates consulted with before going was 41. At the meeting, W. specifically mentioned that his dad did not know about it. Gates, feeling a little guilty, did not reveal that he had already talked to 41.

"It was clear he had not consulted his father about this possible appointment and that, contrary to later speculation, Bush 41 had no role in it," Gates wrote in his memoir.

But then, eight years later, when *41*, W.'s paean to his dad, came out, Gates was surprised to read that 43 had indeed called his father to ask if he should appoint Gates. And the father never told the son he had consulted with Gates beforehand.

After shattering the Middle East, W. devoted his postpresidency to trying to make himself whole. He painted seminude self-portraits set in the shower and bath—like a guilty Lady Macbeth, washing her hands over and over. And he tried to burnish the dented family name, writing his own memoir and the adoring portrait of his father, which he introduced at his dad's library.

"He wanted to atone for his sins a little bit," said one Bush I official.

And to atone for leapfrogging Jeb, W. was the leading figure pushing Jeb to move beyond Bush fatigue—most pointedly expressed by their own mother—and run for president.

Meacham believed that the frail patriarch of the clan was determined to live to see the long-yearned-for Jeb presidency finally come true.

H.W.'s friends noticed that W. even began to talk more reverentially about his father, rather than simply barking "Good man," as he used to do.

"It was as though he couldn't wait to say all the things he wanted to say when he was trying so hard to show how independent he was and that he didn't need anybody," said a family confidante.

But some of what W. said sounded disingenuous.

At the library Q & A to introduce his book, he praised his father for being "the finest one-term president our country's ever had," but then reiterated that he had not wanted his policy advice, just his pats on the back.

"People can't possibly comprehend," he said, "that when you admire somebody as much as all of us admire George H. W. Bush and he offers help or comfort, it means more than any advice he could possibly give."

The more W. said it, the less sense it made.

In an interview with the *Times*'s Peter Baker, 43 said that his father followed Ronald Reagan, "a transformative president, still being quoted by potential candidates," which "kind of obscured his accomplishments."

Of course, W. was the candidate who pioneered lionizing Reagan and obscuring his father. The first thing I ever heard from W.'s advisers in '99 about his presidential run was that he was much more like Reagan than his own father.

It will go down as one of the most astonishing historical ironies of all time that W.'s belittling use of his dad as a reverse playbook ended up, seesaw like, burnishing H.W.'s historical reputation and sparking what Meacham called "Poppy chic."

Although it got him fired by the electorate, H.W.'s tax increase to fix the deficit is now widely seen as paving the way for prosperity in the Clinton era. Whereas W. appointed lame-duck regulators and unshackled Wall Street, H.W. infuriated Wall Street by signing the Financial Institution Reform Recovery and Enforcement Act (FIRRE) of 1989 in the wake of Reagan's Savings and Loan crisis. He went along with FIRRE—which set higher capital standards, empowering financial regulators and tightly regulating lending practices—even though he had been warned that it would spark a small recession and hurt his political fortunes.

W.'s descent into chaos in Iraq made H.W.'s much-debated decision not to go into Baghdad look like the smart move.

For many years, when Jim Baker, Bob Gates and other veterans of the Bush I administration gave speeches, they were met with skepticism on their decision to leave Saddam in power.

"For ten years, every speech we gave, people would stick up their hands and say, 'Why didn't you guys take care of Saddam when you had the chance?'" Gates said. "After March 2003, we never got that question again."

In interviews with Jon Meacham for the 2015 bestseller *Destiny and Power: The American Odyssey of George Herbert Walker Bush*, H.W. had a twilight unburdening to a sympathetic biographer, finally spitting out for the record how he felt about his son's regents, Cheney and Rummy.

Cheney, he said, "had his own empire there and marched to his own drummer," adding: "He just became very hard-line and very different from the Dick Cheney I knew and worked with." He said that the 9/11 attacks had made Cheney "just iron-ass. His seeming knuckling under to the real hard-charging guys who want to fight about everything, use force to get our way in the Middle East." He also blamed the influence of Lynne Cheney, also an "iron-ass" in his opinion.

He did not let his son off the hook for letting his vice president grab so much power, belatedly putting Junior over his knee and noting: "But it's not Cheney's fault, it's the president's fault," adding at another point, "The buck stops there."

W. was surprised to hear his father's criticism, and their dysfunctional, elliptical father-son communication process spilled into full view. It was remarkable that two presidents who went to war with the same Iraqi dictator can bluntly talk to each other only through a biographer.

"He certainly never expressed that dynamic to me, either during the presidency or after," W. said, adding that his father "would never say to me, 'Hey, you need to rein in Cheney. He's ruining your administration.' It would be out of character for him to do that. And in any event, I disagree with his characterization of what was going on. I made the decisions. This was my philosophy."

H.W. took revenge on his old nemesis, Rumsfeld, calling him "an arrogant fellow" and an "iron-ass" who had "a lack of humility, a lack of seeing what the other guy thinks."

Rumsfeld responded in his usual classy way, suggesting that the elder Bush was dotty. "Bush 41," he said in a statement, "is getting up in years."

As one Bush I official said with wry satisfaction: "We look like rocket scientists in foreign and domestic policy, thanks to them."

While once W. distanced himself from his dad, now officials of the dad's administration distance themselves from W.

"You have to look at the said presidencies separately," a top adviser to Bush 41 said, "and you see the father's presidency was quite significant."

In May 2014, H.W. was awarded the Profile in Courage award. He was not well enough to go to Boston and hear JFK's grandson, Jack Schlossberg, say that "America's gain was President Bush's loss, and his decision to put country above party and political prospects makes him an example of a modern profile in courage that is all too rare."

Meanwhile, W.'s reverse playbook of slashing taxes erased a surplus and caused a ballooning deficit that not even Republicans could stand by.

At the 25th anniversary celebration of his inauguration in 2014, held at 41's presidential library, a visitor asked the former president how he felt about the warmer regard bathing him now, as Americans look back longingly at a presidency that was not polarizing and a pol who preferred consensus to shrillness.

"Hard to believe," the former president said about "the legacy thing."

Now, as the country continues to lose faith in its institutions and in politicians frozen in dysfunction, 41's efforts to stay on good terms with those he disagreed with and to split the difference seem like a golden era.

If he sometimes changed positions for political expediency, he also sometimes did it simply because he thought it was good for the country.

He worked across party lines to pass the Clean Air Act amendments of 1990 and signed the landmark Americans with Disabilities Act, after Boyden Gray and Gray's close friend, wheelchair-bound Evan Kemp, the chairman of the US Equal Employment Opportunity Commission, urged him to do the right thing. At the ADA signing ceremony, H.W. saluted his former presidential campaign rival, a senator and fellow World War II veteran who lived with and rose above a disabling war injury.

"Bob Dole has inspired me," President Bush said.

\*   \*   \*

W. went overboard trying to be macho because his dad had been accused of being not macho enough. But H.W.'s former aides think that 41's reputation has grown in part because Americans know that he has a weepy, emotional side to him and that it makes him seem genuine.

Certainly, it was painful for the patriarch of the Bush clan to watch a jeering TV reality star, a man he thought of as an "ass," belittle Jeb as a "low-energy" wimp in the Republican primaries. Bush senior was known to throw his shoe at the TV set when Donald Trump was on.

Despite spending a $130 million war chest amassed with the help of his dad's connections and a barrage of ads, Jeb never broke through in a crowded field. His mother was right when she told the *Today* show in 2013 that "we've had enough Bushes."

The 91-year-old took back those words and gamely tried to drag Jeb over the finish line in South Carolina and New Hampshire. But in the end, there was dynasty fatigue on both sides of the aisle—especially on the Republican side. And Jeb did seem low energy and rusty after a decade away from the arena, slow to strike back at Trump. He was too moderate and reasonable for an electorate that was steeped in fury about the lost American dream. He said he would campaign "joyfully," but most of the time he campaigned dolefully.

With Trump belittling him for being low energy and running to Mommy and Daddy for help, Jeb realized he was in a new world.

At one point, he was reduced to begging a New Hampshire audience: "Please clap."

His brother's muscle-bound presidency led to Barack Obama and the diffident Obama led to a new brand of furious, Tea Party–infused Republicans.

While Jeb was off stage, the whole party and political environment had passed him by. He came back looking very '90s. He was talking about pragmatic government at a time when the drivers in his party were talking about tearing down government.

Jeb got confused. He thought he was still in an era when people had to pay their dues.

"This was my chance," Jeb said after dropping out. "This was the chance and I ran into a storm." Trump boasted to me that even after Jeb spent millions of dollars on attack ads "he got his ass kicked." Salivating over his victory, Trump added, "And 'low energy,' that term just hit, it's amazing. It was over. That thing, that was a one-day kill. Words are beautiful."

H.W. was devastated that Jeb would not be 45, helping to redeem the family name after 43's blunders, and chalked it up to insane politics. Some of his friends were careful not to even bring up the 2016 race when they had lunch with Bush senior after Jeb was trounced by Trump, fearing it would pain him. The two presidents showed solidarity with the vanquished Jeb by boycotting Trump's Cleveland convention. "I'm worried," W. told friends, "that I will be the last Republican president." At least W. could take private satisfaction that, despite his parents' early doubts, he did prove to have better campaign skills than the wonky, lackluster Jeb.

"Trump carried Greenwich, the town that was the beginning of the journey for the Bushes," Meacham marveled to me. "Prescott Bush was the moderator of the Greenwich town meeting. Eight decades on, Donald Trump carried it. That is the end of all things."

I winced for 41 at the news that Greenwich was Trump territory.

Through the decades, Poppy's "madness Richter scale" at me went up and down. "Is pissed off OK," he asked in one note, worried that saying he felt that way toward me sounded too vulgar. But the underlying sweetness was always there.

"Put it this way," he wrote me once. "I reserve the right to whine, to not read, to use profanity, but if you ever get really hurt or if you ever get really down and need a shoulder to cry on or just need a friend—give me a call. I'll be there for you. I'll not let you down.

"Now, go on out and knock my knickers off. When you do, I might just cancel my subscription."

*Rita Beamish and I reminisce with President Bush in his Houston office about our years covering his White House after lunch at his favorite pizza dive in 2011.*

# Jeb Bush's Brainless Trust

I had been keeping an open mind on Jeb Bush.

I mean, sure, as Florida governor, he helped his brother snatch the 2000 election. And that led to two decade-long-and-counting botched wars that cost tens of thousands of lives and trillions of dollars. The nation will be dealing for a long time with struggling veterans and the loss of American prestige. Not to mention that W. let Wall Street gamble away the economy, which is only now finally creeping back.

But, all that aside, shouldn't John Ellis Bush have the right to make the case that he is his own man?

In his foreign policy speech in Chicago on Wednesday, Jeb was dismissive toward those who want to know where he stands in relation to his father and brother. "In fact," he said, mockingly, "this is a great, fascinating thing in the political world for some reason."

For some reason?

Like the Clintons, the Bushes drag the country through national traumas that spring from their convoluted family dynamic and then disingenuously wonder why we concern ourselves with their family dynamic.

Without their last names, Hillary and Jeb would not be

front-runners, buoyed by networks of donors grateful for appointments or favors bestowed by the family. (When Jeb and W. ran gubernatorial races in 1994, they both mined their mother's Christmas card list for donors.)

Yet Jeb is bristling with Jane Austen–style condescension, acting as though he would still be where he is if his last name were Tree. The last two presidents in his party were his father and brother, and his brother crashed the family station wagon into the globe, and Jeb is going to have to address that more thoroughly than saying "there were mistakes made in Iraq for sure."

He says he doesn't want to focus on "the past," and who can blame him? But how can he talk about leading America into the future if he can't honestly assess the past, or his family's controversial imprint?

In his speech, he blamed President Obama for the void that hatched ISIS, which he also noted didn't exist in 2003 at the dawn of "the liberation of Iraq." Actually, his brother's invasion of Iraq is what spawned Al Qaeda in Iraq, which drew from an insurgency of Sunni soldiers angry about being thrown out of work by the amateurish and vainglorious viceroy, Paul Bremer.

Although Jeb likes to act as though his family is irrelevant to his ambitions, Bushworld stalwarts recite the Bush dynasty narrative like a favorite fairy tale:

The wonky Jeb, not the cocky W., was always 41's hope. H.W. and Bar never thought W., unprepared, unruly and with a chip on his shoulder, would be president. His parents' assumption that he was The Golden One got in Jeb's head and now the 62-year-old feels he needs "to try to correct and make up for some of W.'s mistakes," as one family friend put it. The older Bush circle seems confident that Jeb sided with his father and Brent Scowcroft on the folly of letting the neocons push America into diverting from Osama to Saddam.

So for Bushworld, Jeb is the redeemer, the one who listens and talks in full sentences that make sense, the one who will restore the luster of the Bush name. But if you want to be your own person, you have to come up with your own people.

W. was a boy king, propped up by regents supplied by his father. Since he knew nothing about foreign affairs, his father surrounded him with his own advisers: Colin Powell, Condi Rice and Dick Cheney, who joined up with his pal Donald Rumsfeld and absconded with W.'s presidency.

Jeb, too, wanted to bolster his negligible foreign policy cred, so the day of his speech, his aide released a list of 21 advisers, 19 of whom had worked in the administrations of his father and his brother. The list starts with the estimable James Baker. But then it shockingly veers into warmongers.

It's mind-boggling, but there's Paul Wolfowitz, the unapologetic designer of the doctrine of unilateralism and preemption, the naïve cheerleader for the Iraq invasion and the man who assured Congress that Iraqi oil would pay for the country's reconstruction and that it was ridiculous to think we would need as many troops to control the country as General Eric Shinseki, then the Army chief of staff, suggested.

There's John Hannah, Cheney's national security adviser (cultivated by the scheming Ahmed Chalabi), who tried to stuff hyped-up junk on Saddam into Powell's UN speech and who harbored bellicose ambitions about Iran; Stephen Hadley, who let the false 16-word assertion about Saddam trying to buy yellowcake in Niger into W.'s 2003 State of the Union; Porter Goss, the former C.I.A. director who defended waterboarding.

There's Michael Hayden, who publicly misled Congress about warrantless wiretapping and torture, and Michael Chertoff, the Homeland Security secretary who fumbled Katrina.

Jeb is also getting advice from Condi Rice, queen of the apocalyptic mushroom cloud. And in his speech he twice praised a supporter, Henry Kissinger, who advised prolonging the Vietnam War, which the Nixon White House thought might help with the 1972 election.

Why not bring back Scooter Libby?

If he wants to reclaim the Bush honor, Jeb should be holding accountable those who inflicted deep scars on America, not holding court with them.

Where's the shame?

For some reason, Jeb doesn't see it.

# Poppy Bush Finally Gives Junior a Spanking

I visited HBO's *Game of Thrones* set in Belfast last week, and after watching Daenerys Targaryen in firelight for a couple hours, I learned how to say "I have to go to the bathroom" in Dothraki.

I'll never be fluent in that martial language. But I am fluent in mangled Bush-speak.

So I must pull myself away from the Iron Throne and return to the Iron Ass, trading one serpentine family tangle for another. I am here, my puzzled readers, to help interpret the latest Oedipal somersaults of our royally messed up Republican royal family.

Like many uptight, upper-class families, the Bushes seem oddly unable to directly confront tensions and resentments and talk to each other candidly. With other families, the unsaid and circuitous end up rupturing relationships. In the case of the Bushes, it ended up rupturing the globe.

Like Queen Cersei, old King George knows that revenge is a dish that doesn't lose its flavor when served cold. After more than a decade of publicly keeping his lips zipped, Poppy Bush took his full measure of payback in Jon Meacham's new biography, *Destiny and Power: The American Odyssey of George Herbert Walker Bush.*

While W. used to say that what he liked about Dick Cheney and Donald Rumsfeld was their brass appendages, Poppy offered a dimmer anatomical appraisal, calling each an "iron ass."

He said he thought Rumsfeld served W. badly, and Rumsfeld responded with his usual charm, noting, "Bush 41 is getting up in years."

The gentlemanly 91-year-old is not going gentle into that good night. He finally spit out what he had been obsessing about privately for so long: Why did Cheney, 41's loyal defense secretary, turn so belligerent and unilateral, "knuckling under to the real hard-charging guys who want to fight about everything and use force to get our way in the Middle East"? How did the neocons manage to push his son's administration into pursuing their foolish agenda of refashioning the Middle East at the point of a gun?

He ultimately faults his son for the administration's deadly embrace of Cheney and the neocons and for allowing Cheney to create his own national security apparatus, noting: "But it's not Cheney's fault, it's the president's fault," adding at another point, "The buck stops there."

Bush senior, who had been so deferential and dutiful as a vice president that he endangered his chances of being president, with George Will calling him a "lapdog," was offended by Cheney's White House empire-building and upset that his son let his vice president grab so much power.

A surprised W. told Meacham, "He certainly never expressed that opinion to me, either during the presidency or after." He added that his father "would never say to me, 'Hey, you need to rein in Cheney. He's ruining your administration.' It would be out of character for him to do that. And in any event, I disagree with his characterization of what was going on. I made the decisions. This was my philosophy."

Even for a Waspy American family with scorn for introspection and a long tradition of fathers not weighing in, choosing to let their sons make their own life choices, it's remarkable that two presidents who went to war with the same Iraqi dictator can bluntly talk to each other only through a biographer.

If only they were Italian. Maybe the father could have simply said to the son in real time: "Don't screw this up, invade the wrong country and create a power vacuum in the Middle East. Dick's gone nuts."

The sad part is, they probably now agree on Cheney, whom W. has distanced himself from, and Rumsfeld, fired by W. in the second term.

Far from shrinking away from his twilight unburdening to a sympathetic biographer—even though it severely complicates life for Jeb, who is sinking in dynasty quicksand—41 seems eager to get the belated word out. His office in Houston is helpfully sending out bulletins about where Meacham is appearing on his book tour, including a signing hosted by H.W.'s library at Texas A&M University.

At Yale, in military service and in politics, W. chafed at his father's shadow. He drifted, drank and became what James Baker jokingly described to Meacham as "a juvenile delinquent, damn near." He labored under the disapproval of his father. When he sobered up and found his path in politics, he presented himself as the heir of Ronald Reagan, not his own father.

That had to hurt, but Poppy kept it to himself.

W. became president by using his dad as a reverse playbook.

That had to hurt, but Poppy kept it to himself.

In the White House, Cheney brought in his old mentor, Rumsfeld, who had schemed against Bush senior and belittled him as a flighty preppy. W. went along with Cheney and appointed his father's nemesis defense secretary, without asking 41's advice about it. It was like hothead Sonny Corleone going over to the Tattaglia family.

That had to hurt, but Poppy kept it to himself.

As a young man, W. once got drunk, drove back to the family home in Washington, plowed his car into a neighbor's garbage can and then challenged his disappointed father to go "mano a mano."

Now the father, in belatedly putting W. over his knee, has taught the son the meaning of the phrase. If only it could have happened face to face.

# Escape from Bushworld

The Bushes always bristled at the "d" word. And now they don't have to worry about it anymore.

The dynasty has perished, with a whimper. The exclamation point has slouched off.

The Bushes are leaving the field to someone they have utter contempt for: Donald Trump.

And the main emotion in Bushworld is relief. No one could bear one more day of watching Jeb get the flesh flayed off him by Trump.

With his uncanny batlike sonar, sensing how to psychologically gauge and then gut an opponent, Trump went straight for the Bushes' biggest bête noire: wimpiness.

The blustery billionaire painted Jeb as a "low-energy" candidate with a wilting exclamation point who was desperately in need of an infusion of testosterone; a soft child of privilege who had to depend on Daddy's friends for money and Mommy's presence on the trail to bail him out, even as he feared using his surname on his campaign posters; an entitled wonk who pathetically tried to get more popular by taking off his rimless glasses.

When Jeb bragged during the CBS debate about "winning

the lottery" by getting Barbara Bush as a mother, Trump cracked, "She should be running." And indeed, the 90-year-old exemplar of Greenwich granite wrote the epitaph of Jeb's campaign before it even began, noting correctly that, "We've had enough Bushes," and that the same families should not be allowed to pass the White House back and forth.

Starting with 41, the family saga was the arc of blue bloods trying to seem red-blooded. They wanted what they saw as their due, as the royal family of Republican politics. But they also wanted to come across as self-made men, men who struck out south from Kennebunkport and Greenwich to make their way in the world. They all had elaborate mythologies to prove they were their own men, even as they made business deals thanks to the family name and connections and mined Bar's Christmas card list for donors.

The Bush men always recast themselves to woo voters. Poppy Bush shed his preppy striped watchband and pretended that pork rinds, rather than popcorn, was his favorite snack. W. acted like the heir of Ronald Reagan rather than of his own dad, who had alienated the conservative base and failed to win two terms. And Jeb tried to pep up—getting contact lenses and belatedly punching harder against Trump.

When Poppy Bush ran against Bill Clinton, he simply assumed that the public would not choose a draft-dodging womanizer over him. "His ambient reality was that a president was above all a figure of dignity and decorum," Bush senior biographer Jon Meacham said. "Clinton went on Arsenio Hall. Bush 41 probably thought Arsenio Hall was a building at Andover."

Just as the political ground had shifted under his father, leaving him befuddled and looking at his watch, so it shifted under Jeb, leaving him befuddled and tapping his foot.

Despite all the talk about civility, the Bushes threw out the red meat whenever they had to, from Lee Atwater and Willie Horton in

'88 to W.'s supporters whispering in 2000 that John McCain came home from Hanoi with snakes in his head, to the W. 2004 campaign strategy of encouraging gay marriage ballot initiatives to rile up the evangelicals, to Jeb spending a fortune on ads this winter eviscerating the character of the man he deemed the disloyal protégé, Marco Rubio.

Winning was always more important than gentility. That's what happened in 2000, when the family had to pressure Jeb to help purloin Florida. In return, W. came out of his oil-painting exile to try to deliver South Carolina for Jeb.

South Carolina was the place the whole byzantine sibling rivalry drama was going to be made right. The Bushes always thought their sober and studious second son would be president, but the prodigal son shoved Jeb out of the way. Now Jeb would get his due.

Except that the inflammatory Trump, who delights in breaking the fourth wall, was perfectly happy to shatter the convention in Republican circles that W. "kept us safe," as Jeb kept saying.

Trump stunned everyone by pointing out the obvious: W. and Condi were not on the ball before 9/11, when W. was mountain biking and ignoring memos headlined, as Bill Maher dryly put it, "Osama bin Laden is standing right behind you." Then, after 9/11, they played right into Osama's recruiting plans by invading and occupying two Muslim countries, instead of simply going after the guilty party, as W. had promised to do when he yelled through the bullhorn at Ground Zero.

Trump held the Bushes accountable for the trumped-up war. W.'s arrogant and delusional administration pulled the wool over Americans' eyes about the Iraq invasion, which has ended up costing us trillions and killing and maiming hundreds of thousands. Even though Poppy Bush's circle has always assumed that Jeb was on their side, believing that the invasion was a mistake because it would shatter the Middle East, Jeb stumbled around on that question and ended up defending his brother's indefensible war. He even shocked his father's circle by putting out a list of foreign policy advisers for his campaign that included one of the war's woolly-headed architects, Paul Wolfowitz.

The underlying message of Bush campaigns is always: "Trust us. We know best." But that has been proven false.

The country is now aflame with anger and disgust about politicians and bankers who conned trusting Americans and never got punished for it. That fury has led to the rise of wildly improbable candidates in both parties. As the Bush dynasty falls, it must watch in horror knowing that it is responsible for the rise of Donald Trump.

# Interlude

## *A Life of Voting Dangerously*
## by Peggy Dowd

*My sister grapples with the gilded era of Trump.*

As I watched Donald Trump take that now famous escalator ride into the political chaos of 2016, I flashed back to our first encounter.

It was in March 1991. The Washington association I worked for was holding a convention at the Taj Mahal hotel in Atlantic City, and Mr. Trump had agreed to be the general session speaker at his new property. The audience consisted of invited CEOs from 6,000 associations. The speech was business-oriented with an emphasis on winning and deal making and Trump received a standing ovation.

I was on the welcoming committee and I found him to be

courteous and smart, showing no signs of the bigoted, narcissistic, misogynistic bully he is accused of being today.

So as I began to think of a candidate to support, my feelings remained very positive. I would back Mr. Trump even though his road to the nomination seemed nearly impossible—and all the data-mining experts stated unequivocally that we should forget about it.

His competition was formidable. I began to follow him studiously, reading two papers every day, watching every debate and keeping CNN as my go-to. I loved seeing the talking heads completely baffled after each primary win, and it only reinforced my original commitment. I glowed as Trump knocked off his competitors, one by one.

What took me by surprise was the vitriol from my female friends. I didn't expect to have my sanity questioned. I was told it was my duty, as a woman, to vote for Hillary and if I couldn't do that, I should sit out this year and not vote at all.

Voting for Hillary is out of the question. She is too secretive and sneaky. The country would have had more available health care in the '90s if she had just been more open and flexible. She also feels that she is entitled to this position and that no one should challenge her. But the thing that bothers me the most is that, like her husband, she can never own up to mistakes without dragging other people, living or dead, into the controversies. First the Clinton White House raised the specters of JFK and Thomas Jefferson and their paramours to excuse Bill Clinton cavorting in the Oval Office. And then Hillary corralled Colin Powell to excuse her unseemly email setup, even though she was operating under very different rules in a very different Internet climate. Powell was not using his own homebrew server.

I do not want to continuously hear, "Everybody else does it." I want a leader to say, "I did it and it was wrong and I'm sorry." As JFK once remarked, an error doesn't become a mistake until you refuse to correct it.

My sister teases me about my zig-zaggy political trajectory.

I first put my toe in political waters at 19 years old when, like all young Irish Catholics, I was eager to cast my first vote for JFK, who had beaten back all the bigoted contentions that there would be a secret tunnel between the White House and the Vatican and that a President Kennedy would take his orders from the Pope. But then came November 1963 and my chance to cast that vote disappeared with an assassin's bullet. Instead, I found myself standing in the chill in front of St. Matthew's Cathedral listening over speakers as Cardinal Cushing gave his eulogy at President Kennedy's funeral mass.

I was also, remarkably, at the Ambassador Hotel in Los Angeles the horrible night Bobby Kennedy was assassinated. Another Kennedy I yearned to vote for who died far too young.

Not wanting to support LBJ, I joined the Young Republicans and, like Hillary Clinton, became a Goldwater Girl and enthusiastically cast my first vote for Barry Goldwater. My dad had helped me buy my first new car, a white convertible with blue interior, and I was very proud to put a Goldwater sticker on the bumper. It was not on there a week when I came out of a restaurant in downtown DC to find my top slit in several places and vile words written all over the car in lipstick. (A precursor to Internet trolls.)

That campaign was where I learned how vicious TV political ads could be as America watched a little girl picking a daisy as a nuclear bomb exploded in the background—an image LBJ used to convey what could happen with a Goldwater presidency. The ad was revived on cable TV in June when Hillary gave a speech in San Diego about how Trump was too dangerous and erratic to trust with the nuclear codes.

Jimmy Carter won my vote running as a man of the people, but two-hour gas lines and darkened Washington monuments sent me scurrying back to the Republican side. I had lived in California when Ronald Reagan was governor and thought he was excellent in swiftly pulling the state out of the red. So I was more than ready to switch back and give him my full support when he threw his hat in the presidential ring. My dad was a Truman Democrat but after he died, my mom and I became charter Reagan Democrats.

I met George W. Bush when he was governor of Texas, and he quickly became my choice for president. He had that JFK crackle. I worked for him on a West Virginia phone bank and volunteered at the Republican convention in Philadelphia. I crashed in my sister's hotel room but she ordered me to leave my "W Stands for Women" sign in the hall. Over a long sybaritic lunch, the late *New York Times*

*Peggy with W., who inspired her so much she volunteered to work for his 2000 campaign.*

political correspondent Johnny Apple assured me that W. would win the election and be a popular chief executive. But then came 9/11, the Iraq war and Dick Cheney. W. should have listened to his father.

In 2008, I got swept up in Obama fever. I helped my sister throw an inaugural party that was so crowded and chaotic that somehow Tom Hanks got stranded outside in subfreezing weather yelling for a beer. But I got to meet Anderson Cooper while I was making little sandwiches in the kitchen, so it was all worth it. I believed, like everyone else, that Barack Obama's election would ease racial tension in our country. Instead, we seem more divided than ever.

After a trip to Cuba last spring, I became fascinated by Che Guevara, but it was only Che's Irish heritage that enraptured me. And Maureen was astonished that I was going to morph from Democrat to Republican to Democrat to Republican to Democrat to Communist to Socialist to Republican.

I did end up going Socialist briefly. On June 14, in the DC primary, the last in the nation, I cast my vote for Bernie Sanders as the anti-Hillary.

I agree that Donald Trump sometimes goes too far with his rhetoric. And his personal insults make me cringe. But that, in my opinion, is bravado. I have jumped off the Trump train over some of these more personal insults, and returned only after he offered a rare apology for one unneccessary insult about Heidi Cruz in my sister's column. I don't think he meant to be bigoted when he complained that Judge Curiel was biased in the Trump University suit. I think it was a calculated Trump move to put the onus on the judge and get his way.

I yearn to channel Jiminy Cricket to give Trump a new conscience and keep him away from his Twitter account or to whisper in his ear when he is about to attack someone unnecessarily. This is especially true when he attacks members of the GOP.

I'm still going back and forth on voting for him, rocked by each new cherry bomb he tosses out on the Internet and on TV. But as we enter into the final round of this presidential contest, my belief remains that Donald Trump is a good person on the inside and that the outside will eventually fall into place. He would not have the love and support of five exceptional children, as witnessed at the recent GOP convention if this were not true. His family is a tribute to him, so he must be doing something right.

Now he needs to follow their example.

It's a conundrum for me. Hundreds of thousands of men and women have fought and died to give me the right to vote, and I will not throw that privilege away. I will follow my gut when the moment comes.

As of today, I am tuning out the clueless talking heads, refusing to debate politics with righteous friends and hoping that Jiminy Cricket does his job.

# 8

# Unconventional Conventions

# In Paris with Boris, Donald and Lemon Tarts

I did something in Paris last Saturday night that I've never done before.

I went to a restaurant alone for dinner. I know, it's lame that I've always been afraid to go out to public places at night on my own. I tried to get beyond this phobia by going to the movies by myself one Saturday night in Washington, many years ago, after a breakup. But when the lights came up, my ex was sitting in front of me with a pretty date. That cured me of the desire to venture forth solo for another couple of decades.

But I was in France for work for the week and stopped in Paris on the way home. I spent Friday night eating the minibar—salt-and-vinegar potato chips, popcorn, nuts, chocolate and white wine. But by the second night, it seemed too sad to be cooped up in a dark room in the City of Light.

So I worked up my nerve and made it as far as the hotel dining room. I was staying on the Left Bank at L'Hotel, where a depressed

Oscar Wilde came to live in 1898, subsidized by the French government, after his release from Reading Gaol.

He died there at 46, in a room off the lobby that is now a petite mirrored bar with glossies of famous drop-ins like Mick Jagger and Johnny Depp, and a cocktail called "Born to Be Wilde," made with Bacardi, basil, honey, lime juice and Tabasco. Legend has it that Wilde's last words were: "My wallpaper and I are fighting a duel to the death. One or the other of us has to go."

The wallpaper is now ruched gray silk, so Wilde would no doubt like it, and the worn carpet is a suitably wild leopard print. I walked past the bar to the restaurant and trepidatiously asked for a table for one. The response was not comforting. "Madame," the young sommelier said, gently pulling me aside. "This is a *gastronomic* restaurant." I wasn't sure what I was supposed to infer. "Do you mean prix fixe?" I asked.

He shook his head, grabbed a menu and pointed to the prices, which were in the range of a nice Washington restaurant, and gave me a dubious look.

Was it something I wore? I had changed out of jeans and put on a flowered Diane von Furstenberg sundress and a striped seersucker J. Crew jacket. They did clash a little, but clashing prints are supposed to be in. Perhaps not in Paris.

Did he think I should go out for Le Big Mac or a Royale with Cheese? I murmured something about running out of food in my room. "Oh, you're in the hotel?" Valentin, the sommelier, asked. Then he went off to huddle with his boss, Philippe, the restaurant director, and came back.

"All right," he said, pointing to a table with striped love seats. "You can sit here."

As I ate my avocado and yuzu mousse, and braised turbot with aniseed fragrance and maritime aster leaf, accompanied by Valentin's handpicked Burgundy, I looked around. There were 10 tables, nearly all with couples. Maybe Saturday night in Paris was not the best time for bravado.

When I got my Italian lemon meringue, a work of art shaped like sun-drenched teardrops, Philippe kindly explained, "You can eat the gold leaf on top."

"I know," I told him. "I used to watch Martha Stewart's show."

He gave me a blank look.

I was armed with a bunch of newspapers, so I could pretend to study up on the Brexit vote convulsing Europe. Oscar Wilde's bon mot perfectly sums up the continental divorce: "Each man kills the thing he loves."

What better to do when you're alone than contemplate why England wants to be alone? The sexy couple next to me was too busy smooching over red wine for me to inquire about the French attitude toward British solitude.

Parisiens I had talked to were universally disgusted: with David Cameron, for holding the vote; with the British, for Brexiting; and—always unsolicited—with Americans, over l'affaire Trump.

"*C'est impossible,*" they lectured. "*Fou.*"

I pondered the parallels between the world's two most infamous blonds, Donald Trump and Boris Johnson.

They are prolific authors born in New York City to parents of considerable means and known around the planet by their first names. And there's the odd fact that John Oliver called Johnson an orangutan and Bill Maher suggested Trump came from one.

Boris, a Shakespeare aficionado who went to Oxford, is more erudite, witty and disheveled than The Donald.

But, as the *Times*'s Sarah Lyall wrote, Johnson has a sometimes buffoonish "cocktail of charm, bluster and obfuscation." And so does Trump. Johnson is obsessed with his own brand and mocks with a rapier. So does Trump.

Johnson had an extramarital affair that became notorious in

the tabloids. So did Trump. Johnson lies with ease and cavorts in farce. So does Trump. Preferring grandiosity and PR stunts to policy details, Johnson has stumbled on his hubris, lack of preparation and disorganization. So has Trump. Johnson was abandoned and knifed by many in his own party. So was Trump.

"True friends stab you in the front," as Wilde said.

Like Trump, Johnson brilliantly and cynically played to older, white voters and rode a wave of xenophobia, anti-elitist, anti-immigrant, they're-taking-what's-ours begrudging.

As Lyall wrote, Johnson, leading the "Leave" contingent, had a talent for making things up and taking a kernel of information about Brussels's ineptitude and spinning it into a broad negative narrative.

Just so, Trump can amplify a few crimes by undocumented Mexican immigrants and spin them into an indictment of an entire nation.

As with Hillary and the more compulsively watchable Trump, Cameron and the more compulsively watchable Johnson started off as friends and then found themselves in opposite corners for a spectacularly nasty fight.

As with Trump, Johnson was not trusted by many to do the job or seen as having a real plan besides chaos and the fearful message that THEY are stealing everything WE built.

After spinning up his storm, Boris failed to seize the moment, acting sheepish and almost repentant as he backtracked on some crucial Brexit promises.

After spinning up his storm, Donald also failed to seize the moment. He has failed to cement Republican support and raise his game to a mature, knowledgeable level. Trump wasn't sheepish about herding the crowd with demagogy, but he has been looking a bit nervous, confronted with a scenario where he could become a losing brand.

You can write off the success of Johnson and Trump with older, white voters to self-defeating nostalgia.

But there are painful, interlocking identity crises roiling, with young pitted against old and long-simmering resentments against leaders who haven't recognized the pain of globalization or the yearning for national exceptionalism.

Many Brits don't like being dictated to by bureaucrats in Brussels. And many Americans wonder, if we can no longer win any war and build the best stuff, who are we?

Both parties are having identity crises as well. Republicans despairing at a BuzzFeed story about alleged Trump eavesdropping on guest and staff phones at Mar-a-Lago can take heart that Bill Clinton still has a talent for getting himself—and the wife he supposedly wants to help—in trouble.

Bill's having a Phoenix airport 30-minute meet-cute with the attorney general in charge of the FBI investigation on Hillary's emails was a debacle for all three of them.

How could the guy with the gold-plated political instincts not see the problem with trooping across the tarmac to surprise Loretta Lynch with a visit? It's part of a bizarrely predictable cycle of the Clintons: Just when things seem to be going well, they squander the advantage.

"I am just flabbergasted by it," Trump said. "I think it's amazing. I've never seen anything like that before."

For once, he may not be exaggerating.

# The Clinton Contamination

It says a lot about our relationship with Hillary Clinton that she seems well on her way to becoming Madam President because she's not getting indicted.

If she were still at the State Department, she could be getting fired for being, as the FBI director told Congress, "extremely careless" with top secret information. Instead, she's on a glide path to a big promotion.

And that's the corkscrew way things go with the Clintons, who are staying true to their reputation as the Tom and Daisy Buchanan of American politics. Their vast carelessness drags down everyone around them, but they persevere, and even thrive.

In a mere 11 days, arrogant, selfish actions by the Clintons contaminated three of the purest brands in Washington—Barack Obama, James Comey and Loretta Lynch—and jeopardized the futures of Hillary's most loyal aides.

It's quaint, looking back at her appointment as secretary of state, how Obama tried to get Hillary without the shadiness. (Which is what we all want, of course.)

The president and his aides attempted to keep a rein on Clinton's

State Department—refusing to let her bring in her hit man, Sidney Blumenthal.

But in the end, Hillary's goo got on Obama anyhow. On Tuesday, after Comey managed to make both Democrats and Republicans angry by indicting Clinton politically but not legally, Barry and Hillary flew to Charlotte, NC, for their first joint campaign appearance.

Obama was left in the awkward position of vouching for Hillary's "steady judgment" to run an angry, violent, jittery nation on the very day that his FBI director lambasted her errant judgment on circumventing the State Department email system, making it clear that she had been lying to the American public for the last 16 months.

Comey, who was then yanked up to Capitol Hill for a hearing on Thursday, revealed that instead of no emails with classified information, as Hillary had insisted, there were 110, of those turned over to the State Department. Instead of Clinton's assurances that the server in the basement in Chappaqua had never been breached, Comey said it was possible that hostile actors had hacked Clinton's email account. Among the emails not given to State, he said at least three contained classified information.

Hillary had already compromised the president, who feels he needs her to cement his legacy. Obama angered FBI agents when he was interviewed on CBS's *60 Minutes* last fall and undermined the bureau's investigation by exonerating Hillary before the FBI was done with its work, saying preemptively, "This is not a situation in which America's national security was endangered."

Hillary willfully put herself above the rules—again—and a president, campaign and party are all left twisting themselves into pretzels defending her.

Obama aimed to have no shadows, but the Clintons operate in shadows.

After Bill Clinton crossed the tarmac in Phoenix to have a long chat with Lynch, the attorney general confessed that the ill-advised meeting had "cast a shadow" over her department's investigation into his wife and that she would feel constrained to follow the recommendation of the FBI.

"I certainly wouldn't do it again," Lynch said, admitting it hit her "painfully" that she had made a mistake dancing with the Arkansas devil in the pale moonlight.

The meeting seemed even more suspect a week later, when the *Times* reported that Hillary might let Lynch stay on in a new Clinton administration.

The fallout from the email scandal has clouded the futures of longtime Hillary aides Cheryl Mills, Huma Abedin and Jake Sullivan, who were also deemed extremely careless by Comey for their handling of classified information. The *Times* reported that they could face tough questions as they seek security clearances for diplomatic or national security posts. (Not to mention remiss in not pushing back on Clinton about the private server.)

"You've got a situation here where the woman who would be in charge of setting national security policy as president has been deemed by the FBI unsuitable to safeguard and handle classified information," Bill Savarino, a Washington lawyer specializing in security clearances, told the *Times*.

So many lawyers in this column, so little law.

President Obama is not upset about being pulled into the Clinton Under Toad, to use an old John Irving expression. He thinks Washington is so broken that the next president will need a specific skill set to function, and he thinks Hillary has that.

But what should disturb Obama, who bypassed his own vice president to lay out the red carpet for Hillary, is that the email transgression is not a one-off. It's part of a long pattern of ethical slipping and sliding, obsessive secrecy and paranoia and collateral damage.

Comey's verdict that Hillary was "negligent" was met with sighs rather than shock. We know who Hillary and Bill are now. We've been held hostage to their predilections and braided intrigues for a long time. (On the Hill, Comey refused to confirm or deny that he's investigating the Clinton Foundation, with its unseemly tangle of donors and people doing business with State.)

We're resigned to the Clintons focusing on their viability and disregarding the consequences of their heedless actions on others. They're always offering a Faustian deal. This year's election bargain: Put up with our iniquities or get Trump's short fingers on the nuclear button.

The Clintons work hard but don't play by the rules. Imagine them in the White House with the benefit of low expectations.

# Remainder Night
# at the Convention

Fortunately, Donald Trump likes it rough.

The violent incidents at his rallies, he told me once, didn't worry him. He felt it added a frisson of excitement to the proceedings.

So he probably loved Loser Night at his convention.

Three of the men he beat—he would call the final rivals "the remainders" or "the leftovers"—had to suck it up tonight and bow down to the Bling King.

Scott Walker appeared on stage and endorsed The Donald. Marco Rubio gave Trump his due in a video. But then it was Lyin' Ted's turn, and that's when things got ugly.

The bitter roundelay between the men started earlier in the day. As Ted Cruz had a campaign-style rally in Cleveland, with 2020 wafting in the air, Donald Trump's plane flew over and drowned Cruz out.

The Cruz fans erupted in boos at the cacophonous Trump plane and Cruz noted dryly: "All right, that was pretty well orchestrated."

But this evening, the boos were going in the opposite direction.

At first, the crowd was enthusiastic about Cruz. But soon Cruz began to seem like the guy who comes to your book party and starts brandishing his own book. When he had been speaking for quite awhile without endorsing the nominee, only perfunctorily congratulating him on winning the nomination, and when he advised everyone to vote "your conscience" up and down the ticket, the crowd turned ugly.

Suddenly Trump, certainly irritated at not hearing the glorious sound of his own name in an elongated address by a "loser," entered the arena. He was once more soaring in, drowning Cruz out.

All eyes went to Trump as they dimmed the lights on the stage and the nominee regally walked in, a procession of one, to sit with his family in his stadium box with gold-and-black striped railings. The crowd got even more feral toward the former rival suddenly trapped onstage, looking like he didn't know how to finish and finally slinking off.

Delegates near me started booing and jumping up and pointing at Cruz and screaming, "Trump, Trump Trump!" Others shouted, "He's full of baloney!" and taunts pocked with "idiot" and "moron."

Cruz finally escaped with his wife, Heidi, after she was escorted off the floor as a delegate was shame-shame-shaming her with the name of her former employer: "Goldman Sachs!"

Asked about the kerfuffle, Marion Ashley, an alternate delegate from California, summed it up to the *Times*'s Sam Purdy this way: "Trump used 'Lyin' Ted.' It looked like he proved Trump right."

This convention is getting so gladiatorial that Cruz was probably lucky the crowd didn't start screaming "Lock him up!" After getting a little bloodlust, the crowd seemed to perk up, just in time for Mike Pence.

# Trump's Historical Fiction

I could have waited to break the news.

Tomorrow is another day, after all.

But it had to be done.

I sidled up to some South Carolina delegates who had come to watch Donald Trump drop out of the sky in a helicopter.

I happened to be wearing a pink palmetto cap from Charleston, so I got a warm Southern welcome.

Ida Martin, a 61-year-old first-time delegate rocking a flag scarf and a blue shirt with little white stars said she was from Kingstree, "a sportsman's paradise and a woman's nightmare."

"Sort of like this convention?" I asked. She replied with a grin and a nod.

She said she was "worn-slam-out" because they were "ramming a lot into this one thing" but having fun. She liked watching Trump "rarin' down" in his copter.

She wasn't bothered by that little plagiarism episode with Melania and Michelle that kicked off the convention.

"Michelle didn't invent the wheel and she didn't invent all those little words everyone uses, like 'and' and 'the,'" Martin said.

It was time to end the pleasantries and break the news.

Did the Southern delegates know that Trump had told the presidential historian Jon Meacham for a *Time* cover story this week that the Civil War could have been negotiated through the art of the deal? Trump, who once told me that brokering a Middle East peace would be the ultimate exciting challenge for a dealmaker, has found something even yuger.

Based on his experience skipping golf to binge-watch Ken Burns's series on the war, Trump said that he felt that "the South overplayed their hand."

Ida Martin's friend Peggy Upchurch of Lake Wylie, an alternate delegate, also spruced up in red, white and blue and an elephant necklace, blanched.

"The South didn't overplay its hand," she said starchily. "The North overplayed its hand. Abraham Lincoln did not necessarily want to go to war. If he had just waited a bit."

But it all worked out in the end, she said, since she married "a Yankee."

That other Yankee, Donald Trump, doesn't know much about being civil. He probably doesn't know all that much about Abe Lincoln, either, since he told the *Washington Post* that he has never read a biography of a president. "I'm always busy doing a lot," he said. But he knows how to go to war with Republicans.

Now he must figure out how to parley his civil war with his party the way he wanted the earlier one settled: without bloodshed.

*July 21, 2016*

# The Loneliest Man in the Lone Star State

Ted Cruz really is Canadian.

Because if he were a true Texan, he would know, yes, when to hold 'em and when to fold 'em.

We happened upon the El Paso branch of the Texas delegation at the Hyde Park Prime Steakhouse. The delegates, wearing matching white cowboy hats and red, white and blue shirts with a lone star, were still fit to be tied at Cruz's withholding convention speech and truculent meeting with them this morning.

It was a case of Andrew Marvell irritation: Had we but world enough and time, this coyness, sir, were no crime.

Cruz thought his coy, smart-alecky refusal to endorse or even boost Donald Trump in his prime-time speech was a springboard to 2020. Instead, he's riding a bronco called Trump. If he had wanted to stand on principle and not play patty-cake with Trump like Paul Ryan and Marco Rubio, many here felt Cruz should have stayed home.

"I've never seen someone commit hara-kiri on national television," said Mark Dunham. "Mr. Cruz, whether he realizes it or not, he turned himself into Omarosa. It was political suicide. I cannot rationalize his thought process other than he's taking it way too personally and making it more about himself than God and country."

Adolpho Telles, the owner of Rosa's Cantina in El Paso, agreed: "I am so annoyed with him. He should have accepted what occurred and moved on with his life. You've got to support your candidate 100 percent."

The bright side, he said, was that the anger at Cruz had brought the delegates together and distracted them from the worries some have that they are not yet totally in love with their erratic, dictatorial Gotham mogul.

Telles was not buying Cruz's defense this morning to them that he was not "a servile puppy dog" who would tell Trump "thank you very much for maligning my wife and maligning my father."

Telles said he was thinking: "This is not about you or your wife. It's about Trump. And it's about America."

# Of Wine and Avocados
# Women for Trump Speak Up

Much has been said about Donald Trump's reputation as a connoisseur of women—mostly by him.

So it is interesting to see which women—besides the glossy Bond girls in his family—are stepping up to the podium to give testimonials to the Beauty of Trump.

Ordinarily at a Republican convention, you get a lot of pasty-faced white guys droning on about policies that would yank rights away from women. But G.O.P. officials jammed all the Teanderthal "Mad Men" stuff in the platform a week ago.

The Trump convention is a blithely policy-free zone, "the ultimate reality show," as Trump's campaign chairman, Paul Manafort, called it. Some Washington think tanks even canceled their usual policy seminars. What was the point?

In the absence of the usual suspects—G.O.P. stars and a few A-list celebrities from movies where things get blown up—a selection of random women have stepped into the void.

Convention planners are hoping there has to be another way

besides Ivanka to improve Trump's abysmal favorability numbers with women and to provide some counterprogramming to the harsh calls for execution or imprisonment, or both, of the first woman to head a major party ticket.

But delegates sometimes looked a little mystified by the parade of obscure women, some of whom offered no explanation of how or even if they knew Trump.

Somehow, in this unorthodox gathering, an avocado farmer and former soap opera actress who won two awards from Soap Opera Digest for being Outstanding Villainess ended up in prime time, standing before a screen the exact color of guacamole in a Trump Tower taco bowl.

"Many of you know me from one of your favorite soap operas 'The Young and the Restless' and 'The Bold and the Beautiful,'" Kimberlin Brown said, adding that since she had only One Life to Live, she pursued other dreams.

Kerry Woolard, the general manager of the Trump Winery, made Trump's turnaround of the Virginia vineyard sound like Eisenhower at Omaha Beach: "Quickly and decisively," she said, he went "to work replanting the vines."

We also enjoyed the stylings of Michelle Van Etten, a statuesque blonde with a disjointed speaking style and karate-chop hand motion that seemed to alarm some delegates. Balancing out Trump, called the "short-fingered vulgarian" by Spy magazine, Von Etten has unusually long fingers.

She told the traumatic saga of going to her 20th high school reunion. She saw that her former classmates were driving BMWs and "looked like Barbie," while she was 30 pounds overweight and driving a minivan.

"I began to dream again," she said, adding that she started a fashion business in Florida and "after two years, I was able to retire my husband" and he was able to home-school their kids.

Natalie Gulbis, the 441st best female golfer in the world who was in the second season of "Celebrity Apprentice," told the story of how she hit the links once with Trump and he helped her realize her dream of opening a Boys and Girls Club.

"These words previously fell on deaf albeit well-intentioned ears, but that day was different," she told the crowd. "They finally fell on ears that cared enough to take action."

Trump's caring ears must have been burning.

# Not Quite as Scary as 'Game of Thrones'

Q: Many Americans talk about leaving the United States if Trump is elected. Canada, Australia. The Anglophonic world, mostly. Do any of the columnists know how I can leave for the planet on which Westeros and Essos exist? —Deborah San Gee

A: Dear Deborah,

It is true. The Cleveland night is dark and full of terrors. The Red Convention has not yet reached Red Wedding proportions, even though "Ted Wedding" is trending on Twitter after the bloodfest at the hall Tuesday night between Cruz and Trump.

Don't go to Essos because you could become a love slave to a Dothraki prince. And stay away from Westeros because Cersei is about to get into some carnage that will make the Republican chaos look like child's play, and don't forget winter is here with the Whitewalkers.

On an amusing side note, I asked D.B. Weiss, one of the cool creators of the show, whether Trump reminded him of any GOT character.

"Hodor," he replied.

# Ivanka the Fabulous Fabulist

Ivanka Trump glided onstage to the Beatles' "Here Comes the Sun."

It was apt.

She was sun-kissed, her blond hair perfectly sleek, blowing photogenically, no doubt from a fan in the podium. The fashion entrepreneur's blush-pink sheath and stilettos looked Fifth Avenue chic.

The 34-year-old ornament to the Trump brand was like a beautiful sunny morning in the midst of a dark, lashing hailstorm.

She was glossy, both in how she looked and how she spoke.

She glossed over all of her father's ugly rhetoric and incitements, his erratic behavior and lack of any policy depth or even any policy, and offered a gauzy, idealized vision of a Bobby Kennedy-style figure as her father channeled Richard Nixon in '68.

She hailed her dad as a fighter against injustice, a boss who is "colorblind and gender neutral," who hires people of all ethnicities and backgrounds.

She glossed over the entire ideology of the G.O.P. and the regressive party platform for women and presented her father as a feminist who fights for women in the Trump organization and who would fight as president for child care, "affordable and accessible for all," and for women's rights, equal pay and maternity leave.

"I will fight for this, too, right alongside him," she said, serving, once more, as the classy conjurer of the Moderate, Sane Donald in place of the Dark, Ugly Donald.

One impediment to joy, as Ivanka tried to channel Hillary: The Boston Globe's Matt Viser reported last month that men in the Trump campaign earn about 35 percent more than the women in his campaign.

Trump would never make the eat-your-peas pivot to professionalism, comity and civility, so Ivanka did it for him.

She called her father "the people's champion" and "the people's nominee," making him sound like Princess Diana, the people's princess.

She offered sweet anecdotes to personalize her father, but she was so sunny that her portrait of him was almost unrecognizable. More like a jolly Santa than a short-fingered vulgarian.

She said she remembered him, when she was a child playing with Legos in the corner of his skyscraper office, tearing stories out of the newspaper about someone facing some injustice or hardship and writing a note in his black felt-tip pen to find the person and have them brought to Trump Tower, where he could get in their corner when they were down and give them a job or a break until they could feel that life is great again.

She said her father had "empathy and generosity," and threw in "kindness and compassion" for good measure.

Hopes are often reposed in family members. Everyone hoped that Barbara Bush was secretly working to make H.W. Bush more liberal on choice issues. Everyone hoped that Laura Bush was secretly working on W. to get Donald Rumsfeld fired.

But Ivanka Trump has a stupefyingly harder task. Everyone is hoping that with her calm and gracious air, she is secretly working to turn Donald Trump into a completely different being, to make him stop acting self-destructive and crazy and nasty.

She offers herself as that bright promise. But, as much as she might try to steer her willful father, we know that it is not really possible to curb his impulsiveness and narcissism or to moderate and modernize his positions. He is too in thrall to the roar of the crowd, too old to develop impulse control.

So it just turns her into a fabulous fabulist.

She said her father advised her when she was growing up: "Ivanka, if you're going to be thinking anyway, you might as well think big." And what can be bigger thinking than making the most divisive, disliked candidate in modern history seem like noble Atticus Finch—though it would be hard to imagine Atticus saying, as Donald Trump once did of his own daughter, that he would like to date a full-grown Scout if she weren't, in fact, his daughter."

She said he taught his kids to have a moral compass—with a straight face.

Ivanka has, at times, played the charming sidekick to Trump in his more unsavory business dealings. In 2006, she helped sell spots in a future Baja California condo complex that bore the Trump name. While the Trump organization earned $500,000 for their branding and sales efforts, all the people convinced by her and her father's promises lost their money when the outside developer failed to build anything. She denied any fault, telling CBS News that her family had "lived up to our obligation under a license agreement."

In the absence of all the normal political allies a typical candidate has, Trump's family takes on paramount importance as character witnesses. Melania tried to be one for her husband Monday night, saying how inclusive he would be, but the attempt got bollixed up in a speech shoplifting incident.

Ivanka tried again tonight. And in return, her dad came onstage and cupped his hands around her hips and patted them.

# Donald Trump's Disturbia

Like any masterly comic book villain, Donald Trump is reveling in conjuring a dystopia. And it's a natural progression, given that he got this far by reveling in conjuring a diss-topia.

Both of his barbed-wire universes were on display here last week.

Trump did not slay a dragon in the way that presidential contenders did in the old days with laurels from the battlefield. In his mythmaking, he slayed 16 dragons on the debate stage.

Ivanka offered her father's hero-myth at the beginning of her convention speech Thursday night: "He prevailed against a field of 16 very talented competitors."

And how did the political tyro accomplish this seemingly impossible feat?

He dissed all of them, death by a thousand cuts. Jeb Bush was "a one-day kill," as a gloating Trump put it, with the "low energy" taunt. "Liddle Marco" and "Lyin' Ted" bit the dust. "One-for-38 Kasich" fell by the wayside.

Trump bragged on it again Friday morning when he met with his convention volunteers here before flying off on Trump Force One.

"No matter what your feelings, whether you're the governor of Ohio, whether you're a senator from Texas, or any of the other people that I beat so easily and so badly, you have no choice," he crowed. "You've got to go for Trump."

And on the distaff side, we are bound to hear more about "Crooked Hillary" and "Pocahontas" as the ladies celebrate making history in Philly this week.

There is a brutality and harshness about Trump's two worlds: feral insults that "kill" opponents and a convention so feral that Politico's Glenn Thrush said he expected to see wild cats wandering through it.

On Thursday night, the nominee painted a crepuscular "Midnight in America" picture of the "death, destruction, terrorism and weakness" that he claimed President Obama and Hillary had wrought. "Our convention occurs at a moment of crisis for our nation," he said. "Any politician who does not grasp this danger is not fit to lead our country."

America is a disaster but Trump will descend from his gilded skyscraper and sacrifice himself and move to a mere six-story white home to save us.

Ronald Reagan put a charming, smiling face on harsh policies. W. was a genial candidate who gave no hint of the doom to come. But Donald Trump doesn't sugarcoat it. Take him or face dissolution.

Trump told the crowd that he was presenting the facts "plainly and honestly." But his dystopia is fueled by diss-information and diss-tortion, insulting rivals with disturbing exaggerated and cherry-picked facts and unsubstantiated assertions and conspiracies.

The president has put himself forward as the Trump Fact-Checker in Chief. At a joint press conference Friday at the White House with the president of Mexico, Obama pushed back on the Republican nominee he disdains.

"This idea that America is somehow on the verge of collapse, this vision of violence and chaos everywhere, doesn't really jibe with the experience of most people," the president said.

He added: "When it comes to crime, the violent crime rate in America has been lower during my presidency than any time in the last three, four decades. And although it is true that we've seen an uptick in murders and violent crime in some cities this year, the fact of the matter is, is that the murder rate today, the violence rate today, is far lower than it was when Ronald Reagan was president—and lower than when I took office."

The rate of killings of police officers is also much lower since the Reagan years, he said. "Those are facts. That's the data."

Nothing should be remarkable with Trump anymore. But it was still remarkable to see him the morning after his balloon-drop coronation as head of the Republican Party return to trolling Ted Cruz. There's a dissonance in his bleak dystopia and his brash diss-topia as he switches from Dr. Strangelove to Don Rickles.

At their meeting with volunteers, a bemused and wary Mike Pence stood behind Trump, looking at him as if he were a big bottle of nitroglycerin. Trump gleefully got back to diss-topia, dissing Cruz because Cruz dissed him—follow along, readers—by not giving an endorsement in his prime-time speech Wednesday.

"All I did," Trump said disingenuously, talking about Cruz's father, Rafael, "is point out the fact that on the cover of *The National Enquirer,* there was a picture of him and crazy Lee Harvey Oswald having breakfast."

Actually, the picture was of Oswald passing out leaflets about Cuba with a man the tabloid was alleging, through some kind of photo analysis, was Rafael.

Trump said *The Enquirer,* owned by a friend of his, should be "very respected" and should have won a Pulitzer for breaking the John Edwards love child story.

As Pence looked on with smiling trepidation, Trump asked him if he could set up a "super PAC" while he was serving as president to destroy Ted Cruz but didn't wait for an answer.

He then went on to review the whole story again about the diss to Melania, when her "risqué" photo in GQ—"a reasonably respected magazine," he called it—was run in an ad on Facebook by an anti-Trump super PAC and Trump responded by retweeting an unflattering picture of Heidi Cruz.

He called Heidi "a very nice woman and a very beautiful woman" and "the best thing he's got going, and his kids, if you want to know the truth." After more along these lines, he finished with, "So that takes care of the Heidi thing."

The truth is out there, Donald.

*July 26, 2016*

# Bill Clinton Pours on the Estrogen

His life took off, he said, when he fell in love with "that girl."

He told a familiar love story, recounted in his memoir, about springtime at Yale Law School in 1971 and a "magnetic" girl with thick blond hair and big glasses and no makeup and a long, white flowery skirt.

He said when he first saw her in a political and civil rights class that he wanted to tap her on the shoulder, but he knew if he did, he would be starting something beyond his control.

With a sky-blue tie and silvery hair and an easy smile, the sixty-nine-year-old looked healthier than he has on the trail. And he was sharp.

The Big Dog basked in the unique historic moment: a former president and a husband and a wannabe first lad making the case for a former first lady, a wife and a wannabe first woman president.

In an act of amazing self-restraint, the man who relishes the word "I" managed to make the talk, as he prefers to call his folksy speeches, all about her. He was positively uxorious.

She "calls you when you're sick, when your kid's in trouble or when there's a death in the family," Bill said of his partner of forty years.

It has been said that the essence of the Clinton marriage is coming to each other's rescue in critical moments. Or maybe more precisely, their byzantine conjugal dynamic works like this: One of them—usually Bill—creates chaos, and then they get out of it together. Or as a former aide described the Clinton pattern: "Hubris. Funk. Reintroduction."

"You could drop her in any trouble spot, pick one, come back in a month and somehow, some way, she will have made it better," he said, in a line that could have applied to global crises or marital. (An earlier celebrity speaker tonight was Tony Goldwyn, who plays the philandering president in a series inspired by Bill and Monica.)

After the email shaming and a bloodless campaign, tonight it was Bill's turn to rescue Hillary from being the most unknown known person in history. One of the most liked presidents was charged with humanizing one of the least liked presidential candidates.

"One of the most seductive characters we've seen in American politics in our lifetime," as David Axelrod calls Bill Clinton, had to melt the sphinx-like aura of his guarded wife.

The uncontrollable Clinton had to make the tightly controlled Clinton seem less coiled and more endearing. The Protean pol had to take his wife's ever-shifting personas and policies, and paint a cohesive portrait. He rivaled Ivanka in his talent for airbrushing, but he probably won't be offering his convention outfit for sale tonight.

Hill and Bill both have 100-percent name ID, but Bill's task was to reintroduce her as "the best darn change-maker I have ever met in my entire life."

A quarter-century after Clinton aides wrote memos about how to warm up and round out Hillary by raising her profile as a mother, Bill was still trying to drive that point home.

"My daughter had the best mother in the whole world," he said tonight, adding that Hillary was "first and foremost" a mother, "our family's designated worrier" who only worried about Bill's parenting when he took a couple days off with Chelsea to watch all six *Police Academy* movies "back to back." He described Hillary on her knees, lining Chelsea's Stanford dorm-room drawers with paper when their daughter moved to college, until Chelsea told them it was time to leave.

It is another example of the overcorrecting that marks Hillary's career. In trying to feminize and maternalize Hillary, Bill almost went overboard about that "girl," as he called her three times. He poured on the estrogen, presaging his role as helpmeet in the East Wing.

He never mentioned Donald Trump, the man he used to be friendly with and play golf with. He simply alluded to the way the Republican convention had tried to turn Hillary into a "cartoon" villainess. "Life in the real world is complicated and hard," he said, and "a lot of people think it's boring."

"One is real, the other is made up," he said of the caricature of Hillary. "You nominated the real one."

He implicitly compared his wife to her gilded rival, limning her as someone genuinely seeking a life of service. He talked about her summer sliming fish in Alaska and all her work for poor children.

Hillary has said that she never realized how hard it was to be as great a persuader and performer as Bill until she tried to do it herself.

Bill has now given ten convention speeches, and he has had awful moments and great ones. I was there in 1988 when he talked for thirty-three minutes, and the Dukakis delegates began cheering when he finally said "In closing..." And I was there in 2012, when he won raves for selling Barack Obama's agenda, after the articulate-but-aloof president somehow wasn't able to and had to appoint Bill as "Secretary of Explaining Stuff." This speech was slightly over forty minutes.

Donald Trump had a soap opera actress speak at his convention, but the Clintons easily topped that. Their lives have been an astonishing soap opera in which Bill has played many starring roles: the loyal spouse, the betraying spouse and the subconscious saboteur.

This was a night a long time coming for the former moot court partners, a night celebrating the promise that animates the Clinton partnership: She helped him. She moved to Arkansas for him. "I really hoped that her choosing me and rejecting my advice to pursue her own career was a decision she would never regret," Bill said tonight.

She added the Clinton name to Rodham to please old-fashioned Southerners when Bill lost the governor's mansion to help him win it back. Bill told the story tonight about how she engineered his comeback, noting: "My experience is it's a pretty good thing to follow her advice."

Hillary chafed at eight years of the anachronistic role of first lady, even through slights like getting stationery with the restored middle name of Rodham missing as her husband campaigned for the White House. (She sent it back.)

"That girl" put up with the humiliations of Bill's hound-dog ways with "that woman" and others, and let him hide behind her skirt.

And tonight Bill paid her back—and tried to extend his own legacy—even as Trump gets ready to exert more effort dragging the former president through the mud. Jeb Bush had faltered partly on dynasty fatigue, but Bill does not intend to let that happen to Hillary.

Starting tonight and through the fall as he tries to woo back white voters and older voters in the Rust Belt and the South, he is trying to conjure the halcyon days of Clinton peace and prosperity. He does not want to remind people of the shady days of Clinton avarice and deceit, or the parts of his presidency or post-presidency that haven't aged well, like NAFTA, the crime bill, deregulation of Wall Street and the Defense of Marriage Act, the Marc Rich pardon or the unseemly braiding of the Clinton Foundation with Hillary's State Department.

Bill tried to augment Hillary's sparse vision, talking about how she would be the right pilot for "the ride to America's future."

"In the greatest country on earth we have always been about tomorrow," 42 said, urging America to choose Hillary as 45.

In other words: As Donald Trump tries to drag us back to the past—and to the Clintons' past—don't stop thinking about tomorrow.

# Trump's Thunderbolts

*Donald Trump is mad at me. He thinks I've treated him "very badly." But he returned my call on Friday night on his way to a rally in Colorado and agreed to do a lightning round on the Democratic convention. He began, naturally, by bragging about his convention ratings and bounce, but then we got down to specifics.*

**On Michael Bloomberg's speech suggesting Trump is not "sane" and mocking him as a con man:**

"A guy who didn't have the guts to run for president. Little Michael. He doesn't know anything about me. But he never had the guts to run. He probably wished he did but he didn't. He spent millions of dollars on polling but he was missing one thing: guts. Little Michael."

**On President Obama calling him "not really a facts guy" and a businessman who left a trail of lawsuits and people who were unpaid and felt cheated:**

"Obama gave a good speech but not nearly as good as the press would have you believe. Whether it's good or bad, the press will say it's fantastic. In many ways, I like Obama. It's hard to define. There's something about him I do like. I'm embarrassed to admit it. I give him a lot of credit. It's very unique and very hard to do and I give him tremendous credit. He became a two-term president of the United States. He's got some quality going."

**On Bill Clinton's reminiscences about his storybook romance with "that girl," Hillary:**
"He left out the most exciting chapter by far."

**On Michelle Obama, who said you can't boil down the issues a president faces to 140 characters:**
"She gave a very good speech."

**On Chelsea's introduction of her mother:**
"I thought Chelsea was excellent. I thought she was very good. She's very friendly with Ivanka. They like each other and they should continue to be friends. My children were the stars of my convention."

**On the poignant appearance of Muslim lawyer Khizr Khan and his wife, whose son, Humayun, an Army captain, posthumously received a Bronze Star and a Purple Heart and was buried at Arlington National Cemetery after he was killed by a suicide bomber in Iraq in 2004. As his wife, Ghazala, stood silently by his side, Khan held up a copy of the Constitution and asked Trump if he had ever read it and said, "You have sacrificed nothing."**
"I'd like to hear his wife say something."

**On Virginia Gov. Terry McAuliffe saying that Hillary would turn around as president and support the trade deal:**
"He is the only person closer to Hillary Clinton than Bill. I know Terry very well. And he said that Hillary is saying she's against the Trans-Pacific Partnership now, but if she gets in, don't worry, she'll go back to supporting it. She went from calling it the gold standard

to going against it. But if she gets in, she'll change a comma or something and support it again.

**On the hack of DNC emails, with the Russians as the suspected perpetrators:**
"Emails in general are terrible. There's no security. It happens so often. I'm old-fashioned. I put a letter in an envelope and have it hand delivered. My son is 10 years old, and he has grown up computer literate. They start using computers before they can walk. His computer was locked and he unlocked it. And I said, 'Barron, how did you do that?' And he said, 'I won't tell you, Dad.'"

**On former Secretary of State Madeleine Albright talking about how Trump may be "the Siberian candidate," a puppet of Vladimir Putin:**
"Madeleine Albright. Talking about a name from the past. Putin said I was a genius. I do say this: Wouldn't it be wonderful if we actually could get along with Russia and China and some other countries that we don't get along with, and then we go out and knock the hell out of ISIS? Wouldn't it be nice if we cleaned that mess up? Wouldn't it be smart?"

**On Missouri Democratic Senator Claire McCaskill telling Andrea Mitchell on MSNBC that Trump inviting a foreign government to hack our government "violates the Logan Act and he should be investigated." (The Logan Act, passed in 1799, bars private citizens from negotiating with foreign governments without permission.)**
"I said it as sarcasm. There were 200 reporters asking me questions and I wanted to be sarcastic, comparing their questions on the DNC hacking to the fact that Hillary Clinton wiped out 33,000 emails through deletion or otherwise. It's so ridiculous."

**On retired four-star Gen. John Allen hollering, alluding to Trump, that "our international relations will not be reduced to a business transaction" and that "our armed forces will not become an instrument**

of torture, and they will not be engaged in murder, or carry out other illegal activities":

"He's a failed general. He was fighting ISIS? He's not Gen. George Patton. He's talking about me and he knows nothing about me. I have a general—General Flynn. I'll take him any day."

**On Tim Kaine's speech taunting, "Hey, Donald, what are you hiding?" about Trump's refusal to release his tax returns:**

"I never met the guy. I never saw the guy. He proposed raising taxes in Virginia in his first week by $4 billion. He's the exact opposite of Bernie Sanders from just about every standpoint. Sanders people will not vote for Hillary. I will release my tax returns after the audit.

**On Bryan Cranston of *Breaking Bad* and LBJ *All the Way* fame, contending that Trump doesn't really want to be president:**

"I want to make America great again. I can do it. She can't."

**On Joe Biden's speech saying Trump was full of "malarkey" and had "no clue":**

"He tried very hard. He took some shots at me, but I'm fine. I'm getting used to it."

**On Bernie Sanders:**

"I think he wanted to go home and go to sleep. I'd like to hear his wife say something. He could have left one of the great legacies, but he made a deal and now he has buyer's remorse."

**On Anthony Weiner being in the convention hall in bright red pants, calling Trump's convention "a Dumpster fire":**

"I think he's a pervert. It's dangerous to allow him on the convention floor."

**On Roger Ailes getting fired as head of Fox News over cascading sexual harassment allegations:**

"Roger's a friend of mine."

**On his friend Bill O'Reilly getting criticized for saying—after Michelle spoke about the wonder of her daughters growing up in a White House built by slaves—that those slaves were well fed:**

"One thing about Bill, he'll find a way to be just fine."

**On Hillary's big night:**

"I'm feeling she's not going to get in. I have a strong feeling about it. I don't think she has what it takes. I watched her last night. It was hard to watch. I was falling asleep. It beats Sominex every time. She could barely beat Bernie. The system is rigged. It's a terrible thing."

# Thanks, Obama

It wasn't easy for Barack Obama, a skinny newcomer to national politics with an exotic name and scant résumé, to overthrow the voracious Clinton machine.

The 45-year-old had to turn himself into a dream catcher. He had to become an avatar of idealism and persuade Americans that he could take us to a political Arden beyond lies and vanishing records and money grabs and Marc Rich and Monica and Motel 1600.

"We need a leader who's going to touch our souls," Michelle Obama told a South Carolina rally in 2007. "Who's going to make us feel differently about one another."

Obama was going to lift Washington to a higher plateau—not one where the president consulted a pollster to see where he should vacation or if he should tell the truth about his intern/mistress. The young senator from Chicago was going to prove that the White House could be a gleaming citadel of integrity and ethics and exemplary family life.

Watching Bill Clinton and Newt Gingrich go at it, Obama once wrote, "I sometimes felt as if I were watching the psychodrama of the baby boom generation—a tale rooted in old grudges and revenge plots hatched on a handful of college campuses long ago—played out on the national stage."

He presented himself as the ticket to the future. He made us feel good about ourselves, that we could be better, do better.

Making the case against Hillary, he said that America deserved more than triangulating and poll-driven positions and "the same old Washington textbook campaign," more than a candidate answering questions whatever way she thought would be popular and "trying to sound or vote like Republicans when it comes to national security issues."

What about principles, he asked, what about a higher purpose?

Obama was not surrounded by the mercenary likes of David Brock and Dick Morris but true believers like David Axelrod.

The Clintons, infuriated by the raft of Democrats who deserted them during the 2008 campaign, sneered at Obama's hope and change message. Hillary protested, "We don't need to be raising the false hopes of our country." Bill groused, "This whole thing is the biggest fairy tale I've ever seen."

Voters, however, were starved for the fairy tale. For many, the line in an Obama ad rang true: "Hillary Clinton. She'll say anything and change nothing. It's time to turn the page."

Evidently, President Obama folded the corner of that page over so he could go back to it later. Remarkably, he bought us our return ticket to the past, rolling out the red carpet for the restoration of the Clinton blurred-lines White House.

An army of idealistic young people had moved to Iowa in 2007 to help Obama beat seemingly impossible odds. But in this election, Bernie Sanders's idealistic young people were cast as unrealistic dreamers who wanted free stuff or, according to Gloria Steinem, dates.

The same Obama who sparked a revolution has now made it his mission to preserve the establishment for Hillary. He told the Rutgers school paper in May that Sanders supporters needed to stop searching for silver bullets and recognize "we have to make incremental changes where we can, and every once in a while you'll get a breakthrough and make the kind of big changes that are necessary."

Yes we can—incrementally!

The president passed the baton to Hillary, as he puts it, more than three years ago, feeling she's the safest bet to protect his legacy. As Politico's Glenn Thrush reports, Obama wants to create what he calls "a 16-year era of progressive rule" and refocus American politics as the "Reagan of the left," as one of his advisers put it.

Showing his icy pragmatism, the president passed over his loyal vice president because he thought Joe Biden would not be as strong a candidate, given his tendency for gab and gaffes. (That was before Donald Trump made Biden seem exquisitely bridled.) When Biden didn't take the hint, Obama sent his former strategist David Plouffe to break the bad news.

Maybe Obama felt he owed Hillary, after leapfrogging over her to make history as a "first"—with the help of a lot of Democratic luminaries who publicly broke with the vindictive Clintons, only to find themselves having to spend the last couple years crawling back into their good graces.

Besides Biden, Obama threw another loyal former lieutenant, Chicago Mayor Rahm Emanuel, under the bus.

In the DNC video introducing Obama at the convention, the president was built up as a hero on health care. It said Emanuel went to the president and said, "You're going to have to pull the bill, because if you push this legislation, you will lose in 2012."

Emanuel, who was hosting a party at the convention that night, was rightfully upset. It was his job to warn the president of the political consequences, and after Obama decided, it was Emanuel and Nancy Pelosi who had to arm-twist the bill through with no Republican votes.

Before he died, Beau Biden told his father he wanted him to run partly because he didn't want the White House to fall back into the miasma of Clinton family values.

The president made his vote-for-Hillary-or-face-doom convention speech only 22 days after his FBI\ director painted Hillary as reckless and untruthful.

He argued that there is no choice but to support Hillary against a "self-declared savior" like Donald Trump, perhaps forgetting that Obama was once hailed as such a messiah that Oprah introduced him in 2007 as "the one," and it became his moniker.

In the end, Obama didn't overthrow the Clinton machine. He enabled it.

It turns out, who we choose is not really about our souls. It's just politics, man.